The Praeger Handbook of Community Mental Health Practice

The Praeger Handbook of Community Mental Health Practice

Volume 2

Diverse Populations and Challenges

Doreen Maller, Set Editor
Doreen Maller and Kathy Langsam,
Volume Editors

Foreword by Steven Tierney, EdD, CAS

 PRAEGER

AN IMPRINT OF ABC-CLIO, LLC
Santa Barbara, California • Denver, Colorado • Oxford, England

Library of Congress Cataloging-in-Publication Data

The Praeger handbook of community mental health practice / Doreen Maller, set editor.
    volumes ; cm
  Includes bibliographical references and index.
    ISBN 978-0-313-39953-4 (hardcover : alk. paper) — ISBN 978-0-313-39954-1 (ebook)
  1. Community mental health services—Handbooks, manuals, etc. I. Maller, Doreen, editor. II. Title: Handbook of community mental health practice.
    RA790.5.P663 2013
    362.2'2—dc23

                                                                    2012034714

ISBN: 978-0-313-39953-4
EISBN: 978-0-313-39954-1

17 16 15 14 13   1 2 3 4 5

This book is also available on the World Wide Web as an eBook.
Visit www.abc-clio.com for details.

Praeger
An Imprint of ABC-CLIO, LLC

ABC-CLIO, LLC
130 Cremona Drive, P.O. Box 1911
Santa Barbara, California 93116-1911

This book is printed on acid-free paper ∞

Manufactured in the United States of America

Contents

Foreword

Steven Tierney, EdD, CAS

Chair of the Community Mental Health Program,
California Institute of Integral Studies

Welcome to *The Praeger Handbook of Community Mental Health Practice*. If you are reading this, you may be a provider of vital mental health services in your community. You may be a graduate student embarking on one of the most rewarding careers you can imagine. You might be an advocate, collaborating with your colleagues who have written these important chapters. Perhaps you are a consumer of mental health services; we hope that you will find what you read helpful and accurate.

That is what community mental health is—all of us working together to improve the health and wellness of all of us. Each of us brings a unique experience to the practice of community mental health, and each of those is vital. As you will learn in these chapters, the practice is rigorous, well-documented, and practiced with compassion and integrity. We do not think community mental health is a derivative of more traditional modalities and venues. We believe that every man, woman, and child deserves the best prevention, care, therapy, and services possible.

The Praeger Handbook of Community Mental Health Practice offers you sound theory, evidence-based practice, and innovation that meet the needs of our changing profession. We insist that the voices of consumers be at the center of our work and our practice, and you will find those voices articulated throughout this series. It is not a question of whether community mental health can be effective; in a civil society, it must be. These volumes provide the theory and tools necessary to ensure that the highest quality of community mental health services is available for all who need it, want it, and deserve it.

The Community Mental Health Movement has been around for a long time. In the United States, we can trace its roots to at least 1868 when Elizabeth Packard, a former psychiatric patient, became an outspoken advocate for patients (Rosenberg & Rosenberg, 2006, p. 8). That history is important. Then, as now, the mental health system is made up of people who care enough to understand, be creative, and speak out for effective, appropriate services and treatments. We are the community in community mental health: consumers, their families, providers, educators, and policy makers.

The new "community" mental health system can be truly revolutionary. It will not be about where services and treatments are delivered. That definition of community is not enough. It will not be solely about what services are delivered. Evidence-based practices and innovation will need to exist side by side. The vision of "community" mental health proposed in these volumes is built on a foundation partnerships formed to create and deliver a sustainable system of care. Effective and sustainable "community" mental health will require providers and policy makers to become full partners with consumers and their families. The consumers, providers, and family members who form the mental health teams of the future are the community mental health system that will be effective and sustainable.

In the new definition of community mental health, providers will be willing to take a risk and work not from a safe, objectifying distance (Watkins & Shulman, 2008, p. 31) but up close where genuine partnerships with consumers are required. The consumers, providers, and family members who form the mental health teams of the future are the community we must build and support. This new community mental health must involve working together: developing communal processes, imagining different strategies, and using shared evidence to create effective services and treatments. Liberation psychologist Ignacio Martin-Baro proposed these ideas in the 1980s (Watkins & Shulman, 2008, p. 27). It is time now to commit fully to these partnerships and the new mental health system they can create—a true community mental health.

California is one example of a robust approach to mental health service revision. It is presented here so that the reader can see what is possible when consumers, family members, providers, and policy leaders work together. It is not the only example, but it is a useful example to study. The many communities and jurisdictions that are working creatively and in respectful, engaged partnerships are equally important areas for study and are included in other sections of this series.

In California, one in five adults reported a need for help with mental or emotional problems. More than 1 million additional Californians reported symptoms associated with serious psychological distress. Approximately one in three of these adults reported seeing a mental health provider (Grant et al., 2010, p. 1).

In a 2009 editorial in the *Lancet*, Arthur Kleinman called for the kind of transformation that had previously been experienced in HIV-related care: "decreasing stigma and empowering the consumer and his or her family." This type of change in the mental health system has encouraged needs to become the central focus of institutions, professionals, and family movements in the mental health field (Kleinman, 2009, p. 603). Large numbers of Americans report a need for mental and emotional health services and a significant percentage of those adults report a lack of meaningful access. In 2003 the President's New Freedom Commission on Mental Health stated that the failure to make mental health a priority is a national tragedy. In its final report, "Achieving the Promise: Transforming Mental Health Care in America," the commission detailed the virtual collapse of the community mental health system and called for transformation of the system to better serve individuals and families. The commission recommended an infusion of resources to make it possible for services and treatments for people with psychiatric disabilities to be recovery oriented and consumer driven. The cost of this lack of prioritization has been profound:

- Mental disorders are implicated in 90% of the 30,000 suicides and 650,000 suicide attempts in this country each year (Simpson & Jamison, 1999, p. 60).
- Jails and prisons are, de facto, the largest mental institutions in the nation (Institute of Medicine, 2001). The American Psychiatric Association reported in 2000 that one in five prisoners in the United States was seriously mentally ill and that 700,000 mentally ill persons are processed through the prison or jail system each year (Montagne, 2008).

The need for profound transformation in the system will benefit virtually every American family in every state and county of our nation. This is a daunting task because the opportunities for community mental health to address deep-seated and long-term deficits in American mental health care are vast. The special circumstances include the following:

- Our nation's moral and ethical relationship to mental health, disease, and wellness
- Stigma and discrimination as barriers to mental health access and effectiveness
- Race, age, sexual orientation, and gender identification as barriers to care
- The criminalization of mental illness
- The devastating impact of poverty and class on mental health parity
- The economics of health care—individual and systemic implications

Although I present challenges to the development of an effective, sustainable system of community mental health care, it is not my intention to review a litany of the insurmountable problems facing the American or global mental health systems. As in community mental health planning and service delivery, hope is a critical component, and, when combined with responsibility and innovation, real progress can be achieved.

SETTING THE STAGE FOR CHANGE

Beginning in the 1960s, many states moved to close down large, expensive, and ineffective state hospitals and asylums. Between 1970 and 1997, more than 50 state hospitals were closed, and approximately 500,000 patients were released into American communities during this period (American Psychiatric Association, 2000, p. 2). The paradigm that was developed called for patients to be released to supportive community housing and to receive care in community mental health clinics. Almost universally this plan failed because resources, training for community housing programs and staff, and adequate accessible treatment options were lacking.

Journal articles and the lay press questioned the wisdom of community mental health, the states' commitment to and ability to create and sustain a viable mental health care system, and the safety of patients and communities where the patients live, patients who are often not monitored and do not receive the care they need (Murray, 1975, p. 2035). These articles provoked concern, fear, and for some, hopelessness (Talbott, 1979, p. 621). These publications also brought attention from compassionate mental health professionals, wise and empowered consumers (and their families), and public health and political leaders with the courage to promote system-wide change (Smucker, 2007, p. 18).

At the federal level, the report "Achieving The Promise: Transforming Mental Health Care in America" signaled the intention of the administration that the federal government would play a key role in defining, building and supporting an effective community mental health system (New Freedom Commission on Mental Health, 2003).

California is unique in its approach to creating community-based mental health care. Californians have twice gone to the polls to support a major reorganization of the state's mental health care system. In 2004 the voters passed the Mental Health Services Act (MHSA; Mildred, 2008, p. 1). This sweeping bill is a call to change: who is served, who the providers are and need to be, how those providers must be trained, and where they will practice. The law also makes clear the necessity and benefits of partnerships between consumers and providers. The importance of evidence-based practice is defined to make it clear that what we do together works.

The people of California recognize the need for change; even in tough economic times, they have clearly indicated support for the programs and services required to achieve this new paradigm. Those same voters returned to the polls in 2009 to stop the administration from diverting the funds for this system overhaul (Caldwell, 2011). The MHSA generates its own funding through a 1% tax on Californians with annual incomes of more than $1 million (Caldwell, 2011).

Interestingly, as California was embracing a new system of care that is community based, voices inside and outside the mental health delivery system increased the call for better evaluation and evidence of clinical effectiveness (Rosenberg & Rosenberg, 2006, p. 33). The significant cost of these new systems of care encouraged people to ask difficult questions. Elected and appointed state officials looked to the expenses of providing systems of care as a resource for closing state budget gaps (Honberg, Diehl, Kimball, Gruttadaro, & Fitzpatrick, 2011, pp. 7–8). The mental health community needed well-organized advocacy groups that emerged and collaborated to create guidelines for the future of community mental health. The results are encouraging. For those working in or preparing to work in mental health delivery systems, there are several reality checks that will guide mental health services and treatment in the environments in which these services are delivered:

- Community-based care is here to stay. Hospital-based care is simply too expensive to be sustainable in the vast majority of state and local jurisdictions.
- Consumers and their families are now vital players in the design, delivery, and evaluation of mental health services.
- Evidence-based care is here to stay. Fiscal and political leaders will not finance services that cannot be reasonably expected to improve the quality of life for those who need services.
- Evidence-based practices are also required by informed and engaged consumers. If a consumer invests her time, she has a right to know that the interventions she engages in have the potential to meet her needs and improve the quality of her mental health and wellness.
- Mental health systems that intentionally or subconsciously safeguard the status quo will be replaced by new models demanded by individuals and communities that have been left out, marginalized, and underserved.
- Innovative funding mechanisms will be required. The stress of not being able to access care; of having reduced options based on ability to pay; and of being unable to provide for children, aging parents, and others is counterintuitive to sound public health policy.

NEW THEORY TO SUPPORT NEW PRACTICE

Laws are important and encouraging in the effort to build an effective and sustainable system of community-based mental health services. Legislation alone, however, cannot guide, direct, build, or sustain the new system needed to truly enhance and expand the access to mental health services, effectiveness of those services, and the recruitment and maintenance of professional and peer staff who will change the paradigms.

There is significant opportunity for innovation, the creation and testing of new models, and the recruitment and employment of peer and professional staff who share the lived experience of the diverse cultural groups who make up America's population. Traditional therapies, in traditional settings, offered by therapists trained and clinically supervised before the New Freedom Commission and the MHSA have produced some effective results. There must be respect, appreciation, and acknowledgment for what has worked. Starting from scratch is not wise or possible. The hundreds of thousands of people in care need continuity, and the current professionals in the mental health system can provide leadership or barriers in the change movement. Inclusion and collaboration are called for.

WHAT IS COMMUNITY MENTAL HEALTH?

Historically, mental health systems were set up to protect society from those who were considered different and dangerous, and to protect those patients from the dangers of fending for themselves in the cities and towns in which they lived (Grob, 1985, p. 639). This type of institutional and custodial "care" was the basis for mental health services from the establishment of the first U.S. hospital for the mentally ill in Virginia in 1773 until President Kennedy signed legislation to move the responsibility for mental health services away from institutions and into the community in 1963 (Grob, 1985, p. 639). Community mental health has most often been defined by the locations where the services are delivered; large hospitals and clinics versus small community settings including residential programs and/or criminal justice settings. Community mental health can also be defined by those who receive the services and by those who deliver them. Although all of these definitions are valuable and offer historic context, there is a need for a deeper understanding.

What is the role and responsibility of central government in the delivery of care? What role does oppression play in the delivery of community-based care? Americans have indicated a willingness to support a transformation of mental health care systems; what are the people's expectations?

Liberation psychologies offer opportunities to think at the most basic levels about what we do and how we will do it in the future:

> We do not want to assume that the role of psychology is to help individuals and families adapt to the status quo when this present order contributes so massively to human misery, psychological and otherwise. Our psychology should not exist in a vacuum of disconnected theory where classroom, research and clinical encounters are considered apart from conflicts and suffering in society. (Watkins & Shulman, 2008, p. 13)

In the 1980s, Ignacio Martin-Baro conducted research and published articles and books at the University of Central America in San Salvador (Watkins & Shulman, 2008, p. 23). Martin-Baro can be considered the father of liberation psychology. Liberation psychology is a powerful movement that can inspire people to imagine alternatives to their present conditions and play critical and mandatory roles in the design, delivery, and renewal of practices in assessment, diagnosis, treatment planning, care, and evaluation (Martin-Baro, 1994, p. 28). Martin-Baro gave voice to anonymous ordinary people whose voices called for psychology to critically examine itself and become a force for transformation rather than the status quo (Watkins & Shulman, 2008, p. 27). Community mental health must do nothing less.

In its current presentation, community mental health is said to be client centered, based on a recovery model of service delivery including "hope" for recovery as defined by the consumer as a basic tenant (Rosenberg & Rosenberg, 2006, p. 59). These are laudable goals, and the emerging research indicates the power of these practices.

The United States is a nation divided: those who can afford health care and mental health services versus those who cannot. The new system must include those living in such dire poverty that day-to-day survival does not leave time for advocating for appropriate mental health services. The active partners in the new community mental health system must engage those who for reasons of race, ethnicity, language, age, sexual orientation, and gender identification have not had access to appropriate treatment and services delivered by culturally proficient, clinically competent, and qualified caregivers.

We are a nation of immigrants, refugees, and war veterans, returning or arriving from distant shores. The motivation for their travels are often externally imposed, violent, and debilitating. The trauma and posttraumatic impacts are only beginning to be known.

Community mental health can play a critical role in improving the lives of these and other individuals and communities. It cannot do this by reorganizing existing systems. It does this first by working directly with individuals and communities and not on behalf of them. Community mental health must do this by being willing to create new paradigms that are built on inclusion, respect, dignity, and true collaboration and partnership.

In the book *Toward Psychologies of Liberation*, the authors note the difference between speaking "for" and speaking "with" (Watkins & Shulman, 2008, p. 2). Many researchers report the telos of their work as being "to give voice" to the people with whom they were working. Unfortunately, this manner of conceptualization carries a colonial shadow where those with privilege imagine themselves "giving" voice to the "voiceless." Although it is true that some individuals and groups ask for help in creating safe spaces in which they can deepen the process of listening to themselves and expressing their experiences and insights, the voice they develop is not given by another, though it may be nurtured by the process of being listened to carefully (Watkins & Shulman, 2008, p. 176).

Community mental health will be most effective and most rewarding for the practitioners when true partnerships are formed, nurtured, and sustained. It is not a question of cultural competence that can be addressed by the annual diversity-training day. It is carefully listening to and working honestly with people with mental and emotional conditions and their families and support systems. The success will come when the definition of wellness is client generated and provider supported.

In 2003, the President's New Freedom Commission said:

> We envision a future when everyone with a mental illness will recover, a future when mental illnesses can be prevented or cured, a future when mental illnesses are detected early, and a future when everyone with a mental illness at any stage of life has access to effective treatment and supports—essentials for living, working, learning, and participating fully in the community. (New Freedom Commission, 2003, Executive Summary, 1–2)

The community mental health professions are poised to deliver on that promise. It will require the recruitment and training of new professionals and the professional development, support, and commitment to change by existing providers, clinical supervisors, and leaders. Psychologists, social workers, professional counselors, and marriage and family therapists must revise curriculums to reflect the new realities, and new texts such as this book series will need to be developed to reflect these emergent concepts. These professions must also create meaningful access to careers for those who have experienced mental illness and their family members who have worked closely with illness and the road to recovery. The populations who have been underserved—racial and ethnic minorities, the poor, immigrants, and veterans—must be recruited, enrolled, and supported through graduation and licensure. Their voices must appear on both sides of the therapeutic relationship, or meaningful change will not occur.

There has been a common lament among front-line workers in the mental health professions: case management is typically the only "therapy" provided for the poor. This is unacceptable for both low-income and well-resourced individuals and communities; case management and therapy are two separate, useful, and effective activities. Many patients, clients, and community members would benefit from both case management and therapy. When well done, case management looks at the capacity of the individual to sustain his or her desired quality of life (Marion, 2010, p. 8). Assessment questions that can be helpful might include the following:

- Does he have safe and adequate housing?
- Is she able to access the education and training she needs to pursue her job and career goals?
- Does he have access to primary care and pharmaceutical services as needed?

The community therapist exercises her or his option to help the consumer remobilize functioning. Community mental health therapists understand that a mom with hungry kids in the lobby might not be able to actively participate in narrative therapy. A dad with no child care might not focus on the therapist's excellent and probing questions. Many consumers need both case management and therapy.

WHO NEEDS COMMUNITY MENTAL HEALTH SERVICES AND WHO RECEIVES THEM

In a comprehensive new study on mental health status and the use of mental health services by Californians, researchers at the University of California at Los Angeles Center for Health Policy Research found that nearly one in five adults in the state—about 4.9 million people—said they needed help for a mental or emotional health problem. Women were nearly twice as likely as men (22.7% vs. 14.3%) to say they needed help for a mental or emotional health problem ("perceived need"), such as feeling sad, anxious, or nervous. In each of these groups, it is estimated that one in three persons who needed these services visited a professional for treatment (Grant et al., 2010, p. 4).

Although California is unique in many ways, these numbers are similar to other states and jurisdictions (Manderscheid et al., 2010). Part of the challenge is fear of stigmatization; part is lack of insurance coverage (Insel, 2012, p. 1). Approximately 21% of the child and adolescent population receive mental health services annually, 17% from the human service and educational sectors (U.S. Surgeon General Report, 1999). The planning and delivery of mental health services for children and adolescents must be designed with these partners at the table.

OPPORTUNITIES AND CHALLENGES OF HEALTH CARE REFORM

Beginning in 2014 California, and all other states, will be required by the Affordable Care Act (ACA) to expand access to insurance coverage (Healthcare .gov, 2012). Medi-Cal, the state's primary public insurance program, will increase eligibility from 100% to 138% of the federal policy level and allow single adults with no dependent children to be eligible (Insel, 2012, p. 2). The estimated number of potential new consumers is between 1.7 and 3.0 million (Salmon, 2012). The impacts on the systems of care are mind-boggling. The advent of health care reform and its promise of mental health parity make it vital for mental health policy leaders and providers to know who may be coming into the system and what types of services they will need. California provides some basic service to noncitizens, but the statistics are consistent with national data (U.S. Surgeon General, 1999).

This is a young population (Salmon, 2012) poised to start families and to interface with the mental health systems of care. If the community mental health system and therapists provide these clients with effective therapy that includes well-articulated and documented mental health outcomes, these clients can be vital partners in the system. They will share their experiences with family members, friends, and community members. Thus families and communities that have not had access to or have not chosen to access mental health services will have evidence that it can work. It will work when it is culturally and linguistically appropriate, respectful and collaborative, and treats each client with dignity.

The premise here is that best practices in community mental health have begun to emerge, and evidence has begun to demonstrate that Americans want and are willing to support community mental health services, as long as those services work. This is an important time to be actively involved in the community mental health system. The statistics cited previously from the Centers for Disease Control and Prevention and the National Institute of Mental Health make it clear that there is tremendous need for effective, efficient, and culturally competent services.

It is assumed that you, our readers, work in the mental health care systems, are preparing to work in mental health professions, or are a consumer, advocate, or public health policy leader. We can make a difference—we are the community. The system will be changed when respect and engagement begin each treatment and ground each program. The system will be at its best when we stop telling each other and begin to ask each other, genuinely and with interest, "What can we do together to make your life better?"

> "Never doubt that a small group of thoughtful, committed citizens can change the world. Indeed, it's the only thing that ever has."
>
> —Margaret Mead

REFERENCES

American Psychiatric Association. (2000). *Outpatient services for the mentally ill involved in the criminal justice system.* Washington, DC: Author.

Caldwell, B. (2011). California Association of Marriage and Family Therapists blog. Retrieved from http://mftprogress.blogspot.com/2011/02/californias-complex-plan-to-save-mental.html

Grant, D., Wirtz-Kravitz, N., Gaxiloa-Aguilar, S., Scribney, W. H., Aydin, M., & Brown, E. R. (2010). *Mental health status and use of mental health services by California adults.* Los Angeles, CA: UCLA Center for Health Policy Research.

Grob, G. (1985). The transformation of the mental hospital in the United States. *American Behavioral Scientist, 28,* 639–654.

HealthCare.gov. (2012). Timeline for Affordable Care Act. U.S. Department of Health and Human Services. Retrieved from http://www.healthcare.gov/law/timeline

Honberg, R., Diehl, S., Kimball, A., Gruttadaro, D., & Fitzpatrick, M. (2011, March). State mental health cuts: A national crisis. Agency Report March 2011. Arlington, VA: National Alliance on Mental Illness.

Insel, T. (2012, January 26). Balancing immediate needs with future innovation. National Institute of Mental Health Director's Blog. Retrieved from http://www.nimh.nih

.gov/about/director/2012/balancing-immediate-needs-with-future-innovation
.shtml

Institute of Medicine. (2001). "Risk factors for suicide." Suicide: Summary of a Workshop. Retrieved from http://www.nap.edu/catalog.php?record_id=10215

Kleinman, A. (2009). Global mental health: A failure of humanity. *Lancet, 374,* 603–604.

Manderscheid, R., Delvecchio, P., Palpant, R. G., Marshall, C., Bigham, J., Bornemann, T. H., . . . Lubar, D. (2010). Attitudes towards mental illness—35 states, District of Columbia, and Puerto Rico, 2007. *Center for Disease Control and Prevention: Morbidity and Mortality Weekly Report, 59*(20), 620–625.

Marion, C. (2010). *Standards of practice for case management.* Little Rock, AK: Case Management Association of America.

Martin-Baro, I. (1994). *Writings for a liberation psychology.* Cambridge, MA: Harvard University Press.

Mildred, L. (2008). The California Mental Health Services Act: Stakeholder process: Issues and approaches [self-published]. Sacramento, CA. Retrieved from http://www.cimh.org/LinkClick.aspx?fileticket=mgabi_PFNbs%3D&tabid=795

Montagne, R. (2011, September 11). Inside the nation's largest mental institution. National Public Radio.

Murray, J. E. (1975). Failure of the community mental health movement. *American Journal of Nursing, 75,* 2034–2036.

New Freedom Commission on Mental Health. (2003). Achieving the promise: Transforming mental health care in America; Executive Summary. Retrieved from http://www.samhsa.gov/federalactionagenda/NFC_execsum.aspx

Rosenberg, J., & Rosenberg, S. (2006). *Community mental health: Challenges for the 21st century.* New York, NY: Routledge, Taylor, Francis.

Salmon, K. (2012). Health care payment in transition: A California perspective. The California Health Care Foundation. Retrieved from http://www.chcf.org/publications / 2012/01/payment-reform-transition

Simpson, S. G., & Jamison, K. R. (1999). The risk of suicide in patients with bipolar disorders. *Journal of Clinical Psychiatry, 60*(Suppl. 2), 53–56.

Smucker, B. (2007). Promises, progress and pain: A case study of America's community mental health movement. Washington, DC: Center for Lobbying in the Public Interest.

Talbott, J. (1979, September). Deinstitutionalization: Avoiding the disasters of the past. *Hospital & Community Psychiatry,* p. 621.

U.S. Surgeon General, Department of Health & Human Services. (1999). Mental health: A report by the Surgeon General. Rockville, MD: National Institutes of Health. Retrieved from http://www.surgeongeneral.gov/library/mentalhealth

Watkins, M., & Shulman, H. (2008). *Toward psychologies of liberation.* London, England: Palgrave-McMillan.

Set Introduction

Doreen Maller, Melissa Fritchle, and Kathy Langsam

In 1999, the Surgeon General of the United States published a seminal report: *Mental Health in America*. This report clearly articulated the need for progress in both disease prevention and health promotion and suggested that we think of mental health and mental illness as points on a continuum (p. 4). The report identified stigmatization as a social ill that has persisted though history, "manifested by bias, distrust, stereotyping, fear, embarrassment, anger and/or avoidance . . . in its most overt and egregious form, stigma results in outright discrimination and abuse. More tragically, it deprives people of their dignity and interferes with their full participation in society" (p. 7). In its final chapter, *Mental Health in America* identified the need to deliver state-of-the-art treatments into community settings, with treatments tailored to age, gender, race, and culture (p. 22). The report's most significant recommendation obligates early care conduits into the mental health system to "offer services that are responsive to the needs and preferences of their service users and their families" (p. 23).

The Praeger Handbook of Community Mental Health Practice originated from the editors' commitment to identify the building blocks of community mental health care, to present an overview of the changes in care provision, and to discuss the challenges and rewards of providing appropriate and respectful care and support to the millions of people in both the domestic and global community who are affected by mental illness.

The voices of community mental health are many and diverse: advocates, family members, theorists, researchers, individuals seeking care and their care providers, supervisors and administrators, policy makers, stakeholders, and funders.

We invited the books' contributors to share their expertise and experiences and to represent the broad base of community care. From conference rooms to classrooms, consultation rooms, and the open fields of global care, we set out to honor the many contributors to the advancement of care provision. With this work as an educational cornerstone, we intend to participate in the important work of thought leaders and care advocates to reduce societal stigma, help provide awareness and access to appropriate treatment, and open a dialogue around the shifts in the field of community mental health.

We come to these volumes as educators and care providers ourselves; we have personally navigated the trials of internship as novice professionals looking for meaning and structure, as supervisors grooming and training the next generation, and as teachers launching students into their first experiences interacting with consumers of mental health services. We acknowledge the need to train and educate students to the special demands of a career in community mental health as the laws governing mental health provision change on the state, national, and global levels. Core curriculum requirements have changed for some states to reflect these training needs, but there are few texts available that address the unique scope, depth, and nature of community mental health and the challenges to both training and care provision. These volumes intend to address that gap; explain how community work can differ from private practice; and identify the skills that new students, new counselors, and seasoned therapists need to be effective and competent clinicians. Both domestically and internationally, successful community mental health practice requires knowledge of and sensitivity to differences, including culture, language, ethnicity, religion, sexuality, and family diversity.

The demand for sophisticated and integrated mental heath care is great, and yet the complexities of interconnectivity, therapeutic capacity, and the competencies needed to support a multiplicity of issues present a significant educational challenge. Today, new therapists, counselors, and trainees in the mental health field typically work in schools, hospitals, courtrooms, jails, and transitional housing, addressing issues of mental illness, homelessness, addiction, abuse, and trauma. They are often the first point of contact for people entering the mental health system. With their clients often in crisis, those most tender in the field are often responsible for first assessment and case management. Training to deliver interventions at such sites, training long left to the agencies that employ counselors and therapists, is now mandated in California university graduate curricula, with other states starting to follow suit. Regulations now require students to learn the intricacies of community mental health work in the classroom first, preparing them more appropriately for the work they will encounter in the field.

It is our hope and expectation that these volumes will contribute to a more educated workforce, more exposed to and aware of the complexities, challenges, limitations, and rewards of a career in community mental health. These volumes and their chapters' diverse voices expose and educate students to the realities of the work ahead.

Mental illness affects the lives of at least 1 in 4 adults and 1 in 10 children; as many as 60 million people in the United States alone ("About NAMI," n.d.). In this work, we echo the call to action to provide appropriate and effective services and treatment to promote recovery and well-being in a welcoming and emotionally safe environment, domestically and internationally. This book series is not yet this emerging field's definitive text; we invite our readers to use these volumes as a launch point to deepen their own inquiry into effective tools and treatment as they develop and refine their own practices and identify populations that we intend to serve.

The series is constructed in three parts. Volume 1 considers the structures, challenges, and expectations of community mental health to familiarize readers with the meta-organization of the field in an effort toward awareness for opportunities of future practice, requirements, and collaboration. This volume addresses key issues such as service delivery, funding, and key models of intervention and care, including introducing readers to the key concepts of wellness and recovery, grief and loss, and trauma. Volume 2 is an exploration of specific topics and populations that participate in and benefit from community mental health services, including addiction, school-based, juvenile and adult justice, and veterans' services. Understanding the interweaving of these issues, as well as the co-occurrence of them in persons that participate in mental health services, is key for working in community-based settings.

Volume 3 addresses specific needs, considerations, and concerns when working in the global community, including disaster services, trauma, working with children, and training trainers. Preparing for the work, and appreciating the impact one has on participants, as well as the impact on the therapist him- or herself, are stressed in these thoughtful chapters.

All three volumes explore the community mental health system; the sociocultural, political, and economic realities faced; and where and how counselors and therapists work inside a vast array of sites. The series counsels readers to choose best practices to serve people in diverse circumstances, such as families in disaster, teens in the court system, survivors of genocide, immigrants, orphans of war, addicts in recovery, students in special education, people with HIV/AIDS, and the homeless. We also present an overview of global psychology and how to form allies in a new nation, how to work with locals in a foreign land and with embassies, and how to cope with culture shock, form support networks, or foster coalitions for change, whether domestic or international. These books recognize and explain how wide the need for and expectations of appropriately trained mental health workers have become and how we might best meet those opportunities and challenges. All three volumes contain chapters, case examples, and case studies. Please note that specific identifying features and characteristics of the people noted have been changed or obscured to respect privacy and confidentiality.

This is more than a technical manual for mental health professionals; we also call attention to the systemic and interdependent work of community mental health workers and offer information on global mental health services. By featuring the voices of current professionals and the people with whom and for whom they work, we thank and honor those whose work and passion is dedicated to the service of others, and those whose lives are touched every day by mental illness and emotional distress. We hope these books will educate and inspire the next generation of community mental health service providers.

REFERENCES

About NAMI. (n.d.). *NAMI*. Retrieved March 29, 2012, from http://www.nami.org/Content/NavigationMenu/Inform_Yourself/About_NAMI/About_NAMI.htm

U.S. Department of Health and Human Services (1999). *Mental health: A report of the Surgeon General*. Rockville, MD: U.S. Department of Health and Human Services, Substance Abuse and Mental Health Services Administration, Center for Mental Health Services, National Institutes of Health, National Institute of Mental Health.

Introduction

Kathy Langsam and Doreen Maller

In this second volume of *The Praeger Handbook of Community Mental Health Practice: Diverse Populations and Challenges,* we delve deeper into the specifics of delivering appropriate care with a focus on the special populations receiving services in community mental health, especially the challenges and opportunities of working with clients experiencing co-occurring disorders. Although we are aware that it is impossible to address every special and unique population that participates in community mental health services, we believe the collaborative, client-centered, and strength-based interventions and methods presented in these volumes are applicable to other populations and are the essential elements of working in community mental health. No practitioner can be an expert on every population, and most agencies focus on specific modes, theories, and populations; in reality, however, we work with clients who have multiple and complex challenges and do not fit into neat and tidy categories of care and services. The challenge for the modern care provider is to think broadly and systemically, including about issues beyond our personal experiences. Working with individuals and families where each member lives with complex challenges requires an open heart and a bias-free approach to client care. We are big proponents of the humility model, which urges clinicians both new and seasoned to keep an open heart and an open mind and to view each case as unique. In implementing this model, we work *with* clients to co-create solutions toward a more comfortable and fruitful life.

We begin Volume 2 with an exploration and overview of the core concept of the "Sociocultural Realities of Community Mental Health," contributed by Rachel E. Seiler, LCSW, PhD. In this introductory chapter, Dr. Seiler introduces the key concepts of cultural humility, power, and privilege and the tensions of working outside of our cultural norm. In its complementary case study, Therese Bogan, LMFT, shares her struggles with these issues while providing home-based care in the case study "Working with Privilege: Home-Based Interventions."

The introductory chapter is followed by two chapters and a case study, all of which explore addiction services and interventions. In Chapter 2, "We Are All Addictions Counselors Now: Strategies with Problem Substance Use," Annie Fahy, RN, LCSW, shares a historic perspective of addiction work and moves readers toward the need and necessity for addiction awareness and client-specific interventions when working with consumers of mental health services. Harm reduction, brief interventions, motivational interviewing, and how to best partner clients in their own treatment planning are highlighted in this chapter. In Chapter 3, "Come As You Are: Harm Reduction Therapy in Community Drop-In Centers," contributors Jeannie Little, LCSW, Perri Franskoviak, PhD, Jennifer Plummer, PhD, Jamie Lavender, LMFT, and Anna Berg, LCSW, introduce readers to the harm reduction model of addiction and the rewards and challenges of providing community mental health services with clients still actively participating in substance use. This chapter is followed by the case study, "Harm Reduction Groups: Meeting Drug Users Where They Are," contributed by Anna Berg and Jeannie Little, which provides readers with an intimate view of harm reduction interventions, successes, and the challenges of working with co-occurring disorders in group settings.

Chapter 4 explores the concept of therapist as advocate. "Working with the Queer Community: Advocacy as a Therapeutic Intervention," contributed by Danielle Castro and Melissa Fritchle, LMFT, shares the challenges and realities of working with and in the LBGTQ community. Issues of gender bias, sexual orientation, gender identity, and gender expression are defined and explored.

With a government-funding emphasis that favors early-childhood intervention and prevention care, understanding the challenges of children and school-based services is crucial to mental health training and education. School-based services and the challenges for children and families working within school systems are explored in Chapter 5, "Mental Health in Schools: Opportunities and Challenges." Linda Taylor, PhD, and Howard Adelman, PhD, outline opportunities for integrated care provision, preventative services, early intervention, support for chronic and severe issues, as well as opportunities for policy change in school-based services provision. We follow this chapter with a case study by Niki Berkowitz, LMFT, in which the realities of providing such services are explored.

Veteran care and working with posttraumatic stress disorder are emergent fields for master's level care providers. In Chapter 6, "Unleashing Creativity in Veterans," Beryl Brenner, RT/CAT, shares her 30 years of experience providing art-based services to the veterans' community.

Chapters 7 and 8 and their accompanying case studies address issues of working with mental health services in the justice system. Emily B. Gerber, PhD, Jennifer Leland, LMFT, and Karina Wong, MA, address multiple diagnostic issues and complex partnerships in providing comprehensive care with probationary youth. The challenges and rewards of multiple and interdisciplinary collaboration with clients, families, probation, community mental health, and child welfare are explored as well as the race against the clock to provide services before clients age out of the system. The case study "Working with Mandated Juveniles," contributed by Catherine Howland, LMFT, details the unique challenges of this special population. In Chapter 8, "Mental Health with Adult Offenders—Not Another Nurse Ratched: Why More Laughter Is Needed in Community Mental Health," Gardner Fair, LMFT, PhD, provides a glimpse into his work in adult correction and offers an antidote to the despair and frustration of working within the imprisoned adult community. The case study by Steve Podry, MA, CAGS, "A Second Cosmogony: The Image World in an Expressive Arts Prison Program," shares the power of art to provide solace and hope to mothers serving time in prison.

We understand that these eight chapters are but a sampling of issues and circumstances that are present in community mental health, but it is our hope that readers will find these ideas, techniques, and experiences applicable to a broad base of clients and services. We honor our clients and their journeys; they have and continue to be our greatest teachers.

Chapter 1

Sociocultural Realities of Community Mental Health

Rachel E. Seiler

The words on the cereal box taunted her as she leaned on it, filling out her intake paperwork. "Win the American Dream," the contest teased. Over a decade later, I can still close my eyes and find myself there again, amidst the cluttered chaos of the tiny living room—the material remnants of my first client's life. A social work intern on my inaugural home visit, I was struck with the irony that hung like a dense fog all around us; for Veronica and her children, the "American Dream" meant walking an uncertain road away from homelessness and domestic violence toward an equally uncertain future as residents of the supported housing agency where I had been placed for fieldwork.

Issues of oppression, race, and racism had always been part of my consciousness, yet even though I had grown up, and still lived and worked, in a minority neighborhood, these concerns were peripheral to my everyday life. During that home visit, what had previously been intangible became instantly palpable. My desire to relate and connect engulfed me, but I felt capable of only impotent empathy, questioning how I could truly empathize with Veronica's family because their struggles were, in my mind, so inextricably linked to the African American community's long and violent history of marginalization in our nation. This tension stung, sharply. As a middle-class woman possessed of the "power and privilege conferred by White skin" (Barlas et al., 2000a, p. 1) living within the contemporary American power structure and its inherent disparities that systematically replicate and pervade all social systems (Jackson, 2004), where "normal" and White are virtually synonymous and to be Other is "to be the object of the gaze" (Sartwell, 1998, p. 9), I was suddenly unsure of how to reconcile the dissonance I felt with the complex sociocultural realities of engaging in community-based work with diverse populations. In this formative moment of struggle, my professional interest in cultural competence began to seriously coalesce. In its piquant recounting, you get a first taste of some of the major themes of this chapter as it is concerned with what Lee (2008) describes as the *cross-cultural zone*—that charged space a counselor enters whenever his or her cultural background is significantly different from a client's— and the dynamic encounters that unfold there.

This chapter is not intended to be a comprehensive look at all of the sociocultural influences on and implications of community mental health. Rather, drawing on the literature of several related disciplines such as medicine, counseling, social work, and psychology, it addresses some of the direct service-level, social systems and justice issues that seem most relevant to the enterprise of therapy across difference and presents theoretical, conceptual, and practical content pertinent to trainees and counselors who will—or already do—practice within the cross-cultural zone. I use the terms *counselor, trainee, practitioner, professional,* and *provider* interchangeably in this chapter to reflect a varied professional team and readership.

WHY CULTURAL COMPETENCE?

Shifting Demographics

Some things have changed and others haven't since I was a social work graduate student at the turn of the 21st century. One thing that has changed is U.S. demographics. A conspicuous trend is the greater number of minorities in the United States; in 2006, the racial minority population exceeded 100 million and represented about a third of the overall U.S. population. Simultaneously, the White non-Hispanic percentage of the population has dropped (Schiele & Hopps, 2009). These demographic patterns are on track with the ones predicted in the *Time* magazine article, "Beyond the Melting Pot" (Henry, Mehta, Monroe, & Winbush, 1990) and kindle in some a fear of the so-called browning of America, a phrase popularized by that cover story of more than 20 years ago. Pricking the anxieties of White Americans used to thinking of themselves as the Rockwell-esque picture of what it means to be American, the article declared, "In San Jose bearers of the Vietnamese surname Nguyen outnumber the Joneses in the telephone directory 14 columns to eight" (p. 28). A fast-food eatery prophetically opened a microcosmic window on an increasingly diverse American future: "At the Sesame Hut restaurant in Houston, a Korean immigrant owner trains Hispanic immigrant workers to prepare Chinese-style food for a largely Black clientele" (p. 28). These trends and the apprehension they stir are particularly salient, given that in the United States, cultural diversity is still primarily associated with race and ethnicity (Fellin, 2000). Race and ethnicity are often imposed on individuals and groups as the primary basis for cultural identity (LeBeauf, Smaby, & Maddux, 2009), taking precedence over class and gender (Platt, 2002).

In our pluralistic society, culture must be understood more broadly. The diversity seen in contemporary society is reflected not only along racial and ethnic dimensions but is also evident in other aspects of culture such as socioeconomic status, religion and spirituality, sexual orientation, and ability status (Lee, 2008). We all occupy multiple, complex, and shifting social locations at once (Abrams & Gibson, 2007) and any discussion of counseling across difference must take into account these many variables.

Increasing Diversity as Rationale for Cultural Competence

According to Kim and Lyons (2003), the growing number of minorities in the United States during the past four decades has led to an increased attention to the unique needs of these individuals. Hays, Chang, and Havice (2008) wrote that the U.S. population is becoming increasingly heterogeneous with regard to race and ethnicity and highlighted the importance of multicultural competence and training for counseling trainees. Campinha-Bacote (2002) concurred, adding that the long-standing disparities in the health status of people from diverse backgrounds have challenged providers to consider cultural competence as a priority. Theoretical and empirical literature has highlighted the importance of the relationship between counselors' multicultural counseling competence and positive counseling outcomes (Kim & Lyons, 2003). Conversely, absence of skillful and appropriate cultural responsiveness can lead to misdiagnosis, lack of engagement and retention, and poor clinical outcomes (Delphin & Rowe, 2008).

Mental Health Is Ill Prepared for Diverse Clients

Unfortunately, something that hasn't changed since my days in social work school is mental health's general unpreparedness to serve diverse clients. In today's world, community-based providers are challenged to work with "individuals who are economically disadvantaged, who present with multiple basic needs, and who are diverse across the full spectrum of racial or ethnic heritage, gender, age, religious orientation, and housing status, among other dimensions of cultural identity" and must be able to "negotiate intra- and interpersonal cultural dynamics, norms and values to provide services that appropriately address the needs of all clients" (Delphin & Rowe, 2008, p. 182). Yet there is increasing evidence that counselors are unprepared to deal with diverse individuals whose values, attitudes, and lifestyles may be different from and possibly threatening to his or her own (Patterson, 1996). Members of ethnic minority groups are neither users nor providers of traditional psychotherapy in anything close to their proportion in the population (Patterson, 1996). For instance, African Americans account for approximately 25% of the mental health needs in the United States, but only about 2% of the nation's mental health counselors are Black (Gilbert, Harvey, & Belgrave, 2009). Sue et al. (2007) asserted that in the mental health professions, most graduates continue to be White. According to Chu-Lien Chao, Wei, Good, and Flores (2011), they are also disproportionately female—21% of counseling psychology trainees nationwide are men and 79% are women. Graduates also tend to be trained primarily in Euro-Western models of service delivery. As Griner and Smith (2006, p. 532) noted:

> Historically, counseling and psychotherapy have focused predominantly on the therapeutic needs of upper and middle-class European Americans. The pervasive influence of Western values in psychotherapy and the widespread ignorance among psychotherapists regarding others' cultures have not helped to foster trust in mental health services among clients of color.

Indeed, the majority of Anglo-American providers have neither the training nor the experience required for cultural competence (Dana, 1994). What Proctor and Davis (1996) pointed out 15 years ago holds true today: Despite their growth in number, people of color still tend to be segregated from Whites and from mainstream America. Living separately keeps different peoples from knowing and understanding each other; in turn, it may breed distrust. Whites, in particular, know little about the social realities of people of color, and many White practitioners have scant meaningful contact with minorities before seeing them as clients. Additionally, White clinicians receive minimal or no practicum or supervision experiences that address issues of diversity (Sue et al., 2007). Without such exposure, the People's Institute Executive Director Ron Chisom, an Undoing Racism facilitator since the 1970s, asserts that well-intended practitioners can do more harm than good. "They come in the community and they're clueless." They have university training, but some of the universities, Chisom charges, are "racist to the core" (Jackson, 2004, p. 11).

Disparities and Barriers

Minority group clients continue to face barriers to care, receive unequal and subpar mental health services, and experience poor outcomes. In general, minorities experience a higher proportion of poverty and social stressors typically seen as antecedents of psychiatric and psychological disorders than Whites. Yet minority groups are often underserved by high-quality mental health resources (Patterson, 1996). Research suggests that minority groups tend to underutilize mental health services provided by the majority culture (Schnall, 2006), seek therapy only when their problems have become severe (Griner & Smith, 2006), and prematurely terminate from counseling (Kim & Lyons, 2003).

WORKING WITH THE "CULTURAL CLIENT"

Given these realities, Lee (2008) poses salient questions: What are the elements of culture in counseling? What is the nature of culturally competent counseling in the 21st century? As the previous section demonstrates, there is no question that the changing U.S. demographics and historical disparities in the health and mental health status of diverse people have triggered a clarion call from across a broad swath of the helping professions for cultural competence. What's less clear is how cultural competence is to be defined and used in the training of practitioners and the provision of services to clients. The next section explores the meanings and ambiguities of the term and compares and contrasts the concepts of cultural competence and cultural humility.

CULTURAL COMPETENCE

In its traditional sense, cultural competence is seen as containing the three basic elements of cultural awareness, cultural-specific knowledge, and skills (Abrams & Gibson, 2007). According to Delphin and Rowe (2008, p. 183), cultural competence entails the following:

Knowledge and information from and about individuals and groups that is integrated and transformed into clinical standards, skills, service approaches, techniques, and marketing programs that match the cultural experiences and traditions of clients and that increase both the quality and appropriateness of health care services and outcomes.

The main thrust of cultural competence training is to provide skills for effective cross-cultural practice by increasing trainees' self-awareness, encouraging self-reflection, and introducing teaching content about diverse groups (Abrams & Gibson, 2007).

Cultural groups are seen as having unique characteristics and particular needs that are supported by service delivery systems designed expressly for multicultural clients (Fellin, 2000). LeBeauf et al. (2009) call for the counseling profession not only to recognize multicultural and diversity issues but to develop systematic and practical approaches for helping counselors address and adapt counseling practices with culturally diverse clients. For instance, Schnall (2006) suggested using a team approach, with at least one member having expertise in the client's culture, or the client might invite a chaperone who would act as the "cultural bridge." Jackson and Samuels (2011) endorsed changing intake or assessment forms and one's language to allow clients to culturally identify (or not) in multiple, more open-ended ways. Many other recommendations, both general and specific, have been made for culturally competent practice; this section reviews some of them.

First Impressions Count

Reports that the influence of race is waning have been greatly exaggerated. The bottom line is that in American society, "race continues to be a significant social fact" (Fellin, 2000). Race has marked—sometimes volatile—effects on relationships, both in society at large and in professional practice (Proctor & Davis, 1996). In cross-racial helping, the professional faces a formidable challenge; the development of a relationship qualitatively different than either party may have previously experienced with a racially dissimilar other. For effective therapy to occur, a positive coalition must form (McDowell & Garcia, 2006). Proctor and Davis (1996) wrote that respect and professional courtesy are particularly important when forming a therapeutic alliance with minority clients, to whom society frequently gives less. In fact, racial similarity between counselor and client may actually be less important than the practitioner's level of skill in using trustworthy behaviors. Studies suggest that initial encounters have the greatest effect on the development of rapport and continued interaction. Signals of goodwill can be conveyed in several commonsense ways, such as greeting the client warmly, removing physical barriers that inhibit communication, appearing unhurried, and displaying appropriate eye contact (Proctor & Davis, 1996).

Assessment

Campinha-Bacote (2002, p. 182) defined *cultural assessment* as a "systematic appraisal or examination of individuals, groups, and communities as to their cultural beliefs, values, and practices to determine explicit needs and intervention practices within the context of the people being served." Hallmarks of culturally competent assessment also include the use of client's first language and familiarity with various culture-specific assessment tools, such as the *culturagram* (Congress, 2004).

Cultural Knowledge and Practice Modalities

According to Johnson and Munch (2009), counselors should develop specialized knowledge about the history, traditions, values, family systems, and other factors relevant to major client groups served, suggesting that these characteristics (often described as contrasting with those of Euro-Western Americans), if known before meeting the client, would enhance the helping relationship and that counselors should use techniques that "fit" these presumed characteristics (Patterson, 1996). Some traditional approaches have received wide support for diverse clients. On the other hand, many scholars have advocated that such treatments be modified to better match clients' cultural contexts (Griner & Smith, 2006). According to this perspective, problems experienced by minority groups cannot be effectively addressed by relying on practice models emerging from work with non-Hispanic White populations alone (Schiele & Hopps, 2009).

In their meta-analytic review of 76 studies of culturally adapted interventions, Griner and Smith (2006) found that scholars emphasize the need to explicitly incorporate the cultural values of the client into therapy. For instance, African American clients are more likely to remain in treatment when interventions are based on Afrocentric values (e.g., the JEMADARI Program based on a Swahili word meaning "wise companion" for African American men; Gilbert et al., 2009). Other frequently mentioned cultural adaptations included matching clients with therapists of the same race or ethnicity who speak the same native language, outreach to underserved clients, provision of services such as child care designed to increase client retention, and cultural sensitivity training for staff (Griner & Smith, 2006).

Interactional Style

According to Schnall (2006), the clinician and client may have different ideas about the appropriate amount of interpersonal space. They may also be accustomed to using different body movements or facial expressions. For instance, Sharma and Kerl (2002) cautioned that when patients nod in agreement with treatment recommendations then do not follow them, professionals may perceive this behavior as passive-aggressive, not understanding that open disagreement may be culturally prohibitive. LeBeauf et al. (2009) noted that it is important to assess minority clients' level of acculturation. For example, if the level of acculturation is minimal (e.g., immigrants, Native Americans with strong tribal ties), persistent eye contact and direct questioning may be perceived as impolite or even invasive and authoritative. Such clients may prefer circular questioning, analogies, stories related to the issues or problems of concern, and the use of silence. Work with second and third generations of immigrants may require different types of cultural considerations than with first generation (Graham, Bradshaw, & Trew, 2010).

Clients from minority groups are sometimes seen as dependent and desirous of a structured relationship in which the mental health practitioner, as an expert, gives advice and solutions to problems (Patterson, 2004). For example, Schnall (2006, p. 279) wrote that Orthodox Jewish clients have likely discussed a variety of issues with their rabbis, who often supply a *teshuva*, or "response," to a posed *she'ela*, or "question." Such clients may expect counseling to be directive.

Sex, Sexual Orientation, and Gender Roles

Graham et al. (2010, p. 341) wrote that gender is "an important construct in literature related to anti-oppressive and culturally appropriate practice." The more specific a culture is about interactions, beliefs, values, and the like, the more well-defined gender and social roles an individual may have. These roles influence how men and women interact within the family. Families from cultures with a male-dominant hierarchical family structure may encounter conflict in American society, which tends toward more egalitarian gender relationships (Congress, 2004). It is important for clinicians to understand these gender roles and recognize how they can influence an individual's circumstances; interventions that require individuals to operate outside of traditional roles may not be effective. The distinctive communication styles characteristic of each gender should be considered. For instance, females may prefer a conversational style of counseling that allows them to express more personal and emotional feelings. In contrast, males may struggle to identify their emotions (LeBeauf et al., 2009).

Issues of sexual orientation are often overlooked in counseling. LeBeauf et al. (2009) suggested that to be effective in the therapeutic setting with lesbian, gay, bisexual, or transgendered (LGBT) clients, the counselor must consistently communicate genuine empathy and support. Culturally competent counselors should recognize that the mental health problems manifested by members of the LGBT community may not be due to LGBT identity itself. Counselors should also consider the dual discrimination of members of the LGBT community who are also members of other minority groups.

Religion and Spirituality

The cultural diversity literature largely ignores the effects of religion on counseling and psychotherapy (Schnall, 2006). According to Lee (2008), the psychospiritual realm of personality is also often overlooked as a source of empowerment. Spirituality refers to individuals' beliefs, values, practices, and meaning-making processes that indicate a connection with something greater than oneself as opposed to adherence to a specific religious doctrine or paradigm (O'Brien & Curry, 2010). Spirituality and religion are critical components to the well-being and holistic health of many people; approximately 84% of Americans self-identify as being religious or spiritual (O'Brien & Curry, 2010). In many cultural contexts, there is little distinction between religious/spiritual and secular life. For instance, some Muslim clients "adhere strongly and feel bound to Islamic guidelines; their lives are governed by the *shari'a*, or God's teachings" (Graham et al., 2010, p. 340). Therefore, it is imperative that counselors explore their personal experiences and worldview regarding spiritual and religious beliefs and develop tools to examine, analyze, and plan interventions utilizing them as strength-based tools (O'Brien & Curry, 2010).

According to Schnall (2006) mental health workers can liaise with clergy and other faith leaders; this contact will garner credibility and legitimacy. Consultation with religious authorities can prevent clinicians from suggesting activities that conflict with clients' religious views. For example, rabbinic dispensation may aid in meeting the mental health needs of the client, as in the case of a patient who refused to take medication on Jewish fast days. Clergy can also assist in determining whether a client's behavior is within normative religious bounds or is symptomatic of disorder.

It may also be advisable to frame therapeutic ideas in religious terms; some clinicians have actually incorporated religious ritual into therapy (Schnall, 2006). Careful consideration and restraint is due here because volatile and complex issues can emerge from the appropriation or misappropriation of other culture's traditions as alternative sources of knowledge and spirituality in therapy, as Donaldson (2005) cautioned in her discussion of NANA—New Age Native Americanism.

LINGUISTIC COMPETENCE

Outreach, Translation, and Interpretation

Cultural competency involves linguistically appropriate outreach. Agency literature and online content should be translated into the languages most spoken within the community (Keswick & McNeil, 2006). Cultural encounters also involve an assessment of clients' linguistic needs (Campinha-Bacote, 2002). As Dana (1994) noted, language issues trigger ethical considerations, because competent services often cannot be provided in client or provider second languages. This problem is exacerbated by use of translators who speak the language but do not share the culture, resulting in different shades of meaning.

Sharma and Kerl (2002) asserted that the ideal situation is for the clinician to be bilingual, but failing that, Campinha-Bacote (2002) suggested that using a formally trained interpreter may be necessary. The use of untrained interpreters, friends, or family members may pose a problem for many reasons, including their lack of clinical knowledge. Problems with using family as translators can occur even with adult children; clear communication between clinicians and clients can be impaired by the unique relationships and issues that occur between parents and children regardless of age (Sharma & Kerl, 2002).

Caple, Salcido, and di Cecco (1996) explained that there are two contrasting interpretive approaches. In the verbatim style (or instantaneous interpretation) words are translated as closely as possible, and the interpreter's participation in the session's content is minimal. With independent intervention, on the other hand, the interpreter is a cultural bridge enabling the therapist to understand the client's behavior, body language, and perceptions. Interpretation can be most cumbersome when cultural and linguistic differences are greatest. Body language is not universal; it may in fact convey quite different meanings in various cultures and is one of the factors that can contribute to confusion in the interpretation process.

To increase the odds that interpretation will be effective, the practitioner can partner with the interpreter to plan for and debrief the interview. Both must understand the purpose and focus of the contact and agree on the style of interpretation to be used. After the interview, the interpreter may be able to provide subtle information about the client relating to affect, mood, or emotion that may not have emerged during the interpretation process (Caple et al., 1996).

Deaf or Hard-of-Hearing Clients

Sloss Luey, Glass, and Elliot (1996) clarified that *Deaf* means culturally deaf whereas *deaf* refers to an audiological condition or absence of hearing. People in the Deaf community tend to view deafness not as a disability but as a different human experience and alternative culture. Those who become deaf may grieve their loss of hearing and access to spoken communication. The first priority in working with deaf or hard-of-hearing clients is to establish a means of communication. Although speech and writing will almost always be in the person's native spoken language, manual communication has many forms. Some sign systems are manual representations of English. American Sign Language (ASL), in contrast, is a distinct and complete language and the native language of Deaf Americans. Deaf people from other countries may use different sign language and would need a qualified interpreter who knows sign systems other than ASL.

Because most people with hearing impairment are not culturally Deaf, clients with hearing loss will often have a good command of English or the spoken language of their culture. If the client speech-reads, the practitioner can find a quiet, well-lit place to meet and should face the client; speak slowly and clearly, rephrase anything the client misunderstands, and offer to write down key information. Writing is not an adequate accommodation for deaf clients who prefer ASL. Professional interpreters for the deaf are able to use both signed English and ASL and to select the language best suited to the individual and situation (Sloss Luey et al., 1996).

Culturally Nuanced Language

Clients in cross-racial treatment settings often express the concern that the helper does not understand their social reality. A basic part of the failure to understand the client's social reality is a lack of understanding of what various expressions and terms mean to him or her, including slang. Misunderstanding such nuances across racial differences is part of the continuing legacy of segregation. Counselors should immediately acknowledge any difficulties in this regard; this sends the message that the counselor is truly listening and trying to understand (Proctor & Davis, 1996).

TENSIONS AT THE CORE OF CULTURAL COMPETENCE

Clients want a helping relationship in which they feel understood, in which they trust their counselors, and in which they have confidence in the counselor's ability (Proctor & Davis, 1996). Are culture-specific knowledge and approaches required to do that, or must the professional—as Proctor and Davis (1996) recommended—establish credibility through words and actions and address and move beyond the client's diversity-related concerns? Despite calls for "culturally sensitive," "culturally relevant," and "culturally appropriate" techniques (Patterson, 1996, p. 230) that classify clients into groups, each requiring different counseling treatments, and the empirical evidence supporting culturally adapted approaches (Griner & Smith, 2006), cultural competence as it is traditionally conceptualized faces challenges on several fronts.

Knowing a Client's Culture in Advance Is Impossible

No mental health counselor can be prepared in advance to counsel every possible client (Patterson, 2004). As Congress (2004) noted, the myriad diversity of clients' backgrounds, especially in urban areas like the New York City borough of Queens where, in one zip code, families from well over 100 nations are present, makes the prospect of teaching specific characteristics of different populations quite daunting. Moreover, cultural groups are not pure and discrete but overlapping (Patterson, 2004). People do not belong to just one group, but to many. The concept of *intersectionality* refers to the interrelationships among race, ethnicity, and other identities (Johnson & Munch, 2009, p. 226). Only the client can legitimately inform us as to the impact of intersectionality on his or her life. Within each person there resides an almost infinite set of combinations of characteristics. The more multidimensional the counselor tries to make this picture, with the inclusion of the specific challenge or need about which the client requests her or his involvement, the lower the chance of knowing the client's culture in advance. Patterson (2004) posits that attempting to develop different theories, methods, and techniques for each client's infinite cultural permutations would be an insurmountable task.

Overgeneralization and Stereotyping

Descriptions of various groups are generalizations, describing a model person and minimizing the existence of wide differences within groups (Patterson, 1996). Congress (2004, p. 251) wrote that considering a family only in terms of a generic cultural identity, for instance, may lead to overgeneralization and stereotyping. For example, an undocumented Mexican family that recently immigrated to the United States may access and use mental health care very differently from a Puerto Rican family that has lived here for decades. Yet both families are Hispanic. Johnson and Munch (2009) asserted that the tendency to generalize is especially troubling because it frequently entails reducing the rich world of cultural variation to a small number of overly inclusive categories (e.g., "Asian," "Hispanic," "Native American," "African American") that are then contrasted with Eurocentric cultures. This is problematic because differences between groups are not so neatly bifurcated.

Overemphasis on Difference

Patterson (1996) critiqued what he described as the faulty assumption that differences are more important than similarities, writing that all clients are alike in one basic essential: They are all human beings. Surveys of the ethnographic literature show that although differences certainly exist, the peoples of the world share an astonishingly detailed universal psychology. Johnson and Munch (2009) suggested that viewing differences as paramount may have the unintended consequence of distancing the connection between client and counselor, and Fellin (2000) asserted that identification and separation into culturally distinct groups that are treated as "different" does not represent acceptance; it is segregation that leads to injustice. Tension arises when we try to give either the universal or the particular precedence over the other; the former is open to the charge of color blindness.

JOURNEY, NOT DESTINATION

Campinha-Bacote (2002) described cultural competence as the process in which the provider continuously strives to achieve the ability to work effectively within the cultural context of the client. This is an ongoing process, not an event. Tervalon and Murray-García (1998) envision cultural competence as being best defined not by a discrete endpoint but as a commitment and active engagement in a lifelong endeavor. Models of cultural competence that involve a progression in stages from not knowing to knowing suggest a linear development that is open to evaluation. Although instruments measuring cultural competence have been developed, such as the Sex-Role Egalitarianism Scale (SRES) and the Multicultural Counseling Knowledge and Awareness Scale (MCKAS; Chu-Lien Chao et al., 2011), Johnson and Munch (2009) questioned whether the attainment of cultural competence could ever be determined. From this perspective, cultural competence is less of "an easily demonstrable mastery of a finite body of knowledge, an endpoint evidenced largely by comparative quantifiable assessments" (Tervalon & Murray-García, 1998, p. 18) and more of a lifelong personal and professional journey (Delphin & Rowe, 2008).

Person-Centered Generic Practice

Culturally competent practice is, in many respects, simply good practice. For instance, Johnson and Munch (2009) discussed a paper on cultural competence as it relates to Native Americans that concluded that skills for culturally competent work with Native Americans are not radically different from those generally required for practice. In a 2007 study of 186 client and professional views on what cultural competence entails, client responses mostly described generic practice—for example, respect for the individual and prompt service. This suggests an experiential-phenomenological model for culturally competent multicultural practice that is generic; it requires practitioners to situate themselves as learners rather than experts, deemphasizes practitioners' assumptions and previous knowledge, and stipulates full participation of the client in interventions (Graham et al., 2010). Patterson (1996) insisted that such a universal system is not one size fits all but a basis for becoming capable of working with a wide variety of clients—colloquially, for understanding "where the client is coming from."

Patterson (1996, p. 234) sensed a change in the literature on counseling across difference "that could portend a return to recognition of the basic nature of counseling as an interpersonal relationship" based on warmth, genuineness, and empathy. He encourages counselors to

> search for a framework that recognizes the complex diversity of a plural society and at the same time suggests bridges of shared concern that bind culturally different persons to one another . . . that includes the universal and the specific in therapy. The universal is the process, and the specific deals with the content in therapy. (Patterson, 1996, p. 235)

CULTURAL HUMILITY OR ATTUNEMENT

As Tervalon and Murray-García (1998) suggested, these outcomes are perhaps better described as *cultural humility*. Jackson and Samuels (2011, p. 237) used a related term—*cultural attunement*—to counter the "problematic meaning of cultural competence as a potentially presumptuous or oversimplistic professional goal." These concepts emphasize that the knowledge and skill required in practice are intimately linked to the cultural standpoints of others; this requires awareness and acknowledgment of individual and group-based experiences of difference and oppression. The practitioner must be perceptive and make adjustments that account for a client's intersecting identities that shape unique experiences of race and culture (Jackson & Samuels, 2011).

Cultural attunement requires vigilance, humility, and informed critical self-awareness over the course of one's professional development and during one's interactions with clients. It requires practice wisdom that draws from the client's unique cultural experience while also using an empirically, historically, and professionally derived knowledge base. This level of self-awareness must acknowledge that many of our conceptions of racial identity are embedded in dominant and often flawed legacies (Jackson & Samuels 2011). From this point forward, when I use the term *cultural competence,* I am actually referring to the practice of therapy across difference that embodies the best of both cultural competence and cultural humility or attunement.

Not Color-Blindness

Cultural humility should not be equated with the ignorance of global history and current conditions and mechanisms of oppression (Johnson & Munch, 2009) or denial of the social significance regarding race and racism in the United States today (Chu-Lien Chao et al., 2011) that accompanies *color blindness*. Sue et al. (2007) stated that color blindness denies the reality of people of color and lets White people claim that they are not prejudiced. It is a racially biased framework that individuals, groups, and systems consciously or unconsciously use to justify the status quo or minimize inequalities (Chu-Lien Chao et al., 2011). Studies have demonstrated that counseling trainees with higher levels of color-blindness not only score lower on self-reported multicultural knowledge but also potentially distort diagnoses of minority clients (Chu-Lien Chao et al., 2011). Color-blind practice is escapist; the color-blind professional is excused from confronting racial injustice.

Barlas et al. (2000a) equated color-blindness with *power evasiveness*, a discourse many well-intentioned White people in the United States engage in that overemphasizes all people's essential sameness. Barlas et al. assert that such color-blindness from the summit of White privilege perpetuates racism and systems of domination. This notion offers an ideal segue to the discussion of power and privilege within the multicultural therapeutic relationship.

POWER AND PRIVILEGE

Unlearning Racism and Confronting Privilege

Discussing diversity and multiculturalism without a critique of power structures and privilege reinforces the status quo. Abrams and Gibson (2007) asserted that unlearning racism is a long-term process that involves undoing years of socialization and internalized ideologies of racial superiority. Barlas et al. (2000a) described *White supremacist consciousness* as a way of thinking that takes for granted the superiority of White norms and values. That this consciousness is often invisible to those who hold it strengthens it as a force for hegemony while permitting White individuals to deny how White privilege benefits their own lives. People of color, on the other hand, cannot avoid seeing, experiencing, and living the manifestations of White privilege and are, therefore, more aware of its existence and consequences (Abrams & Gibson, 2007). Liu, Pickett, and Ivey (2007) defined privilege as "a special right, benefit, or advantage given to a person, not from work or merit, but by reason of race, social position, religion, or gender." They continued:

Privilege is usually unconscious and invisible to the individual graced with it, and privilege is exercised unknowingly and assumed to be a natural right. We believe that privilege arises from situations and environments wherein one's social identities (i.e., religious, race, social class) are considered normative and therefore not questioned by peers, family, or society. Over time, the individual's insulated worldview is assumed by the individual to be normative, universal, and ubiquitous, and those not subscribing to the privileged person's worldview are considered deviant.

Different, intersecting forms of privilege have an impact on the counseling relationship; these include class privilege, able-bodied privilege, male privilege, and heterosexual privilege (Niehuis, 2005); privileges due to race (Delphin & Rowe, 2008); Judeo-Christian privilege (Liu et al., 2007); and so on.

Schiele and Hopps (2009) asserted that White privilege is not only alive but thriving, and because much of counseling is suffused with White middle-class biases and worldviews and counselors are trained in this milieu, it is likely that counselors will adopt a similar worldview. Because the assumptions that counselors carry into counseling may influence the therapeutic relationship, diagnosis, and treatment (Liu et al., 2007), White middle-class bias and privilege are particularly relevant issues for practitioners of community mental health. Hays et al. (2008) wrote that counselors who examine their privilege and the active role it plays in the therapeutic relationship are less likely to rely on stereotypes and impose their own ethnocentric values. They are also more likely to view problems of minority clientele from a systemic perspective, to seek more personal knowledge from the client, and to recognize and reduce the influence of power dynamics in the therapeutic relationship.

That White privilege awareness is an important construct to process in counselor preparation should seem obvious, yet although young White people are taught not to be "prejudiced," Whites are not necessarily challenged to understand or accept the manifestations of their unearned privileges. Abrams and Gibson (2007) cautioned students against having "empathy" for the plight of people of color rather than having an actual vision of reframing White privilege. Hays, Chang, and Dean (2004) wrote that White counselors' awareness of their personal privilege derived from acknowledging oppressive beliefs and attitudes as well as how they may have benefited from those attitudes could be an important step toward multicultural competency. It takes purposeful effort to develop such awareness. Instruments such as the White Privilege Scale based on the list of privileges in Peggy McIntosh's seminal piece, "White Privilege: Unpacking the Invisible Knapsack" (Abrams & Gibson, 2007), and the White Racial Identity Attitude Scale (WRIAS) can be used to assesses individuals' attitudes about privilege and their race in relationship to their attitudes about people of color.

This is a salient developmental process for Whites, characterized by complex and emotional self-discovery (Abrams & Gibson, 2007). Whites may need a critical event or experience to help them recognize how race operates in their own lives (Barlas et al., 2000a), something on par with Mezirow's (2000) concept of the *disorienting dilemma* that prompts self-examination, resulting in a critical assessment of assumptions and ultimately a reintegration into one's life based on conditions dictated by one's new perspective.

Focusing not on White supremacy in others or in society but in oneself can be challenging, to say the least. Even counselors with a strong personal commitment to uncovering racism must go through a process of interrogating their own racism and privilege, and changes in behavior must follow changes in perception. Depending on their level of awareness, White counselors report anger, guilt, confusion, defensiveness, sadness, and a sense of responsibility and need for advocacy when discussing these topics (Hays et al., 2004).

TRAINING AND SUPERVISION

According to Delphin and Rowe (2008), multicultural training is associated with increased interracial comfort, increased ability to conceptualize a culturally diverse client's mental health issues, and more positive ratings of counselor competence. Continuing education in cultural competence is a key strategy in enhancing provider effectiveness in working with diverse clients. Experiential learning may be particularly useful in facilitating personal reflection, cultural empathy, and increased awareness of one's own worldview and cultural experiences (Delphin & Rowe, 2008). Some popular methods include the use of film (Kim & Lyons, 2003), books, personal stories (Abrams & Gibson, 2007), and music (Tasker, 1999) as a means of helping learners come into contact with and enter the world of the Other.

McBride (2003) stated that encounter with the Other is necessary to produce in us what Martin Luther King Jr. called *creative tension* that unsettledness that leads to awareness and actions of which the goals are peace, justice, and reconciliation. Because many counselors lack direct, authentic experience with minorities, training needs to happen in the diverse communities where counselors will eventually practice (Tervalon & Murray-García, 1998). Patterson (2004) actually encouraged mental health counselors to live in a community of the kind of clients they expect to work with; at minimum, a lengthy internship is necessary.

As Sue et al. (2007) pointed out, mental health training programs must support trainees in overcoming their fears and resistance to talking about difference by fostering safe and productive learning environments that are structured and facilitated in a manner that promotes inquiry and allows trainees to experience discomfort and vulnerability. Supervision may be sought from a culturally dissimilar supervisor as a means of confronting one's own White supremacist consciousness (Barlas et al., 2000b).

Trainees and practitioners alike can be supported to be compassionate with themselves in the face of their own bias and prejudice. Barlas et al. (2000a) found *cooperative inquiry* to be a viable strategy for helping people with power and privilege expand personal consciousness of their privilege and its impact on their lives; it supported the participants in their study to face and transform rather than repress their feelings of shame or distrust regarding White supremacist consciousness, making them sources for learning that in turn prompt changes in behavior through reflection-in-action.

Both White and racial/ethnic minority trainees are involved in multicultural counseling in which their own backgrounds are crucially relevant to interactions with clients. Chu-Lien Chao et al. (2011) emphasized the caveat that whereas multicultural training significantly enhances multicultural awareness for White trainees, for racial/ethnic minority trainees, multicultural awareness remains at similar levels regardless of the multicultural training levels. Present training tends to emphasize helping White trainees improve their counseling of clients of color; counseling psychology programs need to address the training needs of racial/ethnic trainees who may be benefiting less from it.

PARTING ADVICE FOR THE CULTURALLY COMPETENT PRACTITIONER

These closing recommendations are intended to support you, the community mental health practitioner, in your journey toward cultural competence in its most expansive sense: Have the courage to not know, to not always have to be the expert. Remain committed to the tension that diversity can create, knowing that the dynamics of difference often demand being comfortable with that which is uncomfortable (Abrams & Gibson, 2007). Be willing to really look at yourself and your blind spots and develop awareness of your own sociocultural self, including a critical awareness of the social locations you inhabit as well as your culturally situated assumptions, values, and beliefs in relationship to those you serve (McDowell & Garcia, 2006). Remain alert to the implications of oppression, racism, privilege, and the political climate regarding issues such as immigration, poverty, and welfare that may be affecting the psychological welfare of your clients (Delphin & Rowe, 2008).

Work on cultivating personal qualities that may transcend culture: respect, genuineness, empathic understanding, and the ability to demonstrate these to the client. Strive to convey unconditional positive regard and seek to understand the problem from the client's perspective, with the goal of arriving at an individual solution (Patterson, 2004). Try to embody the all-important traits of "comfort, humor, humanity" (Jackson, 2004, p. 8).

Eschew *cultural imposition*, "the tendency of an individual to impose their beliefs, values, and patterns of behavior on another culture." Instead, endeavor to expresses *cultural desire*, "the motivation of the health care provider to *want* to, rather than *have* to, engage in the process of becoming culturally aware, culturally knowledgeable, culturally skillful, and familiar with cultural encounters" (Campinha-Bacote, 2002, p. 182). Finally, remember: When it comes to culturally competent practice, "one size does not fit all" (Delphin & Rowe 2008, p. 189).

REFERENCES

Abrams, L. S., & Gibson, P. (2007). Reframing multicultural education: Teaching White privilege in the social work curriculum. *Journal of Social Work Education, 43*, (1).

Barlas, C., Kasl, E., Kyle, R., MacLeod, A., Paxton, D., Rosenwasser, P., & Sartor, L. (2000a, October 26–28). Cooperative inquiry as a strategy for facilitating perspective transformation. In C. Weissner, S. Meyer, & D. Fuller (Eds.), *Challenges of practice:*

Transformative learning in action: 3rd international transformative learning conference proceedings (pp. 51–56). Teachers College, Columbia University, New York.

Barlas, C., Kasl, E., Kyle, R., MacLeod, A., Paxton, D., Rosenwasser, P., & Sartor, L. (2000b, June 2–4). Learning to unlearn White supremacist consciousness. In T. Sork, V. Lee-Chapman, & R. St. Clair (Eds.), *Proceedings of the 41st annual adult education research conference* (pp. 26–30). University of British Columbia, Vancouver, Canada.

Campinha-Bacote, J. (2002). The process of cultural competence in the delivery of healthcare services: A model of care. *Journal of Transcultural Nursing, 12,* 181–184.

Caple, F. S., Salcido, R. M., & di Cecco J. (1996). Engaging effectively with culturally diverse families and children. In P. L. Ewalt, E. M. Freeman, S. A. Kirk, & D. K. Inouye (Eds.), *Multicultural issues in social work* (pp. 366–381). Washington, DC: NASW Press.

Chu-Lien Chao, R., Wei, M., Good, G. E., & Flores, L. Y. (2011). Race/ethnicity, color-blind attitudes, and multicultural counseling competence: The moderating effects of multicultural counseling training. *Journal of Counseling Psychology, 58* (1).

Congress, E. P. (2004). Cultural and ethical issues in working with culturally diverse patients and their families: The use of the culturagram to promote cultural competent practice in health care settings. In A. Metten, T. Kroger, P. L. Ranhalon, & A. Pohjola (Eds.), *Social work visions from around the globe: Citizens, methods, and approaches* (pp. 249–262). New York, NY: The Haworth Social Work Practice Press.

Dana, R. H. (1994). Testing and assessment ethics for all persons: Beginning and agenda. *Professional Psychology: Research and Practice, 25* (4).

Delphin, M. E., & Rowe, M. (2008). Continuing education in cultural competence for community mental health practitioners. *Professional Psychology: Research and Practice, 39,* 182–191.

Donaldson, L. E. (2001). On medicine women and White shame-ens: New age Native Americanism and commodity fetishism as pop culture feminism. In E. Castelli (Ed.), *Women, gender, religion: A reader* (pp. 237–253). New York: Palgrave.

Fellin, P. (2000). Revisiting multiculturalism in social work. *Journal of Social Work Education, 36.*

Gilbert, D. J., Harvey, A. R., & Belgrave, F. Z. (2009). Advancing the Africentric paradigm shift discourse: Building toward evidence-based Africentric interventions in social work practice with African Americans. *Social Work, 54,* 243–252.

Graham, J. R., Bradshaw, C., & Trew, J. L. (2010). Cultural considerations for social service agencies working with Muslim clients. *Social Work, 55,* 337–346.

Griner, D., & Smith, T. B. (2006). Culturally adapted mental health interventions: A meta-analytic review. *Psychotherapy: Theory, Research, Practice, Training, 43,* 531–548.

Hays, D. G., Chang, C. Y., & Dean, J. K. (2004). White counselors' conceptualization of privilege and oppression: Implications for counselor training. *Counselor Education and Supervision, 43.*

Hays, D. G., Chang, C. Y., & Havice, P. (2008). White racial identity statuses as predictors of white privilege awareness. *Journal of Humanistic Counseling, Education and Development, 47.*

Henry, W. A., Mehta, N. S., Monroe, S., & Winbush, D. (1990, April 9). Beyond the melting pot. *Time, 135,* pp. 28–32.

Jackson, K. (2004, February). Undoing racism. *Social Work Today,* pp. 8–12.

Jackson, K. F., & Samuels, G. M. (2011). Multiracial competence in social work: Recommendations for culturally attuned work with multiracial people. *Social Work, 56,* 235–245.

Johnson, Y. M., & Munch, S. (2009). Fundamental contradictions in cultural competence. *Social Work, 54,* 220–231.

Keswick, R. R., & McNeil, L. G. (2006). Reaching out to the Arabic community: A CMHC takes steps to better reach and serve Arab-Americans. *Behavioral Healthcare, 26,* 32.

Kim, B. S. K., & Lyons, H. Z. (2003). Experiential activities and multicultural counseling competence training. *Journal of Counseling and Development, 81.*

LeBeauf, I. M., Smaby, M., & Maddux, C. (2009). Adapting counseling skills for multicultural and diverse clients. In G. R. Walz, J. C. Bleuer, & R. K. Yep (Eds.), *Compelling counseling interventions* (pp. 33–42). Alexandria, VA: American Counseling Association.

Lee, C. C. (2008). Elements of culturally competent counseling. *American Counseling Association Professional Counseling Digest, 24.*

Liu, W. M., Pickett, T., Jr. & Ivey, A. E. (2007). White middle-class privilege: Social class bias and implications for training and practice. *Journal of Multicultural Counseling and Development, 35.*

McBride, J. M. (2003). Living the question: Privilege, poverty, and faith. In R. J. Whiteley & B. Maynard (Eds.), *Get up off your knees: Preaching the U2 catalog* (pp. 69–74). Cambridge: Cowley.

McDowell, T., & García, M. (2006). Review of *Voices of color: First person narratives of ethnic minority therapists. Journal of Comparative Family Studies, 37.*

Mezirow, J. (2000). Learning to think like an adult: Core concepts of transformation theory. In J. Mezirow (Ed.), *Learning as transformation: Critical perspectives on a theory in progress* (pp. 3–34). San Francisco, CA: Jossey-Bass.

Niehuis, S. (2005). Helping white students explore white privilege outside the classroom. *North American Journal of Psychology, 7.*

O'Brien, E. R., & Curry, J. R. (2010). Preparing emergent counselors to work with spiritually diverse clients: Implications for supervision. *American Counseling Association Professional Counseling Digest, 30.*

Patterson, C. H. (1996). Multicultural counseling: From diversity to universality. *Journal of Counseling and Development, 74,* 227–231.

Patterson, C. H. (2004). Do we need multicultural competencies? *Journal of Mental Health Counseling, 26,* 67–73.

Platt, T. (2002). Desegregating multiculturalism: Problems in the theory and pedagogy of diversity education. *Social Justice, 29,* (4).

Proctor, E. K., & Davis, L. E. (1996). The challenge of racial difference: Skills for clinical practice. In P. L. Ewalt, E. M. Freeman, S. A. Kirk, & Inouye, D. K. (Eds.), *Multicultural issues in social work* (pp. 97–114). Washington, DC: NASW Press.

Sartwell, C. (1998). *Act like you know: African American autobiography and White identity.* Chicago: University of Chicago Press.

Schiele, J. H., & Hopps, J. G. (2009). Racial minorities then and now: The continuing significance of race. *Social Work, 54,* 195–199.

Schnall, E. (2006, summer). Multicultural counseling and the Orthodox Jew. *Journal of Counseling and Development, 84,* 282–286.

Sharma, P., & Kerl, S. B. (2002). Suggestions for psychologists working with Mexican American individuals and families in health care settings. *Rehabilitation Psychology, 47.*

Sloss Luey, H., Glass, L., & Elliott, H. (1996). Hard-of-hearing or deaf: Issues of ears, language, culture, and identity. In P. L. Ewalt, E. M. Freeman, S. A. Kirk, & Inouye, D. K. (Eds.), *Multicultural issues in social work* (pp. 282–291). Washington, DC: NASW Press.

Sue, D. W., Capodilupo, C. M., Torino, G. C., Bucceri, J. M., Holder, A. M. B., Nadal, K. L., & Esquilin, M. (2007). Racial microaggressions in everyday life: Implications for clinical practice. *American Psychologist, 62,* 271–286.

Tasker, M. (1999). You like Tupac, Mary? *Families in Society, 80,* 216–218.

Tervalon, M., & Murray-García, J. (1998). Cultural humility versus cultural competence: A critical distinction in defining physician training outcomes in multicultural education. *Journal of Health Care for the Poor and Underserved, 9,* 117–125.

U.S. Bureau of the Census. (2010). Age and sex composition. Prepared by the U.S. Department of Commerce Economics and Statistics Administration, Bureau of the Census. Washington, DC, 2010. Retrieved from http://www.census.gov/prod/cen2010/briefs/c2010br-03.pdf

Case Study

Working with Privilege: Home-Based Interventions

Therese Bogan

"I live in a slum, I mean my family, we are our own little sick city."
—*Marlene, James' mother*

The agency where I worked as an intern put together teams of professionals in schools, where we provided supportive service in the classrooms, and then therapy in an adjoining office or in the participating families' homes. Our team, pointedly of mixed race and background, would decide which child needed or could tolerate a specific service. In this case, the intervention specialist was a middle-aged, African American man who also worked as a minister. He told the boy's mother where to find me and told me to do as much therapy/home instruction as possible. He explained to me that the mother, Marlene, was cognitively delayed in some way and was a long-term domestic violence victim who recovered from the violence through working as a hairstylist out of her home. We decided that the home structure, even with the number of people and types of interaction going on there, was the place for therapy. The intervention specialist stressed his belief that James's mother would not be able to "take home" anything from therapy except a continued dependence on the school or me. No one seemed to believe that this Marlene could learn or change, even though (if I stuck to my agreement to suspend my privileged worldview), she had to change for her child to thrive.

James was 6 years old when the process started and 8 years old when we terminated services. His mother was excited to begin service. She chased me down on the sidewalk as I entered my office. What she didn't realize was that her Suburban, a full-size vehicle, might scare me when it suddenly sped up and crossed the street into oncoming traffic to grab a parking spot in front of where I was walking. When she popped out of the driver's seat, many other children, including my client, James, who was pointed out by his first-grade teacher, came running out. I won't say I wasn't scared, but I will say I was just as intensely delighted as I was intimidated. James' mother immediately claimed my fear, "Oh I scared you with the truck . . . everyone's scared of that thing and how it sounds."

Without hesitation, she started talking about how I was White, and I must be scared working in this neighborhood sometimes. This directness was indicative of how Marlene talked about our cultural differences, her motivation, her fears, and her reluctance to take an empowered stance in her marriage or the discipline of her children. She remained completely unveiled. I wish I could say that everyone I've worked with of another culture or background had as much comfort with directness and clarity, but she and I both grew to understand it had more to do with a long-standing head injury than her forward thinking or political empowerment. What we built together and used to forge a good working relationship in visitation home-based family therapy was an understanding of our differences in perspective and a suspension of privilege—sort of like a suspension of disbelief when you are watching a movie that you know is a fake unreal story, but you watch it to get that certain kind of laugh. She was willing to take a situation of "dis"-ability and use the strength that it brought to our relationship, and I was willing to recognize the privilege I hold of being a visitor to both her family system and her neighborhood.

Marlene and I met several times in the school and talked about her history, James' life history, and her family before I had the chance to meet everyone else. We talked about what I wear, how I look, and the fact that neighbors might know that I work at the school. Marlene was polite and put most of the emphasis on this idea that neighbors are just nosy, so I had to be direct in pointing out the emotional burden of my entry into her home. I kept my words simple, anticipated her fears or embarrassment, and tried not to leave out any possible part of our potential challenges. Mostly, the simple honesty was for my sake; talking about entering an all–African American home and neighborhood in the evening was new to me, and I was scared.

After committing to home-based family therapy as a possible treatment for her son's rage, she explained her domestic violence, and how she had lost a pregnancy and endured several head injuries. She added that she and her three eldest sons were often homeless until she was pregnant with James and she lied to a neighbor about the boy being his. When she told this lie, she thought she was giving the boy a father and a permanent place to live. However, they moved when James was 3 years old to live with her now husband, when Marlene became pregnant with her fourth child. Recently, she had told James that the man he knew as his father was not his father but just a nice man. Now Marlene wanted her son to accept her husband (his stepfather and the father of two younger half-siblings) as his father. James' baby sister was 1 year old at the beginning of home-based therapy. The family consisted of five biological children, one godchild, and one stepson from her husband's previous union, all living in a two-bedroom apartment. Marlene's mother also lived in the home and provided a grounded supervision in Marlene's marriage and her childrearing.

Before entering the home, we had to agree that we had to face racial and background differences together, accept that there were bad things that happened in Marlene's life that have consequences for her children, and agree on a goal for family therapy in the home. In this case, Marlene said she wanted a safe, loving home and for James to feel "normal" and that her current husband was his parent.

As the therapist, I could make separate goals for James' individual therapy; I did this with Marlene's consent. We established an agreement that James's play therapy was private from the family, including her. This was hard for James because in his family, his class, and small groups of other children was where he came alive, and he loved to tell about everything he played out. Encouraging James not to use a one-up power play with his peers and keep his play in the therapy office private was the first intervention toward helping James establish boundaries for his feelings and behavior.

When he approached my play therapy office, he was polite, slow to warm, and careful when he used toys. My play office was the same size as his living room. The play therapy office was filled with expressive materials, a sand tray, stuffed toys, blocks, puzzles, character toys, animal figures, and more. With a calmer affect than I ever saw when he was anywhere else, he asked, "What do you want me to play with?" Did I leave it up to him what to pick, or did I direct his activities? I chose to explain that this was his special opportunity to play with his worst fear, best friend, hero, worst enemy, most trusted companion, and the person who told him the truth. He picked these characters slowly over 3 months and worked them into his play. Eventually, I worked with him to translate these characters into "family function roles." Over time, this 6-year-old boy was able to craft the working through of interventions for his family and, with my support, slowly regain his empowerment through play.

The characters James crafted were used as roles in the family dynamic, and each family member took turns playing out each of the roles. There was the "blamer," the "'mama caretaker," the "hulk," and the "crybaby." These names sound negative, I realize, but that is why he chose them. As much as there was a loving tone in his mother's intentions for building a family, there was some scary stuff for James to deal with in his home. His youngest sister (age 18 months) was allowed to take off her own diaper and throw it, crawl over the furniture, scream, and punch, which was "all OK" because she was a baby. His 4-year-old brother regularly scaled several pieces of furniture to climb the refrigerator for snacks he wanted, bullied his younger and older siblings, and used lots of curse words. Both parents politely asked for help and explained that they just didn't understand how the children got so out of control, and Grandma wished me luck and explained that she has tried to teach them boundaries, many times. James himself, the "crybaby" of the family, was angry, had violent outbursts, rejected his new father, and often soiled his pants.

After observing family dynamics in the home, getting to know everyone, and becoming a weekly part of the family, I was able to understand the characters coming out in James's play. Although James focused his fear on his stepfather, the adults were able to see, through our weekly family in-home sessions, that his fear was clearly misplaced. James was surviving sibling rivalry and peer pressure in the home by refocusing his fear on his stepfather and participating in the bullying cycle. His parents and grandmother were shocked at this revelation but were willing to try something new to change this family dynamic. The fact that we would "play" with roles, rather than assign heavy homework, was encouraging for the adults and the children. Everyone in the family was worn out, burned out, and overworked, and at the same time, love was consistently shown through their deeply affectionate words, protectiveness, and family pride. We constructed a role-playing game in which roles were assigned and then family members gave each other compliments on how they played the roles. What is important to note is that I always kept the adults in adult roles—even in the crybaby role. When a role-play ended, it was the adult family member's job to deconstruct the family's behaviors, with my support. At first, I deferred to the grandmother, out of respect and because I suspected that the family relied on her to be the disciplinarian, albeit in a passive and codependent way. Quickly, parents became jealous of her power in the room. Grandma and I worked together, mainly with nonverbal communication, to encourage the parents into taking back their power when deconstructing a role-play. This way, the children watched them problem solve and figure out their challenges and responsibilities.

This intervention inevitably produced tantrums in the children but created an opportunity for the parents, with extra hands in the room, to consciously decide how to deal with resetting the boundaries around safety in the home. We started with obvious "no-no's" like climbing on furniture and moved ever deeper into the emotional violence that naturally stems from unhealed trauma. All the family members were living with reactive rage, withdrawing–isolating behavior, vigilance, frozen-numb apathy, and emotional sensitivity. James, the "cry-baby," was able to read the dynamic and lead into a new set of solutions.

After the tantrums settled and the boundaries were reset, I asked the parents, in an effort to exemplify the challenges of their passive parenting choices, to deepen the intervention by giving up their control to the youngest child in the role-plays. I asked the baby to give each family member (or duo) a role to play and initiate play. That was the only power I gave the baby, but the parents were afraid and reluctant. Because we had been playing together for months now and they felt confident about their ability to institute change, I teased them and joked along with them a bit. "Why not let her lead?" I asked, "Don't you let her reset the boundaries between sessions?" Silence. Although this intervention is risky, it worked for this set of parents; their love for their family was deep, and they saw real change in the children's behavior. They wanted to keep that change, and I needed a strong message to empower their motivation.

Here's where cultural, racial, and socioeconomic differences are just no joke. Although there are general codes in cultures, socioeconomic backgrounds, and racial combinations that can be learned or written, the actual experience of crossing over into a safe place with a family of another culture takes regular supervision and consistent ownership of one's own experience. My cultural cues had to take a secondary position to the home culture and the culture of the process. One example in this case was my need to keep a consistent time as a frame of therapy. I was trained to keep the time frame consistent and require the family system to become organized around this. The reality of this frame was that 5:00 p.m. got dark in the winter, and no White people were generally seen in the neighborhood where I was providing home-based family therapy. This made the family uncomfortable. It took me several sessions in the dark with half the family walking me to the car before I worked up the courage to confront my fear and theirs in a way that was helpful and safe for them. Although our solution did not address the very real discrepancies of privilege in America, what I was able to do, with the guidance of a trusted supervisor, was to strategize a way to assist the family in empowering them to tell me, "Come when it's still light out or we can't calm down about what might happen to you, our therapist who is a White woman, who sticks out like a sore thumb in our neighborhood." The grandmother was willing to explain her vigilant functioning and own a "frame" for our work that allowed her to be more comfortable with me in her home.

Once the family set an effective boundary with me, I could then encourage them to set the boundaries needed to keep the peace when the "White watchful eyes" were not present in the house; this led to increased emotional safety in the family. We then used role-plays to act out and work through the active dynamic behind the five characters at play in their family's dynamics. Each family member, from the baby to the grandmother, acted out their most potent and shadow character to the point of working through, with the encouragement of the rest of the family. Communication skills were taught as psychoeducation in the recap after each role-play. Family members were willing to try new skills and practiced them between sessions. Most important, there was heartfelt, intimate repair and forgiveness communication with each family member about the need to create a parenting hierarchy. The parents were able to recommit to parenting their children.

At the end of our time together, James was no longer soiling his pants or forgetting to wash himself after using the toilet. His aggression had turned to enthusiasm. One thing he learned was that his body was strong and that he communicated well with it. So he started running track and playing sports (now 9 years old) and was quickly making friends. He was able to show compassion toward other angry children and became more patient. The real connection for James was to his compassion for his siblings. The whole group of siblings, regardless of biological parent or birth order, created a level playing field together and began collaborating on their codevelopment as a sibling family unit, rather than competing.

This reduction of competition for attention left Marlene with a lot more energy for herself and her husband. They were able to use newly freed up cognitive space for business and education planning for both of them. When Marlene and her husband planned, the two oldest boys had a model and started planning strategies for more social involvement in their high school. Marlene was shocked at first and needed guidance from her mother and me to believe that parenting was so interconnected with and so much more about her caring for herself. She was able to talk through what she saw transforming in her son James, who had seemed like such a problem. What she saw was the way her home was a possible nest for the development of everyone in the family, from the baby to her mother. Marlene deeply respected her responsibility and understood more clearly that she would continue to make mistakes but that her husband and her mother could be her allies in parenting.

Marlene and I were both able to realize our potential as supporters or facilitators of change. Where I needed to stand or sit in the room to support this for the family was not in the center. Positioning myself outside of the position of privilege and on the sidelines was empowering for the family and a gift of clarity for me. As a therapist working with White skin, I must be constantly aware of my privilege as I ask the other person to find his or her willingness to walk outside the norm with me, toward healing. I must remember that these clients take extra steps to work with me and that we both get added by-products of therapy by having crossed racial boundaries. We both come out empowered on the other side.

Chapter 2

We Are All Addictions Counselors Now: Strategies with Problem Substance Use

Annie Fahy

The American landscape of addiction has a "Berlin Wall" that is toppling. The abstinence model, which has dominated our national narrative since colonial times, does not fit all clients. Harm reduction, brief interventions, and moderation approaches create client-centered, practical, and well-timed interventions (Denning, 2000; Denning, Little, & Glickman, 2004; Rotgers, Kern, & Hoeltzel, 2002). Methods of client-centered care for problem substance use (PSU) exist in polarity with abstinence-only approaches and are dividing funding and missions. This gap holds clients and counselors in a limbo of confusion about what works with PSU. Addiction professionals, although creating an impressive bureaucracy for certification, have identified relatively little toward efficacy of methods. As the public demands more explanation and accountability in health care, so counselors working with PSU are expanding beyond abstinence-only programs. Counselors need competency in substance assessment as an ongoing intervention. Acute interventions do not fit every situation but are often attempted first. The therapeutic relationship is the best venue for change and intervention. Counselors today have a wide menu of options for PSU. Withholding interventions until the client signals his or her own readiness and collaboration is as important as delivering them. Fluency in all manner of harm reduction, moderation, and appropriate abstinence modes is no longer limited to specialists. This is largely due to evidenced-based interventions such as behavior change theory, motivational interviewing, and harm reduction techniques, which all require the client in full collaboration with the counselors. Additionally, the treatment business itself is unable to meet the demands of implementing evidence-based practice. Traditional inpatient treatment is disappearing or becoming a niche market for the super rich, while most programs have converted or blended care with other outpatient modalities. Counselors who serve chronically mentally ill and homeless view treatment more for its "time-out" benefit rather than its ability to permanently fix the problem. Traditional treatment is a much smaller piece of the overall care picture than in past decades.

Another factor affecting PSU is the crises in workforce among addiction professionals. In addition to lack of training and supervision in best practices, addiction workers are underpaid and exhausted by constant restructuring. Most public programs cannot pay licensed professionals, have cut back on training, or have joined forces with criminal justice funding. Counselors function as behavior monitors. This complicates the therapeutic alliance with a dual role (McLellan, Carise, & Kleber, 2003). In the 21st century, one size does not fit all in PSU. Shrinking resources combined with competition for these resources add to the equation of an expanding and complex demographic. Pressure falls on counselors to be a "one-stop shop" with expertise in the complicating factors of PSU and the best interventions. Although harm reduction modalities offer a large tent for clients and many strategies for useful client interventions, it can be confusing for the counselor encountering behavior that demands direction and containment due to potential high-risk consequences and utter destructiveness. Intervening successfully with PSU depends on the therapeutic relationship and an accurate ongoing assessment and evaluation of interventions. The key is in the conversation itself. Assessment becomes an ongoing intervention of small steps and changes that the client identifies in collaboration with a counselor. If treatment and containment are needed, then it comes out of this collaboration with empathy and respect. The either–or days of abstinence or failure does not serve clients. The wall must come down so that we can identify, intervene, and shift to what works with individuals.

SWIMMING POOLS, MOVIE STARS

> Amy Winehouse is found dead in her apartment at age 27. (Huffington Post, 2011)

Recorded history is full of tragic stories of a life hurling out of control due to PSU despite wealth, talent, and success. Thanks to the Internet and the 24-hour news cycle, these images are played repeatedly like background music to our own lives. The debilitating effects of unmanaged substance use in high-profile cases (think Lindsay Lohan, Charlie Sheen, Amy Winehouse, Whitney Houston) are excruciating. They perpetuate feelings and beliefs in our culture about untreated addictions. The Internet makes them luridly available, and like a car wreck, we can't help but slow down and stare. Of course, we feel something in the gut when a talented 27-year-old woman dies—perhaps grateful, superior, saddened, and/or enraged. "Why didn't someone *do* something?" Of course it's not that simple. We as a public are not privy to the multiple actions attempted in these or other cases. We know nothing about what Ms. Winehouse herself attempted. Forcing someone into treatment or abstinence with behavioral interventions isn't always effective. Katie Wikiewitz and Alan Marlatt (2006) explore this failure when recounting the intervention that coerced Kurt Cobain into treatment shortly before he left against medical advice and committed suicide. The sad fact is that, as with Miss Winehouse, a client-centered, harm-reduction approach might have saved Cobain.

Go to Jail—Do Not Pass Go

The addiction narrative in this country affects how clients disclose their stories in our offices. Counselor attitudes and beliefs about PSU also affect whether clients decide to risk talking about a highly stigmatized area in their lives. Clients will hold back from discussing substance use because of a fear that they will be labeled an addict, told that they have a disease, and have to quit.

Current research about behavior change with addictive substances supports client-centered interactions that assist clients in setting the pace and creating solutions toward change (Prochaska, DiClemente, & Norcross, 1992). Many treatment programs have combined with criminal justice systems to restructure criminal behavior that involves substances by rewarding abstinence and punishing use (McLellan et al., 2003). Drug or DUI court offers a choice between jail and treatment. Treatment employs traditional abstinence, cognitive behavioral education, and a 12-step component. Persons participating in these programs are externally motivated to try abstinence, and these methods work for some clients. Outpatient programs, however, do not guarantee abstinence. These programs require higher monitoring by the counselor and may cause the client to fake compliance or produce behavior without addressing inner motivation (McLellan et al., 2003). According to a recent study of Scotland drug courts modeled after the U.S. system, "50 percent of drug court offenders had been re-convicted and within two years 71 percent, at an average cost of the equivalent $27,500 per order" (Peele, 2010). When strictly behavioral programs work, everyone is happy. When they do not, we typically blame the client as we send him or her to jail (Chiauzzi & Liljegren, 1993). Strictly behavioral interventions ignore what we understand about lasting behavior change and do not support personal autonomy (Deci & Ryan, 2000; DiClementi, 2003; Miller & Rollnick, 2002; Prochaska et al., 1992).

No one disputes that criminal behavior against property, others, or the community requires meaningful punishment; however, mandated programs, like other abstinence treatment models, often create good liars who are unmotivated or whose PSU does not fit into a neat package because of trauma, mental health, chronic medical conditions, and other factors involved in their presentation (Denning, 2000; Denning et al., 2004).

If Addiction Is a Destination, How Do You Know When You Have Arrived?

"Insanity is doing the same thing over and over again and expecting different results." This Einstein quote describes addiction and ironically also describes addiction treatment. Addiction is an overused term that has lost its clinical meaning in popular culture (DiClemente, 2003; Chiauzzi & Liljegren, 1993; McLellan et al., 2003). Clients and counselors need to clarify language and beliefs surrounding PSU. Addiction, like depression, can actually mean different things to different people (Denning et al., 2004). Ideas regarding overindulgence and the value of moderation can be traced back to the ancient Greeks. America developed an alcohol problem with its independence. One of the first disease definitions came from Benjamin Rush, a noted physician and signer of the Declaration of Independence (Berk, 2004; W. L. White, 1998). It is interesting to note that Rush, like many counselors today, suffered from the drunkenness of his father and a disrupted family life.

Counselors are often attracted to this work by a desire to fix what is wrong in their own stories. Family history and personal relationship to substances needs to be sorted with clinical supervision. Cultural messages imply that some "addicts" are hopeless or unreachable. These countertransferences can be perpetuated among team members who label difficult clients negatively. Messages of hopelessness, judgment, and disapproval transmit to clients when counselors have not managed their own responses. Current views of PSU haven't changed much since Rush first wrote about it in 1784. Interventions are still weighted toward behavioral controls and a moral assessment that calls for an authoritarian (expert) fixing the "broken" client.

Defining addiction and problematic use has shifted from scientific study of behavior and biology to legal, criminal, and psychological definitions that sequester and control behavior. PSU is a disease that often gets punished. No single phenomenon has affected treatment more than Alcoholics Anonymous (AA). Founded in 1939 by two "hard cases," AA draws from Christian principles and adds a structure that has helped a vast number of people (W. L. White, 1998). Its founders, Bill Wilson and Dr. Bob Smith, added many components to a traditional spiritual intervention that has given it greater integrity than earlier incarnations of support groups. Most impressively, the concept of anonymity, attraction rather than promotion, and a fairly egalitarian society have kept AA vibrant (Alcoholics

Anonymous, 2001). AA does not conduct research, so success is anecdotal, but its ideals and rituals have dominated 20th-century addiction treatment. Many believe that all PSU requires abstinence and AA is the cure. Although effective for some, a one-size-fits-all approach is simply not relevant to many presentations of PSU (Chiauzzi & Liljegren, 1993).

Today, people have some awareness that alcoholism is a disease, thanks to AA and a medical model of disease. In 1960, Jellinek wrote a seminal description of the disease concept of alcoholism. Jellinek began to differentiate different types of alcoholism, but he did not include moderate drinkers as a category. It is a relatively new idea to individualize diagnosis including co-occurring factors, medicating use, trauma, or chronic pain. Classic addiction with all its markers may be one of many presentations. Clients themselves must actively determine what meaning to make of their PSU. A public health approach offers counselors more latitude to explore behaviors, potential harms and risks and best-fit interventions (Denning, 2000; W. L. White, 1998). Harm reduction, motivational interviewing, and narrative approaches all stress therapeutic alliance as a means of change (Denning, 2002; Miller & Rollnick, 2002; W. L. White, 1998). Assuming a disease of the mind, body, and spirit as AA proposes may actually cause harm. Counselors unconsciously act on these assumptions as facts because they are so much a part of the dominant cultural definition of addiction. An example of this is that someone may be blamed for a relapse as "not working it" or not wanting improvement, ignoring the idea that relapse is a fairly normal part of lasting behavior change (DiClemente, 2003; Prochaska 1992). These untested assumptions are a damaging force when applied in cookie cutter fashion. Many clients have been told they "haven't hit bottom yet," implying that they should go out and get worse rather than manage their risks for enhanced quality of life. Clients who do not subscribe to the counselor's definition of disease are often labeled as "in denial" or unmotivated (Chiuzzi & Liljegren, 1993; Denning, 2000; Denning et al., 2004). Counselors (perhaps in recovery themselves) can inadvertently or by design pass on false assumptions and beliefs to clients that can damage their inner guidance and self-efficacy toward problem solving (Chiuzzi & Liljegren, 1993; Denning, 2000; Rotgers et al., 2002).

There is evidence that any time out from drug use creates better outcomes (Deci & Ryan, 2000; DiClemente, 2003; Ryan & Deci, 2000; Miller & Rollnick, 1991, 2002). Brief interventions often work if done well (Miller & Hestra, 1986; Peele, 2010; Rotgers et al., 2002). Still, counselors are placed in the role of monitors and reporters rather than offering therapy and consultation. Counselors working with PSU often experience a level of anger and frustration with client choices and frequently suffer with burnout. Miller and others have determined that much of the resistance or defensiveness encountered in PSU clients is engendered and perpetuated by the counselor's attitudes and judgments (Miller & Rollnick, 2002). Counselors working with substance using clients need supervision to manage this and employ a neutral stance while clients arrive at their own solutions.

NOT YOUR FATHER'S ADDICTION

Creating an individualized definition of PSU that may or may not include addiction is an important therapeutic task. Harm reduction proponents do not use the disease concept (Denning, 2000; Denning et al., 2004). Peele (1989) argued persuasively that the idea of a disease limits care and misleads the public to believe that there is a cure. Some theorists believe that PSU is a maladaptation to coping with a situation, emotional and/or physical. Adaptation models support client autonomy and offer a larger menu choices and incremental change (Denning, 2000; Denning et al., 2004; DiClemente, 2003; Rotgers et al., 2002). Harm reductionists point out that most addiction research focuses only on drinking behavior because other substances have the added stigma of criminality. "People use drugs for reasons" (Denning, 2000; Denning et al., 2004). Helping them to understand behavior that is interfering with identity, values, and goals is the intervention that works best, whether you call it addiction treatment or not. Providing education and accurate definitions of addiction versus PSU is one aspect to beginning this process.

Perceptions are shifting. For example, in one study, 59% saw alcoholism as a disease, and 83% saw mental illness as a disease; 43% see alcoholism as a weakness compared with 13% who think that mental illness is a weakness. Most participants in this survey did think that first-time offenders with an alcohol or drug component should receive treatment (*Alcohol and Drug Abuse Weekly*, 2010). Results like these demonstrate that stigma of alcohol and drug issues is different from other long-term chronic conditions such as diabetes and cancer. This is despite the fact that all of these conditions often include a lifestyle or habit component (Covington, 1998).

Although there is rarely cohesive agreement between harm reductionists and traditional counselors, they both favor a biopsychosocial orientation to working with PSU (Denning, 2000; DiClemente, 2003; Donovan & Marlatt, 1988). The biopsychosocial assessment is a holistic view of multiple factors and causes and is easily individualized.

Most definitions of PSU depend on negative consequences in one or more domains. The client is rarely consulted about these criteria. Definitions of dependence include loss of control, tolerance, withdrawal potential, and craving (American Psychiatric Association, 2000). DiClemente (2003) favored a more behavioral view, saying that addictions include the following elements:

1. They represent habitual patterns of intentional appetitive behaviors.
2. They can become excessive and produce serious consequences.
3. There is stability of these problem behaviors over time.
4. There are interrelated psychological and physiological components to the behavior.
5. Finally, in every case, individuals who become addicted to something have difficulty stopping or modifying [their behavior]. (p. 5)

An interesting thing happens when the word *illness* is substituted for *disease*. *Illness* shifts the focus from objective symptoms determined by an expert to a subjective exploration of the client's perception of symptoms.

Current brain research also elucidates areas of the brain that operationalize pleasure and reinforce appetitive behavior. Development of pharmaceutical agents to control and ease physical and affective symptoms of withdrawal is an emerging business. PSU definitions are expanding to incorporate new capabilities to trace gratification seeking and reinforcing chemistry of some substances and behaviors combined with some individual brain and genetic vulnerabilities (Di Clemente, 2003; Koob, 2006). Covington, whose large body of work focuses on women who abuse substances, adds that relational, attachment, and trauma components are equally important when deliberating definition and treatment (Covington, 1998). Client-centered care begins with collaboration about language and terms. Exploration of attitudes, culture, and family narratives makes a rich beginning to this process. Cultural issues and the missing element of minority and other drug research demands that counselors use an individualized approach. Counselors may decide to use a little bit of this and a little bit of that in their own working definition. Covington offers an elegant definition to build on when she writes: "Addiction is chronic neglect of self in favor of something [e.g., substance abuse] or someone else" (Covington, 1998, p. 7).

In addition to using the term *illness* rather than *disease*, there is the shift from an acute treatment model to a chronic illness or public health model that is activated throughout the life span, like any chronic condition. Using a chronic illness model has several benefits over an acute model. Acute care implies a crisis, and not all PSU is a crises. Treatment is typically offered as a fixed dose. Evaluation occurs at the beginning, middle, and end of treatment at arbitrary time frames (usually 6 or 12 months). Success is measured in behavioral terms such as meeting attendance, urine screens, and in self-report about abstinence. These criteria do not reflect incremental behavior change, adaptation to new behaviors, harm reduction, or quality of life improvement. These effects are lost with an acute evaluation model (McLellan, McKay, Forman, & Carriola, 2005).

According to moderation research approximately 1 in 4 persons identified with a problem meets the true medical diagnosis for addiction (Rotgers et al., 2002). These *DSM-IV* criteria are not present in many clients who present with a so-called addiction (American Psychiatric Association, 2000; DiClemente, 2003; Rotgers et al., 2002). This means potentially that three out of four people identified with a drinking problem may have the ability to return to low risk drinking (Rotgers et al., 2002). It is reasonable to assume that this may also be true for drug users. Pushing all clients into abstinence-based treatment without discerning what their individual conditions are creates another problem beyond initial labeling. The client receives a confusing set of failure messages. When clients believe that they have no control, they are more likely to relapse. If clients are taught that they have volition and can learn skills to prevent relapse, they do better (Chiauzzi & Liljegren, 1993; Denning, 2000; Marlatt & Gordon, 1985).

Counselors who address substance use in the context of the life span will have flexibility to start substance-related conversations early, in a prevention context as well as in PSU. With a life-cycle perspective, evaluation offers a chance for more assessment of family concerns, risks, and relapse prevention. Clients at higher risk need to have more frequent contacts and review of potential harms. Chronic substance users are cycled and recycled through the same treatment, and clinicians wonder why it doesn't work. Offering severe substance users safe time-outs from their drug use without insisting on abstinence is compassionate care. Untreated PSU increases risk for many physical conditions including hypertension, cardiac arrhythmias, trauma, gastrointestinal distress, liver disease, as well as depression and anxiety. Utilizing brief interventions and placing the choice and responsibility for healthier decisions on the client takes the "fix-it" burden off the counselor, and it works according to brief intervention studies (Bien, Miller, & Tonigan, 1993; Miller & Rollnick, 1991, 2002; Miller, Rollnick, & Butler, 2008; Rotgers et al., 2002). It is important to note that not every substance problem indicates a need for a chronic illness model, but sequestered care for PSU is mostly gone. A 15-minute empathic conversation can have as much impact as a specialist intervention. Abstinence is not a requirement of effective therapy (Denning, 2000; Denning et al., 2004; Rotgers et al., 2002). Every problem scenario does not require the most drastic treatment (Rotgers et al., 2002). With a strong alliance comes mutual goals. These goals are well summarized by McLellan et al. (2003) as follows:

1. Decreasing substance use
2. Increasing health
3. Improvement in social functioning
4. Reduction in public safety threats (p. 448)

READY OR NOT

DiClemente (2003) has suggested that counselors place PSU in the context of change theory and says that addictions are "learned habits that once established become difficult to extinguish even in the face of at times numerous negative consequences" (p. 4). Behavior change theories help counselors organize and pace interventions. Clients benefit from education about behavior change when they relate it to their own motivation and readiness. The predominant model used with lifestyle behavior change is the transtheoretical model (TTM), also known as the stages of change model. TTM was developed with smokers and is now utilized with much health-related behavior change (DiClemente, 2003; Prochaska et al., 1992).

TTM delineates progressive tasks that clients must solve as they move toward a permanent behavior change. It is especially useful because it normalizes relapse as a natural aspect of lasting behavior change. Most behavior change includes some relapse or return to old thinking. In TTM relapse is feedback rather than failure. Relapse means new coping skills are required. For example, many people can relate when a person explains a relapse after a loved one has died and coping skills for grief are needed. The more complex the changes the higher the potential for relapse back to the previous stage or return to the old behavior and decreased awareness (Di Clemente, 2003; Prochaska et al., 1992).

Precontemplation—"Not Thinkin' About It"

Clients in precontemplation hold themselves apart from the reality of the distress that the behavior brings. They dream out the need for the change or actively push back attempts to focus them on the change. They are simply not ready to hold the conversation about change. Often these clients are labeled "in denial," and traditional treatment calls for confrontation of that denial. Actually confronting a person who is exhibiting any defense mechanism creates more resistance within the relationship. Resistance is feedback that the counselor is moving too fast or has tried to fix something for the client (Miller, n.d.). The client's resistance could mean, "I'm not ready for that," "I don't know if I can trust you," or "I don't know if I am confident enough," or "Change isn't important now."

In this stage, clients must increase awareness of reasons for change and decrease defenses such as denial. Counselors must become trusted collaborators to explore the change, minimize resistance, and address potential harms with respect (Miller & Rollnick, 1991, 2002).

Contemplation—"Thinkin' About It"

Clients in contemplation explore and solve ambivalence. Sitting with ambivalence can induce counselors to fix and solve ambivalence by offering solutions, advice, and referrals for the client. In this stage, the counselor supports the client to sort through the ambivalence, which builds motivation. Clients often say, "Yeah, but" as in "I want to change my drinking, but I would lose all my friends." Counselors facilitate exploration and support the client to move at his or her own pace while not becoming stuck or resistant to a premature solution. Counselors also hold important pieces of the story for review and promote a decisional balance or cost benefit analysis of making the change versus maintaining the status quo.

Preparation—Baby Steps or the Google Phase

Clients in preparation usually have made a provisional decision and are taking steps toward the larger change. This is a delicate stage and looks different in different clients. Miller, Yahne, Moyers, Martinez, and Pirritano (2004) discussed the possibility of quantum change in which clients decide and act based on some internal guidance. Confidence to make or sustain the change can be an important aspect of this stage. A fear of failure may come from past attempts or other factors. A common clinician mistake is to overload the client with multiple interventions, because any action feels good after ambivalence; however, it is important to let the client try on the change with small actions. Equally, it is important not to go too slow here if the client is ready and confident (Miller & Rollnick, 2002; Miller et al., 2004). Clients must envision their change, and counselors can assist with this.

Action

Clients in action are called "good clients" because they embody the change. Action involves energy and momentum. Clients actively engage in all aspects of change and utilize maximum resources and referrals. They often do not see relapse potential at this point, but relapse planning is an important part of the action stage. Counselors offer maximum support toward change and provide cognitive and other interventions. Appropriate relapse prevention assessment fits in all stages but is especially important here.

Maintenance

Clients in maintenance are learning to sustain the change through natural life events. They are active in relapse prevention and have developed coping skills to manage cravings and other challenges. Counselors assist with developing natural supports and higher-level coping skills for relapse prevention. If a relapse occurs, the counselor will have predicted this possibility and taken steps to normalize it and keep it short lived.

SELF-DETERMINATION

Many harm reductionists prefer self-determination theory (SDT; Deci & Ryan, 2000; Deci et al., 1994; Ryan & Deci, 2000). SDT is derived from the philosophical view that all people are striving toward a more unified integrated self and that certain basic psychological needs must be relatively satisfied to support change. SDT is elegant in its application across cultural, age, and class boundaries. It explains two types of motivation: internal and external. External motivators are those outside of the person such as working for a paycheck or studying for a grade. Internal motivation is connected to the inner values of a person or guidance from within. Often clients present with a combination of internal and external forces pushing for change. The clinician wants to explore both, but finding an internal motivator is like finding treasure when working with behavior change.

SDT describes three basic psychological needs that must be in relative stability before a person can move into complex behavior change. In addition to exploring internal and external motivators, SDT asks questions about these needs and how a person is doing in these areas.

The first area to explore is *competence*. How able is the client to effectively meet goals through his or her abilities and resources? The second area is *autonomy*. Is the client able to author his or her own life? "Autonomy refers to volition—the organismic desire to self organize experience and behavior and to have activity concordant with one's integrated sense of self" (Angyal, 1965, de Charms, 1968, Deci, 1980, Ryan & Connell, 1989, Sheldon & Elliott, 1999, p 231). The third area to consider is *relatedness*, or the feeling of being connected and cared for in the world by others and to care for others (Deci, 2000). Clinicians who use SDT can target and offer reflective conversations that elicit a client's own awareness about how these concepts are operationalized in their own life to increase understanding and motivation. Also, if a client struggles in meeting basic needs, then more complex behavior change may not be possible until that crisis is solved.

IT'S A CONVERSATION—A CONVERSATION ABOUT ALCOHOL AND DRUGS, MOTIVATION AND CHANGE

The most important feature of any health-related behavior change is creating a collaborative empathic respectful working relationship (Miller & Rollnick, 1991, 2002; Miller et al., 2004). Building trust often comes out of a counselor's own natural style and warmth. However, clients with social difficulties, mental health diagnoses, or who have been hurt or betrayed by others may be more difficult to work with.

In therapeutic relationships, the most important vehicle is the structured conversation about behaviors and meaning. Old-style treatment was most concerned with data collection. In fact, many treatment programs are required to collect 2 to 4 hours of assessment (McLellan et al., 2003). Good counselors start with the person and work backward into paperwork. Gathering information becomes a relational process of exploring client material—not so much so that the counselor can find the facts but rather so that the client can experience his or her stories from a new perspective. Data are often important to the agency, and if this is artfully done, the client can often reduce his or her risks and harms.

Emphasizing relationship supports autonomy and client self-determination (Deci & Ryan, 2000; Miller & Rollnick, 1991, 2002; Miller et al., 2004). Of course, risks must be addressed, and one method of doing this without harming the alliance is to ask permission to voice a concern or give feedback (Miller & Rollnick, 2002). Clients cooperate with these discussions because the counselor has put the relationship first. Also, they find value in the conversation because they have never talked about their substance behavior like this before. Often, the only conversations about substance use that clients have experienced have been in the context of use with other users, which only highlight the pleasure, or in "Just Say No" interventions, which have limited effectiveness and oversimplify the issue (Werb et al., 2011). Reality television now offers confrontation "gotch-ya" interventions with rosy outcomes.

The power of compassionate investigation cannot be underestimated. An empathic connection is most important for facilitating change (Miller & Rollnick, 2002; Miller et al., 2004). One way to elicit this conversation is to develop proficiency in *motivational interviewing* (MI). Strategies and techniques in this model utilize reflective listening, open questions, and waiting for client signals of readiness before offering assistance, guiding direction and suggestions collaboratively. Skilled use of reflections can expand and direct the conversation to salient points, and testing for readiness inspires confidence and speaks to the importance of the work at hand (Miller & Rollnick, 2002). MI is simple, but it is not easy. Practitioners use it to enhance client trust, readiness, and awareness of ambivalence. MI is also an effective guiding strategy. Miller and Rollnick identify specific language that predicts behavior change or maintains the status quo. Attention to change talk and other directional strategies separate MI from other client-centered counseling.

Change talk is language that clients offer as they are moving toward behavior change. Clients will speak of *desire and ability to change, reasons and need for change*, and *commitment to change*. According to numerous studies in MI, increasing client opportunities to explore these aspects enhances likelihood of change. MI takes skill, time, and practice to learn effectively (Miller et al., 2004). Ethical practice with MI asks clinicians to use MI collaboratively on target behaviors that would contribute to the well-being of the client. MI is ultimately a conversation that offers a client a place to think out loud about his or her own values and goals and reasons for change. Once this happens, the counselor can shift into planning, offering interventions and relapse prevention (Miller & Rollnick, 1991, 2002). Counselors who wish to learn MI generally do so in stages with formal training and then also with individual or group coaching and feedback from a skilled trainer (Miller et al., 2004).

Assessing and Addressing Harms

Another assessment tool favored by many harm reductionists is *Drug Set Setting*, which was developed by Zinberg in 1984 and refined for clinical assessment by Denning (2000, Denning et al., 2004). This visual assessment uses a triangle as its scaffolding. The conversation targets drug use behavior and details (*Drug*), biopsychosocial factors (*Set*), and environmental details (*Setting*) to create an interactive picture of a person's current situation. Conversation evokes opportunities toward harm reduction and incremental behavior change in any area. Clients also identify connections among emotional states, people, living situation, biology, and substance use.

Like MI, Drug Set Setting focuses on guiding toward changes that the client sees as relevant: Exploring substance use (the how, when, where, and with whom) and the set or the bioemotional make up of the person (the "cards that they got dealt in life"), and the settings in which they live and act. This is the primary assessment tool recommended by Denning and colleagues to assess potential areas of harm as well as other factors (Deci et al., 1994; Deci & Ryan, 2000; Denning, 2000; Denning et al., 2004; DiClemente, 2003).

Counselors may be directive with harms and risks identified. Asking permission to speak of concerns or create a harm reduction plan works here. Most clients will take actions to reduce harms if autonomy is respected and the risk is perceived. Harms might include high-risk sexual behavior, potential for violence and trauma, driving under the influence, liver and other health complications, and dangerous using practices such as sharing needles. Some PSU has a binge component. The best intervention could be to postpone, delay, and even plan a binge event. For example, starting use later in the evening if a binge is predicted can develop more awareness for the client while promoting safety. If PSU is for medicating or relieving, then addressing the stressors needing relief is indicated. Moderation Management recommends a time-out of at least 30 days (Denning recommends a longer break with significant use history) before attempting low-risk use goals. Many clients become motivated to take this break if they are motivated to see if moderation is possible for them (Denning, 2011; Rotgers et al., 2002).

This assessment elicits vivid detail substance use behavior. "Where do they get drugs? What risks are involved? Who is there? How do they use it? How do they take care of safety? How do they mix or time substance use and for what purpose?" It sounds simple, but it is often tricky for a counselor to hold these conversations in a neutral curious way. Often information will present that sounds dangerous or is shocking. The clinician needs to listen attentively and wait for all the information to ask the client what changes he or she might make or to recommend one to the client (Denning, 2000; Denning et al., 2004). There is a fuller explanation of this assessment and a method for clients to use for themselves in the book *Over the Influence* (Denning et al., 2004).

The Drugs That You Prefer Are Like a Brain Chemistry Fingerprint

Counselors should explore drugs and their effects. Clients know what they like and what they don't like. Often these details come woven in with other information. Counselors may avoid these explorations for fear that they will trigger craving and or increased use. There is a taboo about discussing pleasurable effects of drugs with clients that comes from the belief that exploring pleasures instigates relapse (Chiauzzi & Liljegren, 1993). Clients may experience euphoria when discussing drug use in a therapeutic context and learning important facts about their brains. Pleasure comes from the brain, not the drug. Clients often attribute the pleasure to the substance when really all the substance does is express an innate aspect of the brain's biology (Denning, 2000; Denning et al., 2004). When clients discuss their preferences, they are also giving a perspective of how they are wired and what biochemical forces they may be wrestling with. People use drugs for reasons, and those reasons are both well known and mysterious. Clients may explore self-medicating natural challenges such as a long-standing depression or bring home the reality that the positive benefits of using are gone. There is also an opportunity to assess withdrawal, tolerance, craving, and overdose issues and intervene as necessary with education and coping support. Tolerance is a feature of expanding drug use with amounts and frequency to gain the same or desired effects. This feature is noted with many substances, especially opiates. Most opiate users can describe the effect of tolerance and the necessary actions taken to accommodate the biochemical fact that the body needs more to achieve the same desired effect. For instance, many opiate users begin doctor shopping, visiting emergency rooms, or buying illegally when an MD cuts them off from a prescription.

DETOX AND WITHDRAWAL

Various substances also produce significant acute withdrawal. Of these, alcohol and benzodiazepine withdrawal may be life-threatening if unmanaged and may require medical monitoring. Opiates, although not usually life-threatening, produce a constellation of uncomfortable symptoms and often require significant support, medically and psychosocially. This is more complicated when chronic pain is present. Chronic pain clients are some of the most isolated. Often such clients are difficult to work with. They have learned to maneuver in the world to get their needs met. The worker experiences this as manipulation. Some of these clients often bring up anger, frustration, fear, and hopelessness in the worker. These situations as well as many others may require more compassionate directive attention and sometimes hospitalization and medical management. Suffering from a distressing detox does not increase motivation toward change (Denning, 2000; Denning et al., 2004; Wikiewitz & Marlatt, 2006).

To find substance withdrawal time frames check the Substance Abuse and Mental Health Services Administration website (SAMSA, 2010).

In addition to acute withdrawal, clients can experience significant psychological withdrawal based on knowledge, beliefs, and reasons for the PSU. Protracted withdrawal is a real concern. Discomfort and physical and psychological symptoms can occur as the brain shifts from gratification by the substance to replacement brain chemistry or alternative behavior. This brain shift takes time and can be affected by situational, physiologic, nutritional, and other factors. Common symptoms for protracted withdrawal may include the following:

- Anxiety
- Hostility
- Irritability
- Depression
- Mood instability
- Fatigue
- Insomnia

- Difficulties concentrating and thinking
- Reduced interest in sex
- Unexplained physical complaints, especially of pain

These symptoms may wax and wane and can be intense, making a better case for assessing readiness and adequate supports before pushing someone into a premature abstinence (SAMHSA, 2010). Many substances used in complicated patterns have also replaced other attachments, or been adapted to become primary attachments; this may create a deep alienation if changed too abruptly without planning and preparation (Flores, 2001).

"If I Get Drunk and Drink All Night Long, It's a Family Tradition" (Hank Williams Jr., 1979)

In the United States, most drug experimentation begins in adolescence and continues, depending on social and cultural factors, with peaks and moderations influenced by life circumstances. Substance use is assessed on a continuum with markers indicating experimentation, exploration, adventure, abuse, habitual use, problem use, dependent use, and chaotic use. Narrative therapy (NT) creates conversations that externalize problems such as PSU (M. White & Epston, 1990). The cornerstone of NT is that *the person is not the problem, the problem is the problem.* NT asks for "the news of difference," for example, when was life different from now? What was it like when the problem wasn't there (M. White & Epston, 1990, p. 61)? Solution-focused brief therapy (SFBT) is derived from NT (Berg & Miller, 1992) with a focus on problem solving. Narrative approaches evoke conversations that shake up the status quo by focusing on strengths, values, and innovations. Clients are often unaware of their strengths because the problem gets all the attention. NT explores family risk factors and dominant stories perpetuated through generations. SFBT begins with the well-known "miracle question": If you woke up this morning and the problem was miraculously gone, how would you know that this miracle had happened (Berg & Miller, 1992)? Also when a solution fails, a narrative approach says it was the wrong solution rather than making it the client's failure.

Intervention Is a Show on Television, and One Size Does Not Fit All

The recipe for good treatment is fairly simple. It involves a combination of relapse prevention with a full complement of skills training and life skills. Good treatment also includes stress management, relationship counseling, self-regulation skills, finding housing, assisting with finding or keeping work, vocational training, medical and mental health care, relapse prevention, and replacement of one type of pleasure with other, healthier activities (McLellan et al., 2003; Miller & Hestra, 1986). These interventions are true for abstinence or moderation interventions.

Treatment offers prescriptions for social connectedness with meetings and groups. Making changes in substance use affects attachments and relationships (Flores, 2001). Some people need a meeting, and some don't. When AA is a good fit, it's an easy referral because meetings abound. Clients may seek secular recovery or Moderation Management meetings. The Internet also has numerous resources (Rotgers et al., 2002). Evidenced-based practices such as MI, harm reduction, and SFBT, as well as medication advances such as Suboxone blend with traditional psychoeducation and cognitive-behavioral methods. Counselors need adequate training and supervision to develop these proficiencies.

PSU provokes people around it to demand abstinence, contracts, vows, inventories, remorse, and accountability. For 50 years, the treatment business has delivered a service based on a disease concept. Client-centered care and the need for efficacious methods makes the debate between abstinence only and harm reduction approaches moot. As funding shrinks and clients become educated consumers of care, the community counselor will need more flexible skills to meet the challenge PSU presents. Not all clients need abstinence as a first intervention. Ultimately, clients are in charge of the changes that they make. Exploring these changes in collaboration is the new work of counselors. Ongoing assessment in the context of a collaborative relationship is the method to ensure that care is meaningful and client centered.

REFERENCES

Alcohol and Drug Abuse Weekly. (2010). 22:1–8. doi:10.1002/adaw.20220

Alcoholics Anonymous. (2001). *Alcoholics Anonymous big book* (4th ed.). New York, NY: Alcoholics Anonymous World Services. (Also available online http://www.aa.org/bigbookonline). Original work published 1939.

American Psychiatric Association. (2000). *Diagnostic and statistical manual of mental disorders* (4th ed., text rev.). Washington, DC: Author.

Berg, I. K., & Miller, S. D. (1992). *Working with the problem drinker: A solution-focused approach*. New York, NY: Norton.

Berk, L. R. (2004, Fall). Alcohol, temperance & prohibition. Temperance and prohibition era propaganda: A study in rhetoric. Retrieved from http://dl.lib.brown.edu/temperance/essay.html

Bien, T. H., Miller, W. R., & Tonigan, S. (1996). Brief interventions for alcohol problems: A review. *Addictions, 88*, 315–336.

Chiauzzi, E. J., & Liljegren, S. I. (1993). Taboo topics in addiction treatment: An empirical review of clinical folklore. *Substance Abuse Treatment, 10*, 303–316.

Covington, S. (1998). Approaches in treatment of our most invisible population. *Women and Therapy Journal, 21*, 141–155.

Deci, E. L., Eghrari, H., Patrick, B., & Leone, D. R. (1994). Facilitating internalization: The self determination perspective. *Journal of Personality, 62*, 119–142.

Deci, E. L., & Ryan, R. M. (2000). The what and why of goal pursuits. *Psychological Inquiry, 11*, 227–268.

Denning, P. (2000). *Practicing harm reduction psychotherapy: An alternative approach to addictions.* New York, NY: Guilford Press.

Denning, P., Little, J., & Glickman, A. (2004). *Over the influence: The harm reduction guide for managing drugs and alcohol.* New York, NY: Guilford Press.

Denning, P., & Little, J. (2011). *Practicing harm reduction psychotherapy: An alternative approach to addictions* (2nd ed.) New York, NY: Guildford Press.

DiClemente, C. C. (2003). *Addiction and change: How addictions develop and addicted people recover.* New York, NY: Guilford Press.

Donovan, D. M., & Marlatt, G. A. (1988). *Assessment of addictive behaviors.* New York, NY: Guilford Press.

Flores, P. J. (2001). Addiction as an attachment disorder: Implications for group therapy. *International Journal of Group Psychotherapy, 5,* 63–81.

Koob, G. F. (2006). The neurobiology of addiction: A neuroadaptational view for relevant diagnosis. *Addiction, 101*(Suppl. 1), 21–30.

Marlatt, G. A., & Gordon, J. R. (1985). *Relapse prevention: Maintenance strategies in the treatment of addictive behaviors.* New York, NY: Guilford Press.

McLellan, A. T., Carise, D., & Kleber, H. D. (2003). Can the national addiction treatment infrastructure support the public's demand for quality care? *Journal of Substance Abuse, 25,* 117–121.

McLellan, A. T., McKay, J. R., Forman, R., & Carriola, J. (2005). Reconsidering the evaluation of addiction treatment. *Addiction, 100,* 447–458.

Miller, W. R. (n.d.). Addiction treatment efficacy reviews. Albuquerque, NM: Center on Alcoholism, Substance Abuse, and Addictions. Retrieved from http://casaa.unm.edu/ater.html

Miller, W. R., & Hestra, R. K. (1986). In-patient alcoholism treatment: Who benefits? *American Psychologist, 41,* 794–805.

Miller, W. R., & Rollnick, S. (1991). *Motivational interviewing: Preparing people to change addictive behavior.* New York, NY: Guilford Press.

Miller, W. R., & Rollnick, S. (2002). *Motivational interviewing: Preparing people for change* (2nd ed.). New York, NY: Guilford Press.

Miller, W. R., Rollnick, S., & Butler, C. C. (2008). *Motivational interviewing in healthcare: Helping patients change.* New York, NY: Guilford Press.

Miller, W. R., Yahne, C. E., Moyers, T. B., Martinez, J., & Pirritano, M. (2004). A randomized trial of methods to help clinicians learn MI. *Journal of Consulting Psychology, 72,* 1050–1062.

Peele, S. (1989). *Diseasing of America: Addiction treatment out of control.* New York, NY: Lexington Books.

Peele, S. (2010, June 10). Drug courts: You'd think they would work. Retrieved from http://www.huffingtonpost.com/stanton-peele/drug-courts-you-would-thi_b_619681.html

Prochaska, J. O., DiClemente, C. C., & Norcross, J. C. (1992). In search of how people change: An application to addictive behaviors. *American Psychologist, 47,* 1102–1114.

Rotgers, F., Kern, M. F., & Hoeltzel, R. (2002). *Responsible drinking: A moderation management approach for problem drinkers.* Oakland, CA: New Harbinger.

Ryan, R. M., & Deci, E. L. (2000). Self-determination theory and the facilitation of intrinsic motivation. *American Psychologist, 55,* 68–78.

Substance Abuse and Mental Health Services Administration. (2010, July). Protracted withdrawal. *Substance Abuse Treatment Advisory: News for the Treatment Field, 9,* 1–8. Retrieved from http://kap.samhsa.gov/products/manuals/advisory/pdfs/SATA_Protracted_Withdrawal.pdf . http://samsha.org

Werb, D., Mills, E. J., DeBeck, K., Kerr, T., Montaner, J. S. G., & Wood, E. (2011). The effectiveness of anti-illicit drug public service announcements: A systemic and meta analysis. *Journal of Epidemiological Community Health, 1.* Retrieved from http//jech.bmg.com/65/10/834

White, M., & Epston, D. (1990). *Narrative means to therapeutic ends.* New York, NY: Norton.

White, W. L. (1998). *Slaying the dragon: The history of addiction treatment and recovery in America.* Bloomington, IL: Chestnut Health Systems/Lighthouse Institute.

Wikiewitz, K., & Marlatt, G. A. (2006). Overview of harm reduction treatments for alcohol problems. *International Journal of Drug Policy, 17,* 285–294.

Wiley On-Line Library. According to Ohio survey. http://www.Alcoholism and Drug weekly. Alcoholism and Drug Abuse Weekly (accessed August 2, 2011).

Zinberg, N. E. (1984). *Drug, set, setting: The basis for controlled intoxicant use.* New Haven, CT: Yale University Press.

Chapter 3

Come As You Are: Harm Reduction Therapy in Community Drop-In Centers

Jeannie Little, Perri Franskoviak, Jennifer Plummer, Jamie Lavender, and Anna Berg

By the time I reached the bottom of the stairs, I had already heard the moaning coming from the bathroom at the back of the building.

"I've been trying to help her out but she's having trouble pulling herself together," said Joe, one of the community center staff. That she needed something was his on-the-spot assessment, and I nodded, concurring with his judgment. I asked her name, but Joe didn't know. She's been coming in fairly regularly, he said, and is usually in chaos, but never this bad.

After several more minutes, during which I introduced myself through the closed door, the door flew open, revealing a woman with wet hair, missing a front tooth, flinging herself against the walls and screaming, "Don't look at me! Don't look at me!" then apologizing for her outburst in the next breath. A pair of wet pants lay crumpled on the floor. She picked them up only to throw them down, then picked them up again and lifted the hem of her flimsy, delicately flowered shirt to reveal her naked backside.

I looked away as she screamed that she was moving as fast as she could, following this outburst with another apology. She pulled the pants up her legs in a series of jerky movements, then flung her head back as she kicked first one leg then the other straight out in front of her.

As I followed her through the community center, I wondered how I could get her to slow down long enough to speak with her. But talking was not on the agenda, as she hurled herself out the front door and onto the sidewalk. She began flailing, her face contorting first into a grimace, then relaxing, and then crumpling into a worried frown. After a quick glance toward the oncoming traffic, she made her way across the street and into the corner market. I watched the erratic dance of her limbs as she crossed the threshold and disappeared into the store.

How had this woman come to this moment in her life, here in San Francisco's Tenderloin district, clutching a plastic bag of wet clothes and the crumpled pack of cigarettes that I'd picked up off the floor and handed to her as she left the center? Her brain, no doubt propelled by a combination of chemicals—some endogenous, some ingested—was experiencing a war of impulses. She'd be vulnerable on the street, a woman in a neighborhood where manipulation and violence are primary forms of interaction. It was no accident that she'd come to the community center, to a place where people reached out when she showed up, no matter what kind of state she was in. She knew, even if not consciously, that she was welcome here.[1]

Perri, the "I" in this story, is a therapist at the Harm Reduction Therapy Center (HRTC), as are all of the authors of this chapter. The woman, "Susan," is a client of a large homeless drop-in center in San Francisco's Tenderloin district. Susan typifies the people that we work with in our many community-based harm reduction therapy programs. Although not always so chaotic, our community clients are always poor and often homeless mentally ill drug users.

The HRTC and colleagues elsewhere in the United States have developed a new paradigm in addiction and dual diagnosis treatment. Harm reduction psychotherapy, or harm reduction therapy as it is more commonly called, is part of the larger international harm reduction movement, which began in Europe in the early 1980s as a public health approach to working with drug users. The goal was to

---

1. This vignette was originally published in Little, J., & Franskoviak, P. (2010). So glad you came! Harm reduction therapy in community settings. *Journal of Clinical Psychology*, *66*, 175–188.

reduce the transmission of blood-borne diseases, specifically hepatitis B and HIV. Needle exchange, the most well-known harm reduction intervention, has proven that drug users do not have to quit using drugs to reduce harm (Goosby, 2001); it is far too important to save lives by offering immediate practical interventions than to be concerned about whether people should or should not be using drugs. As harm reduction researcher Alan Marlatt (1998) has said, "Harm reduction is founded on a set of pragmatic principles and compassionate strategies designed to minimize the harmful consequences of personal drug use and associated high risk behaviors" (p. 3).

Currently in the United States, harm reduction remains controversial. Historically, reactions to intoxication have led to a more prohibitionist culture than in many other countries. Thus, in the United States, in addition to public health strategies such as needle exchange, nondiscriminatory access to health care, overdose prevention, and drug substitution therapies (for example, methadone and buprenorphine), we also have need of advocacy—legal efforts to reduce the harm done by the War on Drugs: decriminalization of drug use, fair sentencing laws, medical marijuana, and other sane drug policies. Finally, harm reduction therapy is a dual diagnosis treatment model for anyone who uses drugs, regardless of the status of their drug use, regardless of whether they think they have a problem, and regardless of their goals for future use. "Come as you are" and "any positive change" are the fundamental principles of harm reduction and harm reduction therapy.

Already a low-threshold model because it welcomes active drug users, harm reduction therapy has become even more utilized in the past 10 years as the authors have integrated treatment programs into five drop-in centers in San Francisco neighborhoods where the most complicated and marginalized dually diagnosed people live. This chapter describes harm reduction therapy and its application to specific problems that we work with in our community-based programs. We use the term *therapist* throughout the chapter, but the information and guidance we offer is relevant and useful for anyone offering clinical services to drug users.

HARM REDUCTION THERAPY

Harm reduction therapy was developed in the 1990s by several therapists (Denning, 2000; Denning, Little, & Glickman, 2004; Little, 2002; Marlatt, 1998; Springer, 1991; Tatarsky, 2002). Over the past 20 years, it has become a significant alternative to treating people with drug and alcohol problems. Harm reduction therapists work simultaneously with drug, mental health, and social problems *without demanding abstinence as a condition or as a goal of treatment*. We offer a menu of options for behavior change and encourage clients to make their own decisions about the goals, the structure, and pace of treatment. Although we recognize and support abstinence as a worthy goal of treatment, it is by no means the only one, and it is only a legitimate option if chosen by the client.

Of greatest concern in the development of harm reduction therapy were dually diagnosed people, for whom street drugs and alcohol have real or perceived medicinal benefits for the suffering that they experience as a result of mental illness. Dual diagnosis is the rule, not the exception. It is well documented that people with mental illness develop problems with drugs at far greater rates than those without (e.g., see Kessler, Crum, Warner, & Nelson, 1997). Harm reduction therapy was driven by the needs of people who are turned away from both substance abuse and mental health programs because of chaotic drug use and untreated symptoms of mental illness. Sometimes called "revolving-door patients," dually diagnosed people have the poorest rates of abstinence and the highest rates of poverty, homelessness, medical illness, and psychiatric crisis of any group of people.

GUIDING PRINCIPLES OF HARM REDUCTION THERAPY

The following principles serve as a guide for therapists and counselors, as well as for doctors, nurses, public health workers, and social service providers who work with active drug users:

- People *use* drugs for reasons. All drugs enhance pleasure, reduce pain, or alter perception. New learning in neurobiology supports the fact that people, especially those with physical, mental, or emotional illness, get significant relief from street drugs.
- Drug *misuse* is a health issue, not a legal or a moral concern. In the oft-spoken words of Ethan Nadelman, executive director of the Drug Policy Alliance, "There should be no punitive sanctions for what a person chooses or refuses to put into their body" (Nadelman, 1992).
- People don't have a disease (addiction); they have a *relationship with drugs.* As in all other relationships, there are benefits, and there are drawbacks.
- Incremental change is normal. The stages of change model (Prochaska, DiClemente, & Norcross, 1992) is based on the reality that all behavior change (leaving a relationship, changing sexual habits, losing weight, accepting psychiatric treatment, taking HIV medications, or reducing or quitting drugs or alcohol) requires a process of decision making. Change is most solid if we work through the stages one at a time, thoroughly, and in order.
- Clients must lead the goals, the structure, and the pace of treatment (Denning & Little, 2011). Harm reduction offers a menu of options, giving clients autonomy to drive their own change process.

WORKING WITH ACTIVE DRUG USERS

Unlike traditional substance abuse treatment programs, mental health agencies and many therapists that exclude people who actively use alcohol and drugs, harm reduction welcomes active drug users. Just as we wouldn't refuse lifesaving treatment for someone with diabetes who continues to eat ice cream, we do not turn people away from treatment because they are using drugs. We work with drug use as we would with any other problem behavior, and we respect the medicinal properties of alcohol and drugs. Edward Khantzian (1985) first referred to the attempts of substance users to deal with painful emotions as "self-medication." Therapists need to acknowledge the self-medicating aspects of each person's drug use and honor his or her attempts to cope.

Motivational interviewing (Miller & Rollnick, 2002) is the well-established evidence-based model for counseling people toward addictive behavior change. As Miller & Carroll (2006) said, "No one is unmotivated. The question is what a person is motivated *for*, what he or she values, and what reinforcers are effective for him or her" (p. 136). In general, people are not unmotivated to change drug-using behavior. They are more often ambivalent about *whether* to change and *what* to do differently. Ambivalence and resistance are normal and expected parts of any change process, to be *understood*, not confronted. Motivational interviewing, now applied to many fields including mental health, offers many counseling interventions that help to move people through the stages of change.

DROP-IN HARM REDUCTION THERAPY IN COMMUNITY CENTERS

Developed by the authors for people who will not or cannot go to established programs, with their often cumbersome intake procedures and limited tolerance for difficult behaviors, drop-in harm reduction therapy is community mental health at its most profound. Rather than invite clients to clinics set up for the express purpose of providing mental health or substance abuse treatment, we go to the neighborhoods where people live and offer treatment in community drop-in centers. We are the visitors, the interlopers who, upon arriving, do not find a clientele ready and waiting for our treatment services. We must learn the rules of engagement. We must figure out how to meet people, learn how to talk to them, and only then market what we have to offer. We must work side by side, as colleagues, with center staff, case managers, and outreach workers, many of whom are themselves community members and former clients. In early contacts, treatment typically does not take place in an office. Rather, it happens in short exchanges in the drop-in center, on the sidewalk, or standing in a doorway. Only if the client deems those unscheduled contacts suitable will she agree to come in and sit down to begin treatment in earnest.

When clinicians have to figure out how to fit into the culture of the neighborhoods where we work, rather than clients having to fit in with clinic culture and program structures, clients are placed firmly in the driving seat. They choose their own treatment goals—whether, and how, to change their relationship with drugs and whether to take psychiatric medications—and they "dose" themselves with treatment in the same ways that they dose themselves with drugs, on the basis of immediate need, desire, or impulse. It is the job of the therapist, nurse, or doctor to compete with each person's well-established coping mechanisms. To compete successfully, we need to be *more* helpful. This is the true meaning of "client-driven services."

TREATMENT SERVICES

The authors have set up treatment services—crisis intervention and assessment, individual therapy, group therapy, clinical case management, and psychiatric treatment and addiction medicine—in five community and homeless drop-in centers in San Francisco. As in our host agencies, all services are offered on a drop-in basis. We truly "meet people where they are at." The first step to being able to treat someone in a community setting is to engage him in a relationship.

Engagement

Harm reduction therapy is a relational model of treatment. For most clients, significant interpersonal relationships have gone awry due to histories of trauma, leading to an impaired sense of self and a lack of trust in caregivers. To compound the problem of establishing trust, clients are accustomed to being cared for conditionally in institutions and have suffered many transgressions at the hands of past providers. Thus, engagement is a delicate process for both the therapist and the participant. This knowledge informs the need for a style of engagement that both respects each client's capacity for personal interaction and is paced according to his or her comfort level (Little & Franskoviak, 2010).

The first step to effective engagement is compassionate and consistent outreach. We walk around the agencies in which our programs are located, greeting folks, smiling, making eye contact when invited, and stopping to chat when it seems clear that someone has something to say. With some people, we may spend months saying hello on the sidewalk or offering a daily cup of coffee to someone who sits alone day after day. For others, outreach might mean asking permission to sit with them as they wait to see the doctor and, while there, asking about his or her life, being curious, and expressing interest in hearing more, so that treatment becomes a conversation rather than an appointment or a session.

The goal of the first contact or session with someone is to ensure that we have a second. If we can meet clients where they are, join with their experiences, collaborate with them on their treatment, and understand that even the most problematic behavior likely started as an attempt to cope, we have a good chance of seeing someone more than once.

Crisis Intervention and Assessment

Often the first opportunity for engagement is when we intervene in a crisis. In an effort to be helpful to both our host agencies and the clients they serve, we are always on call to deescalate difficult, chaotic, or emergency situations. The episode with Susan is a classic first meeting with a client. Joe, the community center worker, had called Perri to investigate the level of danger of the woman in the bathroom. If she had not fled, Perri would have sat down with her and assessed whether she was in danger. If so, she would have attempted to establish safety, or she might have been forced to hospitalize her. Many clients have come to us this way, and we have gone on to have successful treatment relationships.

Individual Therapy

Individual therapy is almost infinitely flexible. Sidewalk conversations, chats in the drop-in center, and doorway talks eventually become individual therapy sessions. Office visits occur most often on a drop-in basis. At some point, many clients stabilize to the point where they want regular appointments. The evolution from "meeting and greeting" to individual therapy is an organic process, and therapists need to stay loose to evolve with prospective clients as they develop trust and move toward a therapy relationship. Despite this flexibility, charts are opened, often with only a street name, so that documentation of visits can be captured.

Once clients are engaged in therapy, it is of utmost importance that they lead the development of their treatment plan. The therapist will ask about those things that seem to be causing trouble and ask what they might like to change. So that we can genuinely listen, we have to trust that people know what they need, which requires that we contain our own agenda and resist the impulse to become too active. Some clients are ready to move right into changing the behaviors that make their lives chaotic, others may not be able to articulate this for a long time. If a client's goals regarding change are unclear, we tease out what she *is* interested in—a clean set of clothes, a bus token, or a place to live—and help her get it.

Clinical Case Management

In community mental health, therapy and case management are inextricable. We must understand the systemic nature of the problems our clients bring. Often these are as or more important to the presenting problem than intrapsychic or interpersonal history or problems. This understanding should fuel our desire to help clients find immediate help with whatever practical resources are available. The most pressing case management needs are usually the following: help obtaining benefits such as supplementary security income/disability, linkage to medical care, and support to gain housing subsidies by providing documentation of mental illness. Therapists, regardless of our professional discipline, need to develop a social worker's knowledge of community resources, make referrals that smooth the way for clients to use them, and network with social workers.

Group Therapy

Groups present a powerful opportunity to "bridge" people into a community. This is especially important for people who are among the most shunned, isolated, and scapegoated in society. The authors offer daily drop-in groups in the neighborhoods where we work, and we include absolutely everyone who chooses to walk in the door. Called harm reduction therapy groups (Little, 2002, 2006; Little, Hodari, Lavender, & Berg, 2008), these groups are supportive and therapeutic. Our groups utilize motivational interviewing (Miller & Rollnick, 2002) to help people move through the stages of change regarding their drug use. More important, they enlist the wisdom and strengths of group members as co-consultants, which helps people to find their voices and experience themselves as resources rather than drains on the community. Everyone, no matter how intoxicated or psychotic, has insight to share with others.

Psychiatric Treatment and Addiction Medicine

As therapists, our job is to advocate for compassionate and nondogmatic medical and psychiatric care. The use of medications to treat alcohol and other drug problems in combination with psychotropic medications for clients with co-occurring psychiatric disorders is a relatively new field. There are many biases about what drugs should or should not be prescribed for people who have substance use problems. These biases are not always based in science. Often, drugs with abuse or dependence potential, such as benzodiazepines for anxiety or opiates for pain, will not be prescribed because of a client's current or *previous* drug problems, but blanket "do's" and "don'ts" are neither helpful nor accurate. A medication may be safe to use with a person who is actively abusing a substance, or it may not. For example, benzodiazepines are efficacious as treatment for anxiety, but as central nervous system depressants, they are risky to prescribe for someone who is using other central nervous system depressants such as alcohol or opiates. Benzodiazepines are not risky, however, for people who use stimulants. If safety is *not* an overriding concern, then the question becomes, "Will this medication work for someone who is using this drug or that drug?" A well-worn myth is that antidepressants won't be effective in the treatment of depression in a heavy drinker. Our clinical experience is that such medicines can work well. It is different for each person. Because these medicines sometimes work well, clinicians who have blanket policies of "no antidepressants for alcoholics" or "no medications for drug users until they are abstinent" deprive dually diagnosed patients of efficacious and desperately needed treatment. Most important, a doctor's or nurse's concerted efforts to achieve symptom relief and comfort for substance using patients is a strong message of caring and of willingness to partner with patients. Caring is one of the best medicines a medical professional has.

UNIQUE TREATMENT CHALLENGES IN LOW-THRESHOLD COMMUNITY SETTINGS

Some issues are particularly salient for people who frequent community drop-in centers: Poverty is one of the driving forces in their lives; most have histories of trauma and lives fraught with violence and danger; most are active drug users and often come in intoxicated; and more than one third are actively psychotic. The world is viewed through the lens of poverty, trauma, and the perceptual disturbances caused by intoxication and psychosis. These issues present unique treatment challenges, over and above the treatment of substance misuse and mental illness. To add to this volatile mix, therapists bring to the treatment relationship countertransference reactions that are rooted not only in our responses to what our clients bring but also in our own histories and attitudes.

Poverty and Homelessness

Although the vignette about Susan doesn't specifically mention poverty or homelessness, several details allude to these issues: She is in a drop-in center in an urban neighborhood notorious for poverty, drug use, manipulation, and violence; she's missing a front tooth; and she seems to be bathing and/or washing clothes and/or using drugs and/or "being high" in the bathroom. We are called on to respond sensitively to the circumstances in which people live.

Survival Comes First: Esteem the Ways People Are Surviving

Poverty means suffering of many kinds, but it also means having survival skills and other strengths that therapists working with the poor need to esteem. Although this doesn't mean patronizing people for how well they're doing, it does mean recognizing the extra things people must do, and the skills they use, to manage the activities of daily living without enough money. Transportation, communication, obtaining medicines, getting food, finding free goods and services, arranging child care—the less money one has, the more complicated these get, and the more skill is required to get them. It is also important to honor the community's altruism and strength: Often poor people help each other out in amazing ways—and acknowledging their contribution can relieve some of the shame of being "needy."

"The Homeless" Are as Individual as Anyone Else

The term *the homeless* groups together an incredibly diverse array of people, and although for most people without housing, poverty is a shared factor, there may be few other similarities. The experience of poverty differs from person to person: Some fare better than others, with resilience, community supports, help from friends and family, and other factors that alter the severity of the impact; others find the constant struggle to survive miserable, desperate, and intolerable. Some people were born into multigenerational poverty; others were made poor by misfortune—loss of work, a medical crisis, or a debilitating mental health condition, including problems with drug use—during their own lifetime. It is important for the therapist to get to know each person's history, especially what his or her life was like before becoming homeless.

Drug Use Carries Greater Risk and Consequences

Drugs are used by poor people for the same reasons as everyone else, but the poor face bigger risks. Because they more often use in public places, they are caught more often. The lack of access to good legal representation leaves them more vulnerable to felony conviction and incarceration, with the attendant consequences: difficulty getting jobs and, in some states, denial of their right as citizens to vote. Homeless people lack sanitary places to use, thus increasing the risk of infection and disease. The poor in public housing don't fare much better—the more squalid the hotel, the seemingly less stringent the prohibition, but subsidized housing and single-room occupancy hotels often have search and seizure policies that allow police to conduct warrantless, spontaneous searches of rooms. Finally, poor people don't have access to as many treatment options as those with money and insurance. To get any treatment at all, they must rely on publicly funded or charity-based programs, most of which use "treatment as usual" abstinence-only, rigidly structured, disease model, and/or religious-based philosophies. Harm reduction therapy offers all drug users, regardless of socioeconomic status, the same quality of treatment and the same freedom of choice.

Trauma

Not everyone wants to work with trauma. Some of us may feel drawn to it, and others of us feel pretty sure we aren't cut out for it. Regardless of our wishes, those of us who work in community mental health settings must learn to work with trauma survivors—someone much like "Susan" could walk through the door at any moment.

We don't know Susan's story. We don't know what might have led her to seek safety in the community center bathroom. What we can know, if we pay attention, is that Susan's words and body tell a story, and that story is most surely rooted in trauma. First she yells at Perri, then she apologizes. She screams, "don't look at me!" yet her thrashing makes it hard to look away. These seemingly contradictory behaviors may indicate *splits*, a common trauma symptom referring to divisions within the mind or between mind, emotion, and body. We can be "of two minds" about something or feel that our mind wants one thing while our heart wants another and our body yet a third. For example, a drug user receives his social security check on the first of the month. In his mind, he knows he should pay the rent, in his heart he wants to please his case manager, but his body is compelled to get high. This process is analogous to *ambivalence*, which is a key theme in working with drug users (Denning & Little, 2011; Miller & Rollnick, 2002). Less conscious is *splitting*, a common defense in borderline personality disorder that presents as a desire to be close to others while at the same time pushing them away, often with extremely difficult behaviors. Other trauma survivors say, "It's over, I'm fine, I'm not going to let this get to me" while suppressing or "pushing down" other feelings or urges (rage or the desire to scream or cry; Haines, 2007; Levine, 1997; Palmer,

1999; Rothschild, 2004). The difficulty of working with splits and the confounding, alienating, and impulsive behavior they produce makes it imperative to remember that splits are rarely conscious. The client is not *trying* to be difficult; she is acting in the only way she knows how in an ongoing attempt to cope with what feels like a dangerous world.

Trauma-Informed Treatment: Exploring Drug Use and Bumping into Trauma

Almost all of the people with whom we work have histories of trauma and many have complex posttraumatic stress disorder. Trauma violates a person's sense of safety, bodily integrity, and control. Many survivors feel invaded. Traditional substance abuse treatment methods are often intrusive and abusive. We start from a position of *not* doing several things. First of all, we do *not* want to remove a person's drugs from them (as if we could!) until we have a clear understanding of the meaning and purpose of their drug use. Second, we do *not* want to remove ourselves from our clients (by kicking them out of treatment) just because they continue to use or to engage in myriad other behaviors that one might disapprove of. We do not want to create the dilemma in which the user has to choose between us (the treatment) or their drug. The drug, being more familiar and thus more trustworthy, is the obvious choice. As with any defense, a therapist should not attempt to remove it without having something to offer in its place. Third, we do *not* require people to tell their story, or to tell us anything for that matter, sometimes even their names. So what *do* we do?

As therapists, our first priority must be to help survivors establish safety by building on the coping mechanisms that helped them survive. We now understand that helping people identify their strengths and the strategies they have used to keep themselves safe (including and especially drug use) is the foundation of efficacious treatment. It is not helpful to ask someone to recall her experiences; talking about them can be retraumatizing. We remember the first principle of harm reduction: *People use drugs for reasons.* We ask, "What do you think got you through?" or "Tell me what you do now when you feel unsafe?" and "How have drugs helped?" We help people identify their "trauma brakes," ways of stopping traumatic memories or reenactments by learning to build on their survival and coping techniques (Rothschild, 2004). Finally, offering opportunities in which clients call the shots, including honoring the client's right to control the "dose" of treatment, helps to reinstate feelings of control and competency and facilitates a collaborative treatment relationship.

Intoxication

In drop-in centers, where people come in for reasons ranging from a visit to the bathroom, a bus token, or a shelter referral to employment services, medical care, or mental health treatment, people are as likely to be high when they come in as not. Restrictions are placed only on *behaviors* that disrupt others' safety or ability to participate in services. What this means is that, on any given day, harm reduction therapists work with many intoxicated people.

Treat People Who Are Intoxicated as Respectfully as Anyone Else

Regardless of how high, people remain sensitive to how they are treated. They might not remember the content of their interactions, but they do remember the emotional quality. When we assess that a full-length session would not be useful, we make sure to have a pleasant exchange with the client and let her know we are happy that she came in and that we look forward to seeing her next time. If we have to escort someone out because she is disruptive, we urge her to come back another time.

Psychosis

There are many psychotic disorders. We believe that it is most helpful for therapists to concern ourselves with symptoms and functioning rather than diagnosis, especially in settings where we have little access to client history and where accurate reporting is difficult. We commonly see people who have had no mental health treatment in a long time, if ever. They present with delusional thinking, disorganization, bizarre (sometimes sexual) behaviors, anxiety, agitation, social withdrawal, as well as aggressive behaviors. In the case of Susan, we don't know the genesis of her symptoms. We don't have enough information to know what diagnostic category she may fall under, but we have more than enough information to know that she is likely to respond better to us if we utilize particular interventions.

Adaptation and Flexibility: "Dancing" with Psychosis

Working with people with psychosis is like dancing. Some of us aren't particularly predisposed to dancing, but even if we are, this dance is difficult. It isn't a predetermined style, with familiar steps and patterns—it's improvised and spontaneous, the steps dictated by another person whose movements are unpredictable and not intuitive to us. With each psychotic partner, the dance is different. We have to adapt to psychosis, it doesn't adapt to us. This means that a flexible structure of service provision is crucial not just to engaging but also to successfully treating people with psychosis. Creating an environment that makes it as easy as possible for psychotic individuals to feel that they belong and are welcome involves designing services that do not require immediate intakes or appointments. It involves offering multiple "doors" that clients enter—support groups, a medical clinic, the restroom, or the telephone. Once inside, it is important that they encounter therapists who fully embrace their right to be there, no matter if they are "talking crazy" or toting five bags of moldy and malodorous food and newspapers.

Therapists must stay loose so that we can engage with psychotic people at their pace. We must tolerate behaviors—for example, smoking cigarettes, drawing while talking, showing up right at closing time demanding food or bus tokens, lack of interpersonal boundaries—that might be less acceptable for other clients but that serve to relieve psychotic anxiety. We stop and say hello to someone even if we're late for an appointment. We sit down next to a withdrawn person and start a conversation, even if it remains one-sided. We titrate the duration and intensity of treatment interventions, especially when stimulating, difficult, or traumatic topics come up. If we notice someone getting restless or agitated, we end the interaction or change the subject. We use positive reinforcement and support to encourage appropriate social behavior: "Gosh, Susan, I wish we had a private bathroom for you to use, but we have to share this one with other people. Can I help you clean up?" Not only does this approach help to facilitate the development of a therapeutic relationship, it also helps create a welcoming environment that can reduce anxiety and fear.

Finally, we don't have to understand the content to respond to the message; emotional tone, gestures, and other non-verbal forms of expression tell us something about a client's communications. In return, we can respond with emotional resonance that indicates warmth and understanding.

COUNTERTRANSFERENCE

Clients like Susan induce many reactions, including such thoughts as, "Oh, it's just Susan again" or "A drug addict. Come back when you're in your right mind." One might have an impulse to turn away, only to look on in fascination and horror. Finally, one might feel one's chest tightening as helplessness takes over.

Countertransference is currently understood to mean all of the thoughts, feelings, and sensations a therapist experiences in response to his or her clients (Dalenberg, 2000; Geltner, 2006). Earlier definitions of countertransference were more restrictive, attributing countertransference to the therapist's unresolved conflicts or personal issues. Freud (1912) saw countertransference as an impediment to treatment, something that must be "overcome" for the analyst to perceive the client objectively and to make accurate interpretations that would help the client solve the problems that brought her into therapy. Today, theoreticians and clinicians view countertransference as an inevitable and essential component of therapy. Countertransference is a source of information. What we think and how we feel when with a client always reflects information about the client's emotional experience, and it may provide a flavor of how the client affects others in his life.

Countertransference Pitfalls

Working with clients who are impulsive, high, psychotic, or who split and whose lives are chaotic and fraught with danger induces many difficult feelings and reactions in therapists, feelings that must be understood and managed. Here are a few countertransference hazards that require vigilance and support.

The Urge to Control, Punish, or Reject

When we work with clients like Susan, we often have the impulse to *do* something (Unger, 1978). One option is to exert control. This might take the form of citing program rules: "You can only take five minutes in the bathroom." Or we might decide that we know what's best for a client—going to drug treatment is typical— and make that the first goal of treatment. We might also be induced by a difficult client to punish or reject. Most individuals with histories of trauma, mental illness, and substance misuse are ashamed about who they are. They expect to be rejected, either because that is how they are usually treated or because they know on some level that they are unworthy of inclusion. Such clients often induce in the therapist the desire to punish. Clients might do this by acting in an unsafe or disrespectful manner, causing the therapist or program staff to restrict them from services: "If you don't come out next time we ask, you'll have to take a break from services for a week," "I will only talk with you if you don't scream at me," or "Come back when you aren't high" are heard dozens of times a day in community mental health settings across the country. It is important that we stop long enough to analyze our reactions, understand them in relation to the client's life and history, and figure out how to respond according to what the client needs.

Taking Sides with the Part of the Client That Wants to Change

Another typical response is to jump too quickly on the client's professed desire to change. This is often expressed as eagerness to provide helpful, but perhaps premature, solutions. Many people come to us, desperate to save a job, a relationship, or their sanity, saying they have to quit. What does not get expressed is their ambivalence about change. How will they cope with painful memories or overwhelming feelings without their drugs or other behaviors? Who will they spend time with if not the people with whom they have been using? Our job is to resist the temptation to cheerlead change. Rather, we need to ask these questions to help the client recognize the other side of their splits, or ambivalence. In this way, ambivalence can be resolved and authentic decisions made.

Compensating for Clients' Poverty and Deprivation

For those of us who come from backgrounds of poverty, we might reexperience the fear and anxiety that our own poverty caused us and overextend ourselves because we "know how it feels to be poor." We might struggle with the status that a professional role has brought us. For those of us from more affluent backgrounds, we might feel guilt at having more privilege than our clients and find ourselves on one hand pitying our clients and on the other blaming them for their economic problems ("if he would just get a job . . ."). Regardless of background, any of us can experience the fear of poverty and aversion to the poor; all it takes to become homeless is to lose a job, lose connection with family to rely on in tough times, have a medical emergency with overwhelming bills, or become disabled. It is essential that these and other countertransference responses to our clients be explored thoroughly.

Managing Countertransference

To have countertransference feelings is positive, because it means that the therapist is attuned to the client and has access to emotional and sensory information about the client. This is not to say that therapists do not have reactions to clients that are based in our own histories, personalities, and attitudes, but the more we clarify these in *our* therapy and in supervision, the more we can be attuned to the feelings that the *client* is inducing in us, and the more we can understand what the client's life is like from the point of view of her or his history, thoughts, and feelings.

RECOMMENDATIONS FOR PRACTICE IN COMMUNITY DROP-IN SETTINGS

Although this chapter is full of recommendations for community-based harm reduction, we would like to highlight practices that we think maximize the likelihood of success and satisfaction. The clinical skills that we most recommend are in the area of self-management are as follows:

- Be neutral—in both affect and opinion.
- Be curious—especially about why people use drugs—and get comfortable with drugs and the idea of intoxication.
- Be flexible—get comfortable with people not making appointments/not showing up—and never let go of the hope that they will.
- Be real—let clients know when you are concerned.
- Be comfortable not knowing—when you don't know what to do, ask and listen.

The most important intervention is to pay lots of compliments—nothing does more to restore someone's ego functioning. Congratulate people for every act of creativity, for every survival success, and even for every adaptive use of drugs.

Trainings that we most recommend include the following:

- Harm reduction therapy, including reading *Practicing Harm Reduction Psychotherapy* (Denning & Little, 2011), which summarizes all of the foundational models

- Neurobiology of street drugs, common terminology for them, and how the reward-incentive pathway works
- Trauma, trauma and substance use, and somatic treatments for trauma
- Motivational interviewing

Above all, this work cannot be done without regular, strong, supportive supervision. A low-threshold community mental health setting needs to include structures that facilitate what Saakvitne and Pearlman (1996) called the ABCs—awareness, balances, and connection—of maintaining a viable mental health care practice. Any institution designed for low-threshold services has an ethical obligation to provide the means through which each staff member may attain these three elements. A therapist must be able to talk in supervision about all countertransference responses without fear or shame, as well as have opportunities for self-reflection and connection with colleagues throughout the day. Through these activities, we become more aware of what we are experiencing, and the feelings that get activated during sessions with our complicated clients can be integrated into our overall experience and learning. Without these three elements, therapists practicing in low-threshold settings risk becoming vulnerable in ways that harm both their clients and themselves.

CONCLUSION

At HRTC's community programs, we work with hundreds of clients each year. We practice the many strategies presented in this chapter. Over time, most of our clients stabilize—the level of crisis diminishes, drug use comes under more conscious control, psychiatric medications ease the worst symptoms of mental illness, and helpful relationships develop between community members who meet each other in our drop-in groups. Our therapists have remained vital for 10 years by taking great care to support each other and by receiving enormous amounts of training and supervision. Most of all, we enjoy and appreciate our clients—for their creativity, their humor, their willingness to try yet another relationship with a caregiver, and their phenomenal ability to survive.

REFERENCES

Dalenberg, C. J. (2000). *Countertransference and the treatment of trauma.* Washington, DC: American Psychological Association.

Denning, P. (2000). *Practicing harm reduction psychotherapy: An alternative approach to addictions.* New York, NY: Guilford Press.

Denning, P., & Little, J. (2011). *Practicing harm reduction psychotherapy: An alternative approach to addictions* (2nd ed.). New York, NY: Guilford Press.

Denning, P., Little, J., & Glickman, A. (2004). *Over the influence: The harm reduction guide to managing drugs and alcohol.* New York, NY: Guilford Press.

Freud, S. (1912). *The Dynamics of Transference. The Standard Edition of the Complete Psychological Works of Sigmund Freud,* vol. XII, 1911–1913.

Geltner, P. (2006). The concept of objective countertransference and its role in a two-person psychology. *The American Journal of Psychoanalysis, 66*, 25–42.

Goosby, E. P. (2001). *Evidence based research on the efficacy of needle exchange programs: An overview.* Unpublished manuscript prepared by the Office of HIV/AIDS Policy, San Francisco Department of Health.

Haines, S. (2007). *Healing sex: A mind–body approach to healing sexual trauma.* San Francisco, CA: Cleis Press.

Kessler, R., Crum, R., Warner, L., & Nelson, C. (1997). Lifetime co-occurrence of *DSM-III-R* alcohol misuse and dependence with other psychiatric disorders in the National Comorbidity Study. *Archives of General Psychiatry, 54*, 313–321.

Khantzian, E. (1985). The self-medication hypotheses of addictive disorders: Focus on heroin and cocaine dependence. *American Journal of Psychiatry, 142*, 1259–1264.

Levine, P. (1997) *Waking the tiger: Healing trauma.* Berkeley, CA: North Atlantic Books.

Little, J. (2002). The sobriety support group: A harm reduction group for dually diagnosed adults. In A. Tatarsky (Ed.), *Harm reduction psychotherapy: A new treatment for drug and alcohol problems.* Northvale, NJ: Jason Aronson.

Little, J. (2006). Harm reduction therapy groups: Engaging drinkers and drug users in a process of change. *Journal of Groups in Addiction and Recovery, 1*, 69–94.

Little, J., & Franskoviak, P. (2010). We're glad you came: Harm reduction therapy in community settings. *Journal of Clinical Psychotherapy: In Session, 66*, 175–188.

Little, J., Hodari, K., Lavender, J., & Berg, A. (2008). Come as you are: Harm reduction drop-in groups for multi-diagnosed drug users. *Journal of Groups in Addiction and Recovery, 3*, 161–192.

Marlatt, G. A. (Ed.). (1998). *Harm reduction: Pragmatic strategies for managing high risk behaviors.* New York, NY: Guilford Press.

Miller, W. R., & Carroll, K. M., (Eds.). (2006). *Rethinking substance abuse: What the science tells and what we should do about it.* New York, NY: Guilford Press.

Miller, W. R., & Rollnick, S. (2002). *Motivational interviewing: Preparing people for change* (2nd ed.). New York, NY: Guilford Press.

Nadelman, E. (1992). Thinking seriously about alternatives to drug prohibition, Part 1. *Daedalus, 121*, 87–132.

Palmer, W. (1999). *The intuitive body: Aikido as a clairsentient practice.* Berkeley, CA: North Atlantic Books.

Prochaska, J. O., DiClemente, C. C., & Norcross, J. C. (1992). In search of how people change: Applications to addictive behaviors. *American Psychologist, 47*, 1102–1114.

Rothschild, B. (2004). Applying the brakes. *Psychotherapy Networker, 26*, 42–46.

Saakvitne, K. W., & Pearlman, L. A. (1996). *Transforming the pain: A workbook on vicarious traumatization for helping professionals who work with traumatized clients.* New York, NY: Norton.

Springer, E. (1991). Effective AIDS prevention with active drug users: The harm reduction model. In M. Shernoff (Ed.), *Counseling chemically dependent people with HIV illness* (pp. 141–158). New York, NY: Harrington Park Press.

Tatarsky, A. (2002). *Harm reduction psychotherapy: A new approach to treating drug and alcohol problems.* Northvale, NJ: Jason Aronson.

Unger, R. (1978). Sustaining transference in the treatment of alcoholism. *Modern Psychoanalysis, 3*, 155–171.

Case Study

Harm Reduction Groups: Meeting Drug Users Where They Are

Anna Berg and Jeannie Little

The Harm Reduction Support Group begins in its usual way: doors to the group room open at 1:30 p.m., with coffee, chairs, and facilitator ready and waiting. I welcome the group with an introduction that many have heard before while group members get coffee and mill about, getting settled. During the session, 13 people join us.

"Hello! Welcome to the Harm Reduction Group. I'm Anna, and we meet every Monday, Wednesday, and Friday from 1:30 to 2:30 p.m. in this room. This is a harm reduction group, so everyone is welcome just as they are, whenever they get here—even if they join us 5 minute before we end! There are no real rules for this group, other than you can come and go as you need to—whether you need to pee, take a drug break, just aren't feeling it, or you have some other place to be, you make the call. Also, we call everyone here as they introduce themselves. Lastly, we do not allow threats of any kind in this group—this is harm reduction! *Help yourself to coffee or juice and let's start with check-ins. Anyone want to start us off?"*

Casey, a 40-year-old IV drug user who has advanced HIV and bipolar disorder, jumps right in, directing his comments to the facilitator while wriggling in his chair, his foot tapping on the floor. "I really need to check in about my landlord. I think he knows I use and wants to kick me out. When I signed my lease it said, "no drug use of any kind" or they can evict you. Do you think he knows? I put towels under all my doors and windows."

Kurt, a 55-year-old veteran with a traumatic head injury, rolls his eyes toward Casey. "Yeah, man. Of course they know. This is the Tenderloin—the F-in' drug den of the world! He probably just wants you to share." At this, he kicks back his chair and goes to get coffee as Tasha enters the room. Casey continues to wiggle in his chair, almost as if he were vibrating.

"Hihihihi everybody!" announces Tasha, a mother of three in her 40s, although she appears much older. *"I just got to get in here, make some room for me, here I come. I can't get in . . . oh, OK, thanks."* Tasha typically enters group this way—announcing herself and asking others to make room for her. Tasha has multiple sclerosis, which many group members know, as well as posttraumatic stress disorder; as a woman, she is extended courtesies that many male members would not extend to each other. Franco moves his chair so that Tasha can sit close to the door. I welcome Tasha and, to help the group stay focused, let her know that we were checking in with Casey.

Casey continues to verbalize his worry about his landlord, this time directing his questions to Kurt. They get into an argument when Kurt uses the phrase *"Damn straight."* Casey is gay, Kurt knows this, and he laughs awkwardly at the misunderstanding, while Casey revs up.

Franco jumps in to help. Franco is a slight man with schizophrenia who speaks English as a second language; group members often have a hard time understanding him. Today, he seems to be more organized. *"It's OK, man. He just means maybe your landlord thinks you use medical marijuana or something. Maybe he don't know about the speed."*

Franco's intervention calmed Casey down long enough for Kyle to jump in. Kyle, in his 50s, is diagnosed with schizophrenia and is a heavy speed user. He wants to talk about medical marijuana. I interrupt him so we don't get derailed and ask his permission to pose a question to Casey before answering his questions about medical marijuana. Kyle agreed, although he had challenges sticking with this agreement and needed gentle reminding.

I tried to draw out the meaning behind Casey's sudden anxiety about his landlord. *"Casey, you seem really upset about your landlord and worried that he might evict you. Would it be helpful to say more about what is bothering you so much today?"*

After a long pause, Casey disclosed that his drug connection had trashed his apartment the night before, causing damage to the building. This resulted in complaints from neighbors to the landlord. Casey was interrupted by Tasha, who wanted to know what drug Casey used, and by Kurt, who began to talk about the futility of harm reduction. I reminded Tasha and Kurt that in the Harm Reduction Support Group, we ask people for their permission before we give them feedback and encouraged them to get Casey's OK before commenting on his situation. Casey continued, saying, *"The feedback's OK. It's OK that Kurt said harm reduction is dumb. I know I should quit; my doctor says I need to quit—I only have four T-cells."*

DJ, a large, soft-spoken man with an extensive history of trauma, commented that he tried abstinence and it didn't work for him. He suggested to Casey that just because his doctor wanted him to quit, that probably wouldn't be enough to motivate him.

Following DJ's lead, I reminded the group that in harm reduction, what works for one person doesn't always work for everyone. Each person has his or her own

reasons for using and reasons for wanting to change; we call this the decisional balance. *I asked the group if they could help Casey think about the pros and cons of
speed, with lively results. Kurt joined the side of Casey that wanted to change his use,
pointing out that he was jeopardizing his housing and health and may be the victim
of violence because his connection seemed to be unpredictable. Kellie, a round-faced
woman in her early 50s who had previously seemed checked out from the conversation, offered to help Casey clean his apartment, suggesting that he "make use of"
his high by cleaning up. Tasha sided with the part of Casey who worried about his
health, sharing her own stories of struggling with crack and MS, and Kyle joined with
the side of Casey who liked getting high, talking about medical marijuana and the
benefits of getting high "to get away."*

*The discussion proceeded while an unfamiliar young man in the corner nodded
out on opiates and Franco got more coffee. Vaughn entered the room, thumping a
Bible. "Here I am!" he shouted. "I brought the word with me too!" Kyle became impa-
tient to check in and hear from others, and others in the group grumbled that we were
running out of juice.*

*"You're right! We need to check in with other folks. There are many pressing needs
in this group. Can we find out first if we have helped Casey resolve his dilemma?"
Casey reported that he felt less pressure to make a decision about his relationship
with speed and a little less anxious that he might be evicted.*

*The group proceeded, as it usually does, with attention to various issues such as
the virtues of marijuana; a female member's current domestic violence situation; a
biblical lesson from Vaughn, which the group barely tolerated—always with people
coming and going, getting coffee and juice, and both supporting and irritating each
other.*

DECONSTRUCTING WHAT HAPPENS IN A HARM REDUCTION GROUP

Drop-In Groups Are All-Inclusive

*Drop-in groups are the lowest threshold form of group treatment and, as such,
welcome some of the most chaotic and complicated clients in community mental
health. Many clients are not able to keep appointments or follow behavioral expectations of closed session groups nor are they able to tolerate prolonged contact with
others. (Think of Kyle or Vaughn in this case study.) In a drop-in group, people attend
as they need or wish. They are thereby able to "dose" themselves with treatment,
much as they dose themselves with drugs; such a model affirms that the client is
the expert and knows her or his needs. This, in turn, lowers resistance and allows
us to avoid potential power struggles by placing authority in the hands of the client.
Furthermore, drop-in groups replicate the organic, nonlinear change process identified by the stages of change model (Prochaska, DiClemente, & Norcross, 1992). They*

also support client self-efficacy, a key ingredient for motivation to change (Miller & Rollnick, 2002).

Harm Reduction Groups Accept Everything

The primary challenge to promoting acceptance of the adaptiveness of drug use is the cultural dominance of the disease model of addiction. The disease model insists that abstinence is the only rational response to out-of-control drug use. This attachment to the culture of "clean and sober" has created challenges to treatment because people who are most at-risk due to problematic drug use are frequently screened out of care. This encourages clients to lie about their drug use if they don't want to be rejected. As a result, people are not accustomed to talking openly with a therapist about the details of their drug use, and many have a challenging time sharing about their use in groups.

The leader of a harm reduction group must create a counterculture of acceptance of drug use by constantly reinforcing that people use drugs for reasons and by asking group members to talk about those reasons. To create an environment of acceptance—or radical acceptance as a Buddhist might say—the leader models empathy and respect for each person's chosen means of coping (think about the differences in coping methods seen in Kurt, Casey, and the nodding-out young man in this case study). The leader does much reframing to combat the conventional view that continued drug use represents failure. The idea is to lower clients' resistance to change by encouraging them to accept their present circumstances and each other.

Group Members Are the Experts

In harm reduction groups, members tell their own story. No one's relationship with drugs is the same as anyone else's, and no one's story (or drug) is better than any other's. By not defining problems from any particular perspective, such as the disease model of addiction, harm reduction groups create conditions that encourage each individual to explore his or her own experiences with drugs. The practice of not demanding any particular behavior, including attendance, affirms each person's autonomy and builds self-efficacy. As members of the group often say, "each of us knows what we need, including whether to be here or not. No one else can tell us what we need."

Members Talk About Whatever They Want

To reinforce that group members are the experts, the leader of a harm reduction group must not set an agenda. In other words, it is not for the leader to decide what is important. Group members can decide in advance what topics are of interest to them so that the group leader, or a designated member, can come prepared with information on those topics. The group can also be structured in such a way that topics of interest are arrived at spontaneously during the course of a check-in. Typically in harm reduction groups approximately 50% of group time is devoted to talking about drug use and change. Members also talk about emotional issues, struggles to survive, relationships, family, and treatment (e.g., HIV or psychiatric) adherence.

And There Are Almost No Rules

A harm reduction drop-in group must operate with few, if any, rules to accommodate the most chaotic, complex, and at-risk drug users. Most people who experience problematic drug use have severe emotional challenges (Denning & Little, 2011), and people who come to community mental health centers are even more complicated. The only rules are those imposed on the leader: Successful drop-in groups always start and stop on time, are rarely canceled, are held in the same location whenever possible, and begin in the same way each time. This structure helps contain anxiety by helping clients know what to expect. It also helps clients learn that they can count on the help provided by the drop-in group and encourages them to add group attendance to their list of coping skills. By offering a structured group with few rules, there is less opportunity for punishment or feelings of failure if one does not or cannot abide by the rules, thus increasing self-efficacy and helping to build momentum for change. By eliminating rules, the group builds its own norms and has to work actively to include challenging members. (Think of Vaughn, Kyle, or Tasha in the group example.) This is crucial not to just engaging vulnerable people, but also to providing client-centered, efficacious treatment.

REFERENCES

Denning, P., & Little, J. (2011). *Practicing Harm Reduction: An Alternative Approach to Addictions* (2nd ed.). New York, NY: Guilford Press.

Little, J. (2002). The sobriety support group: A harm reduction group for dually diagnosed adults. In A. Tatarsky (Ed.), *Harm reduction psychotherapy: A new treatment for drug and alcohol problems*. Northvale, NJ: Jason Aronson.

Miller, W.R., & Rollnick, S. (2002). *Motivational interviewing: Preparing people for change* (2nd ed.) New York, NY: Guilford Press.

Prochaska, J. O., DiClemente, C. C., & Norcross, J. C. (1992). In search of how people change: Applications to addictive behaviors. *American Psychologist, 47,* 1102–1114.

Rotgers, F., Kern, M., & Hoeltzel, R. (2002). *Responsible drinking: A moderation management approach for problem drinkers*. Oakland, CA: New Harbinger.

Saladin, M. E., & Santa Ana, E. J. (2004). Controlled drinking: More than just a controversy. *Current Opinions in Psychiatry, 17,* 175–187.

Chapter 4

Working with the Queer Community: Advocacy as a Therapeutic Intervention

Danielle Castro and Melissa Fritchle

WHO IS THE QUEER COMMUNITY?

We have chosen the term *queer* consciously because of its inclusive nature. This reclaimed word, reclaimed because it was previously used as an insult, has sociopolitical connotations that are important. Queer is not simply synonymous with LGBTQ (lesbian gay, bisexual, transgender, and questioning), although it is often used that way. The queer community includes gay, lesbian, bisexual, and transgender people; it recognizes the spectrum of transgender identity and expression, including transsexuals, drag kings and queens, cross-dressers, androgynies, and intersex people as well as a large spectrum of sexuality and sexual expression, sometimes being used to represent people whose sexual activities place them outside the mainstream. It can also include people who choose relationship and family structures that differ from traditional monogamous expectations. Queer can be an identity claimed by anyone who feels oppressed or limited by heteronormatively, the gender binary, and traditional relationship structures. It can include allies and advocates as well. In its diversity, the term *queer* breaks down boundaries and can pull a community together in support of personal freedoms. In truth, what it means to be queer is different for each individual and needs to be self-defined.

Because of the diversity of the queer community, competent treatment and understanding includes awareness of that diversity and also the interlocking systems of identity at play for any individual. The queer community has members who are old, young, of any race or heritage, members of any socioeconomic bracket or religion, and in any stage of life-cycle development. Queer people will be a part of any community you enter, any system of care in which you take part. Supporting the queer community means supporting family members and friends of the queer individual and educating yourself regarding issues of impact.

Because of the limitations of this chapter, we focus on LGBTQ representations of queer. We believe that building cultural competence to effectively understand and address the needs of the queer community is a priority and has been historically lacking in the mental health field. For communities that have been unrepresented or face discrimination, advocacy must be seen as a part of the healing process. In this chapter, we strive to give readers an overview of issues and systems that have an impact on the queer community and suggest ways for therapists to provide inclusive, informed, transformative mental health programs for this community; these ideas can be extended to your work within the broader queer community.

THE COMPLEXITIES OF GENDER AND SEXUAL ORIENTATION

The Gender Binary

We feel it's important to begin with some key concepts that provide a framework to better understand the complexities that affect the queer community. In a heteronormative world, the concept of gender is limited to two categories, male and female, but in reality, nature has manifested itself as a spectrum of genders that aren't constrained by our societal beliefs. When a baby is born, the first question parents have is, "Is it a boy or a girl?" Usually the child's gender is assigned by the attending physician based on a limited physical examination of the genitals (Dragowski, Sandigorsky, & Scharrón-del Rio, 2011). To put it bluntly, if a child has something that resembles a penis, then the baby is assigned male. Conversely, if the child has genitals that resemble a vagina, the child is assigned female. There is no chromosomal, hormonal, or extensive testing done to label a child with a lifelong gender marker that will dictate his or her reality for the rest of their life.

Many children have been misgendered by this common practice, in particular, children born with disorders of sexual development (DSD) or those who are intersex. According to the Intersex Society of North America (2008), DSD is a term to describe individuals who are born with reproductive or sexual anatomy (either internal or external) that do not match the definitions of male or female. Children born with DSD can be misgendered and undergo gender confirmation surgery, also known as sex reassignment surgery, to match their assigned gender. Regardless of ethical reasoning or laws, until recently this radical practice was performed without parental consent (Gearhart & Reiner, 2004), and of course the child has had no say because he or she did not have the capacity to make decisions at birth. There are only two options considered: One must be either male or female. This is the gender binary. To understand the concept of gender we must step outside our own beliefs or misconceptions about what gender is supposed to be and be willing to explore what it really is.

Sexual Orientation

As with the gender binary, society tends to compartmentalize its understanding of sexual orientation as a binary system. Most people feel pressure to identify as either gay or straight, and the therapy community has often served to increase this pressure. Well-meaning therapy interventions have seen someone questioning their orientation as either in denial, rebelling, or going through a phase and have pushed clients to settle on a clearly defined (by the binary) sexual orientation. There has been a dismissal of the possibility of bisexuality or a more fluid sexuality that may not be defined by a gender to which one is attracted. Studies are beginning to propose that for many people, their sexual orientation and who they are attracted to throughout their life is fluid and can change (Butterworth & Diamond, 2008).

Gender Identity

Gender identity is better described as the gender people feel they are internally and innately regardless of physical characteristics. Most people say this internal sense of who they are was clear to them by the ages of 3 to 5 years old (Shaffer, 2009), although there are many ways in which one's gender identity may evolve and change throughout one's life—for example, gender queer, transgender, female, gender fluid, transsexual, male, and much more. As a society, we make assumptions about gender identity based on what we see: how people are physically represented. Because gender identity is a self-identifiable, internal process, these assumptions about another person's gender identity can be limiting. For this reason, it is critical to check with the person what their preferred gender identification is and what pronouns they might prefer, for example: ze, zir, them, they, him, her, she, or he.

Gender Expression

Gender expression refers to the way people express their gender identity through the way they dress and walk, the jobs they take, their hobbies or interests, and more. Gender expression can be masculine, feminine, or a mix of both, and it may change often or not at all for each person. For example, a person can identify as a transsexual woman but may express her gender in a very masculine way by taking on a more traditionally masculine role. People that step outside the gender binary and heteronormative gender expression tend to be outcast and often are victims of crimes perpetrated against them because of the narrow social bias that exists (National Coalition of Anti-Violence Programs, 2010). The feminist movement created a cultural jolt and challenged expectations in the realm of gender roles and rules, but clearly more work needs to be done before our world can become a safer place that accepts all people regardless of gender identity or expression.

SPECIAL CONCERNS FOR THIS POPULATION

Discrimination and Stigma

Discrimination against the queer community is extremely prevalent. Currently 75 countries criminalize same-sex relationships, and seven of those countries actually punish those found to be having same sex relationships by death. Although the United States is one of the more progressive countries when it comes to queer legislation and human rights, the rates of bullying and hate crimes here are alarming. According to a study conducted by the Human Rights Campaign in 2009, sexual orientation ranks as the third-highest motivator for hate crime incidents (Wilson-Stronks, 2009).

In February 2011, the National Center for Transgender Equality found that out of 6,450 trans-identified individuals from throughout the United States, 63% reported having experienced a serious act of discrimination, including loss of employment due to bias, eviction due to bias, school bullying or harassment so severe that the respondent had to drop out, being bullied by an instructor, physical assault due to bias, sexual assault due to bias, homelessness because of gender identity and/or expression, lost relationships with partner or children due to gender identity and/or expression, denial of medical services due to bias, and finally incarceration due to gender identity and/or expression (Grant et al., 2009).

People are threatened by what they do not understand, and unfortunately hate crimes against the queer community are an example of what people are capable of when acting out of this gender binary based hatred. Homophobia is described as hatred or rejection of gay, lesbian, or bisexual people. There have been many cases of gay bashings or brutal attacks made on queer people. Regardless of the label, all of these phobias are the result of ignorance, lack of understanding, and beliefs based on the gender binary system.

Internalized Stigma and Homophobia

Over time stigma, discrimination, hatred, homophobia, and transphobia can become internalized and can cause queer individuals to think negatively about themselves. This may lead to self-shame, depression, anxiety, social phobia, and even suicide. Suicide attempt rates among the general population in the United States are 1.6% (McIntosh, 2002). The suicide attempt rate among trans-identified individuals is 41% (Grant et al., 2009), and lesbian, gay, and bisexual individuals are more than twice as likely as the heterosexual population to report a suicide attempt (Beautrais et al., 2010).

Queer communities are forced to cope with their internalized emotions and can turn to substance use as a way to escape intense feelings. There is little research specific to substance use within the queer community, but the information that does exist finds that the odds of queer youth using substances was 190% greater than heterosexual youth and 340% higher for bisexual youth (Bukstein et al., 2008). Substance use is a prevalent problem in the queer community, and there is continued need for research and resources.

Family Issues: Safety in the Home

Discrimination and stigma can happen in any context, including at home. Most people think of home as a safe space to which they can retreat when the world becomes overwhelming. Queer identified individuals, whether they are children, adults, or elders, often do not have a place that they can call "home." Families may reject their queer family members and sometimes estrange themselves completely. The emotional traumas caused by rejection are countless but can include depression, anxiety, anger, resentment, suicidal ideation, stress, use of illegal drugs, and many more negative health outcomes (Diaz, Huebner, Ryan, & Sanchez, 2009).

Family rejection has a great impact on a child's mental health and well-being. According to Hammer, Finkelhor, and Sedlack (2002), 1,682,900 youth under age 15 were forced out of their homes or ran away sometime during 1999. Although it is challenging to estimate how high the prevalence of homelessness is within LGBTQ youth communities, we know that these youth are more likely to be thrown out or run away from home (Whitbeck, Chen, Hoyt, Tyler, & Johnson, 2004). Once queer youth are homeless, they have to find ways to survive. Survival sex work may then become a means to an end and puts queer youth at higher risk for homophobic and transphobic hate crimes, HIV and other sexually transmitted diseases, illegal drug use, and death (Hyatt, 2011). The overrepresentation of queer homeless youth is a growing problem in the United States (Clark, Desai, Rabinovitz, & Schneir, 2010) that needs to be addressed and researched to facilitate healing and wholeness.

Relationships and the Coming-Out Process

Decisions related to "coming out" and sharing their sense of self and relationships create ongoing challenges and concerns for the queer community. Coming out is a lifelong process that will be revisited not only at home but in other social contexts such as new relationships, school, work, places of worship, and other social settings. It is not a one-time event. Society is still heterocentric and holds the expectation that people will be straight. This social pressure creates a tense environment for anyone who is queer identified. Coming out as gay, lesbian, or bisexual can feel like a daunting task that causes anxiety and concern. The thoughts that run through a person's mind are fear of rejection, isolation, potential verbal or physical abuse, fear of abandonment, and many other frightening ideas. Coming out is a reaffirmation of one's own sexual orientation, relationships, sense of self, and gender identity. It can carry a lot of meaning for people coming out and those around them; however, there are real risks related to all of these, for example, risks of losing family members' support, long-term relationships, homes, custody of children, or membership in social or religious groups. Depending on the circumstances, though, coming out can be a positive experience that offers individuals the freedom to be their authentic selves.

Trans people can and often do have a difficult time coming out as well. When LGBQ individuals face the coming-out process, they have choices about who and how much to disclose because sexual orientation is not immediately apparent to an outside observer. Each individual can decide in each setting whether it is safe to disclose about themselves or not. Trans people disclose their gender identity and expression, which can be external expressions of self, and once someone begins transitioning, their changes are visible to their peers and loved ones. Queer people can go through many challenges when coming out or transitioning. The diversity of experiences is as diverse as the queer community itself.

Employment Issues

Employment discrimination and underemployment are major issues for the queer community and should be considered in clinical settings. In the United States, discrimination based on sexual orientation in the workplace or gender identity is not illegal. Some states have adopted their own laws to help protect their queer workforce, but most have not. It is estimated that gay men earn 16% less than heterosexual men (Allegretto & Arthur, 2001). The General Social Survey conducted by the National Opinion Research Center at the University of Chicago found that 27% of lesbian, gay, and bisexual respondents had experienced sexual orientation–based harassment in the 5 years leading up to 2008 (Mallory & Sears, 2011). This adds another layer of challenge for queer people. Many are forced to hide their true identities because of fear of losing their careers or jobs.

Even in more progressive states like California, despite having laws that protect queer communities, discrimination still occurs. A 2009 survey conducted by the Transgender Law Center in San Francisco revealed that 70% of the transgender community reported having had experienced workplace harassment or discrimination directly related to their gender identity (Hartzell, Frazer, Wertz, & Davis, 2009). The report also highlighted that many trans people have a college degree but are still unable to find gainful employment after transition. It is challenging for trans people to find a job, particularly if they do not pass as their gender identity or identify with an ambiguous gender. Many businesses will choose not to hire trans people because of their own biases and beliefs. Although this is considered discrimination under California law, it still happens (Guardian & Transgender Law Center, 2006).

CONSIDERING INTERLOCKING SYSTEMS

Health Care Issues: Lack of Competent Care

Access to health care is a big concern for all communities; however, members of the queer community have many barriers to accessing competent health care that is sensitive to their diverse needs. The heightened need for health care professionals skilled in queer health was brought to the forefront by the rise of AIDS in the 1980s. The wake of AIDS left behind a ripple effect that later became the beginnings of a movement to educate health care providers about the needs of the queer community. A recent study by researchers at the Lesbian, Gay, Bisexual and Transgender Medical Education Research Group at Stanford University found that American and Canadian medical schools reported on average medical training consists of just 5 hours related to LGBTQ care and a third of the schools admitted to spending no time on this population (American Association of Sex Educators, Counselors, and Therapists, 2012).

The medical community has made great strides since the start of the 21st century to be as inclusive as possible; nonetheless, the LGB community continues to experience health disparities that need to be addressed. Accessing health care can be challenging for LGB adults, and most will delay making an effort to access critical health care services because of the discrimination and lack of provider competence that exists. According to the Center for American Progress, 29% of LGB adults postpone seeking health care as compared with 17% among heterosexuals (Krehely, 2009).

The issue of health insurance is another barrier for LGB communities. Some states do allow for domestic partnership, but this does not necessarily mean that health insurance companies have to provide coverage for domestic partners or their children. The issues that the LGB community is faced with are devastating and can lead to negative mental health outcomes. Clinicians need to be prepared to offer support and process through frustration, depression, anxiety, and fear.

The transgender community has a unique struggle when it comes to health care. In 2009 a survey conducted by the National Center for Transgender Equality along with other collaborative partners found that 28% of respondents were subject to harassment in medical settings, and 2% were victims of violence in doctor's offices (Grant et al., 2009). Therapists should not be surprised when their trans clients express distrust of the medical system and have actively worked to avoid and bypass medical care settings.

Another unique aspect of health care for transgender-identified individuals is the process of physical transition. If a person wishes to go through any type of medical intervention to transition to another gender, most have to go through a pathology-based model that requires transsexuals to seek mental health care services to get special permission to move forward. This process could take anywhere from 1 to 2 years. To understand the emotional distress caused by this process, one can stop to think of what it would be like to have to prove to someone that you are a man or woman to be able to have a healthy life.

If a transsexual wants to have any kind of gender confirmation surgery (e.g., breast removal, breast augmentation, creation of a vagina or penis, feminizing surgeries, or masculine-enhancing surgeries), there are standards of care that are recommended by the World Professional Association for Transgender Health (WPATH, 2011). Most health insurance companies specifically exclude transition-related health care. The cost of surgeries, hormones, and transition-related health care can be prohibitive as it ranges from $45,000 to $60,000 (Horton, 2008). The prohibitive costs, stigma, discrimination, and other barriers for trans people leaves some with no other option than to turn to the black market for their transition-related medicines and surgical procedures, which are not always safe or regulated and can lead to negative health outcomes such as deformity, serious injury, and death (Center of Excellence for Transgender Health, April 2011). Having turned to illegal means to seek hormones or body modification, trans people may fear disapproval from medical providers, which creates another reason to avoid the medical system.

HIV's Impact on Queer Community

HIV is one of the worst pandemics in history. The queer community was hit particularly hard by AIDS; at the beginning of the pandemic, the disease was believed to predominantly afflict gay men. Society quickly came to the conclusion that the illness was a "gay cancer." This unfortunate response was a historic example of societal discrimination, stigma, and homophobia. It was later determined that AIDS was in fact a sexually transmitted disease that affects everyone.

Queer people who were alive during the beginnings of the AIDS pandemic experienced tremendous loss of friends, lovers, family members, and colleagues. People were dying at alarming rates, and the queer community was left to take care of their own. Some medical institutions were willing to work with patients who were HIV-positive or had AIDS, but many refused to provide health care services. The tragedy of AIDS brought the community closer together and also provided a massive platform to fight for equal rights as a queer community (Bell & Binnie, 2000). Today, AIDS is no longer a death sentence. It is, however, a life-threatening illness that infects one person every 9.5 minutes in the United States (Centers for Disease Control and Prevention, 2009). Medications exist that allow HIV-positive people to live longer, but they come with severe side effects and require taking medications several times a day on a rigid schedule, which has its own set of challenges.

Living with AIDS and HIV is a tough battle for everyone. The issues surrounding coming out as queer are many, but they are multiplied if a person is HIV positive or has AIDS. The question of when and with whom to disclose HIV status is challenging. Stigma and discrimination of those infected is still a big problem in society, which adds another layer of difficulty for those infected with HIV. HIV/AIDS is still represented in catastrophic proportions in the queer community, especially for gay and bisexual men (Centers for Disease Control and Prevention, September 2011). It is also estimated that one in four transwomen of color are HIV-positive, and African American transwomen are at highest risk with more than 50% being HIV positive (Crepaz et al., 2008).

Incarceration

Prison is an especially harsh environment for queer people. It is estimated that 67% of all incarcerated LGBTQ people in California are victims of sexual abuse while in prison (Jenness, Matsuda, Maxson, & Summer, 2007). This rate is 15 times higher than the overall population of the incarcerated survey participants. Some prisons and jails have developed policies or common practices that they use to protect queer inmates (Brook, 2004), but this is not the norm. Homophobia and transphobia permeate most of these practices and the common approach is to place queer people in solitary confinement (Just Detention International, 2009).

Trans people are housed in gender-specific prisons according to their genitals. Most trans people cannot afford costly surgeries, and some do not want them; however, this does not mean that they do not have a clear and important gender identity. Transwomen with penises are forced to be housed with men, and transmen with vaginas are forced to be housed with women. Even if transwomen have had breast augmentation and present as outwardly female, if they have a penis, they get housed with men. Routine strip searches, showers, and other activities are done alongside other inmates, and trans people are endangered (Just Detention International, 2009).

There is some hope for reform in the correctional system. More and more correctional facilities are providing transition-related health care for trans people (National Center for Lesbian Rights, 2006), but the services are limited. To be eligible for hormones while incarcerated, trans people need to have had an existing prescription before incarceration. This can be challenging for the trans people who relied on the use of black-market hormones because of their lack of access or distrust of the medical system.

Education and School Settings

Schools are meant to be a safe learning environment, but for queer students, they can also be a setting where bullying, harassment, discrimination, and other forms of hatred take place. Queer youth are exposed to bullying from elementary school all the way through high school and beyond. In a study of adolescent LGBTQ students, out of 533 participants, 81% experienced verbal abuse because of their sexual orientation, 22% had things thrown at them, 38% had been threatened with physical violence, 6% were assaulted with a weapon, and 16% reported being sexually abused (D'Augelli, 2006). Most schools are equipped with policies that are meant to protect their students from any discrimination based on age, ethnicity, religion, and sexual orientation but do not include gender identity or gender expression in these protected categories.

This means that schools are an extremely unsafe environment for queer youth. It is critical to consider the high rates of suicide among queer-identified youth. According to Eisenberg and Resnick (2006), 47% of gay and bisexual adolescent boys reported suicidal ideation, and about 73% of lesbian and bisexual adolescent girls reported suicidal ideation. Compare that with heterosexual adolescent boys, who were found to have 35% suicidal ideation and 53% of heterosexual girls reporting suicidal ideation (Eisenberg & Resnick, 2006). In a study conducted in New York City, 45% of 55 transgender youth reported having thoughts of wanting to take their own lives, and 26% had attempted suicide (D'Augelli & Grossman, 2007). Although the research is limited, suicidal ideation and attempts will be prevalent in clinical settings.

Queer students from elementary though university find their community excluded from educational material with little to no representation of queer history, issues, role models, and so forth. This invisibility has its own profound impact on queer youth, who may feel isolated and stigmatized even more.

EFFECTIVE MODELS FOR WORKING WITH THE QUEER COMMUNITY

Be an Ally: Providing Safe Space

As a mental health practitioner, it is important to provide a queer friendly and safe space by having inclusive literature in the waiting room, intake forms that have space for queer identities and relationships, and nongendered bathrooms. An office or agency should have posted policies that are reflective of diverse sexual orientation, gender identity and expression, intolerance of discriminatory language, and an ability to provide support if someone does experience discrimination in your facility. However, being an ally is more than that.

It is important to stay informed on news and issues affecting the queer community. Do not wait for your clients to educate you; make an effort to follow political and social issues that are relevant. In 2008 during campaigning and elections related to California's Prop 8, referring to the right of same-sex couples to marry, queer clients were exquisitely aware and affected by each event reported in the news and each vote. It was critical to be up to date and prepared to discuss this historical moment with clients.

Many graduate and training programs for mental health professionals do not specifically cover queer issues. Make an effort to seek out training and read books related to this community. Take this seriously as a part of your competency responsibilities. As Joe Kort noted, "It is prejudice to be only gay friendly. You must be gay informed" (2008, p. 18).

Client-Centered Nonpathologizing Therapies

It is important for clinicians to recognize that queer clients have faced stigma and discrimination from the psychology community and have good reason to be hesitant in engaging with a new therapist. They may have fears about their gender identity or sexual orientation being seen as something to be fixed or as pathology. They may have tired of working with therapists who seemed unaware or uneducated about queer issues.

Trans people have historically had to prove to clinicians their need for gender-confirming procedures to be allowed to express themselves freely and move forward with medical regimens such as cross-hormone therapies, gender confirmation surgeries (sex reassignment surgeries), and living full-time in their gender identity. We believe gender dysphoria (GD) should be a temporary diagnosis that facilitates the process of physical transition to the individual's true self. The reasoning behind this is that once people undergo gender-confirming procedures successfully, they can go on with their lives free from pathology. In addition, if a transgender person needs follow-up care specific to GD, the provider can then fall back on this temporary diagnosis. The clinician's role in this process is to provide emotional support as the individual goes through their transition period. The transition period can last from a year to several years for the individual and is a process of reintegrating into all relationships after coming out to family members, coworkers, and loved ones.

Lesbian, gay, bisexual, and transgender individuals may have been through a harmful therapeutic practice called *reparative or conversion therapy*. This intervention is based on the assumption that being queer is a pathology that needs to be cured. Even though the American Psychiatric Association (2000) released a statement opposing use of reparative or conversion therapies, some clinicians currently attempt to reorient their clients' sexual orientation and/or gender identity. This can perpetuate denial of one's true self and has proven to be ineffective (Maccio, 2011). When a client comes in for services, the pain caused by this historical regimen needs to be acknowledged and discussed. The discussion should involve a sincere processing and apology about harmful or unfair treatment by anyone in the psychological profession to establish trust through honest communication. Then together you can establish a treatment plan that is right for this client.

Once rapport is established, the clinician should cultivate a safe environment in which the queer person can allow his or her true sexual orientation, gender identity, and expression to flourish without resistance. It is also important not to assume that the client's main concerns will be related to sexual orientation or gender identity. Like anyone else, clients may be going through different life stages and phases that they would like to explore. Depression, anxiety, and other difficult emotions may arise in therapy, but it is important to keep in mind that these are sane responses to lack of external societal support. The queer experience is really a lifelong process that can be celebrated and enjoyed. Just as any human being goes through a process of gender exploration and definition, so does a queer individual. This evolution of life is natural and ongoing for any person and is to be encouraged. Appropriate psychotherapy approaches and interventions will be as varied as the therapists themselves; effective therapy will rely on an informed compassionate stance of advocacy for the individual's rights and growth.

Support Groups

Support groups can be another way for queer community members to feel empowered, heard, and part of a larger community that shares similar struggles. Writer John Preston wrote about the important place stories from the queer community had in his life, "These stories became as important to me as the stories my mother told me about my family, because they were also about my heritage and they were about my place in the world. They were all the more important because there were so few other stories to be heard that could help me" (Preston, 2001, p. 383). The group can also provide a sense of consistency in an individual's life because many queer community members may have a lack of consistent support from peers or family. A support group can provide the sense of belonging to something greater than one self. This can in turn reduce stress, reduce symptoms of depression, improve coping skills, provide an opportunity to speak openly and honestly about feelings that an individual may not feel safe discussing in other contexts, and provide a forum for practical advice from other queer community members (Brown & Rounsley, 1996).

It is also important to consider that support groups may have more success if they are not targeting a broad spectrum of individuals. It may seem ideal to have a queer support group, but the queer community is made up of many sexual orientations, gender identities, cultures, and issues. For example, having an all-trans support group might prove challenging because a transwoman may not feel comfortable talking about her sex life in front of transmen. The opportunity to feel heard and understood is undermined if this happens, so it is important to try and strategically offer more than one type of support group. One way to decide what types of support groups are needed is to conduct several focus groups or surveys that can provide you with that information.

Referral Networks

Support your queer clients by actively searching out appropriate referral sources from the medical community, other mental health professionals, alternative treatment practitioners, massage therapists and more. Also consider finding other professionals who are allies for the queer community. This will show your clients that you understand the risk they take in seeking support and also ensure that they will receive better treatment.

COMMUNITY MOBILIZATION

One of the most important and empowering experiences for queer people is that of building community to address social issues such as transphobia, homophobia, access to health care, educational gaps, and other community-identified issues. Often individuals are informed about the barriers they are experiencing but do not have strategies to overcome them. As members of a hidden minority, queer people may have found it difficult to find peers and role models. Research has shown that an important part of identity formation is to seek out individuals with similar stories and life experiences. By belonging to a larger community, one can develop a sense of pride in both their identity and how others perceive their identity (Cass, 1979). What can seem like a daunting task, becomes, through mobilization, an organized effort to create positive change.

Through the formation of task forces, coalitions, or work groups, people can identify community needs, identify existing resources, identify areas that need more resources, and create strategies to address those gaps. With a collaborative strategic plan for social change, a community group can advocate at a local level for social change. All policies and laws start with an idea and grow from the unified voices of like-minded individuals. In this same light, a queer community group can influence the direction of local resources.

Community groups are made up of not only queer community members, they also include partners, allies, family members, loved ones, local government officials, service providers, and other key stakeholders. When everyone's expertise is brought to the table, a community group has the ammunition needed to move forward with a collaborative agenda.

There are many great models for community mobilization in existence, but for the purposes of this chapter, we look at some best practices from our experience that can be used to establish community groups or coalitions.

Ensure diverse community participation. A community group or coalition must be made up of individuals who are affected by community-identified issues. The queer community is diverse, so it is critical to include individuals that represent all queer identities. Within the diverse representation, there needs to be racial diversity, and all ages should be included. More diversity will ensure that all community perspectives have a stake in the planning process and will build a larger web of support for clients.

Include diverse areas of expertise in the coalition. It is critical to have a broad spectrum of expertise and strengths. Coalitions can identify needs and gaps in services that may seem unchangeable. Having a broad spectrum of people from different arenas can ensure that a variety of solutions are proposed. For this reason, coalitions should include health care providers, social service providers, community members, government officials, educators, advocates, activists, and any other community representatives with different professional and nonprofessional backgrounds.

Include existing task forces or work groups. Most communities have existing government task forces, community advocacy groups, religious groups, and social groups. These groups can have networking opportunities and different skill sets that can support or collaborate with a newly forming coalition.

Continue capacity building. It may be helpful to invite people with experience in coalition building to come and share their experiences with the community group. They can share lessons learned, leadership development, and strategies for creating sustainable change; how to conduct a community driven needs assessment; and many other helpful ideas. It may be important to teach and promote nonviolent communication skills and work with the groups to have an established guide on how to handle conflict and disagreements. This ensures that the community group will have opportunities to grow and increase their own skill set.

Promote record keeping and evaluations. Keeping track of accomplishments, challenges, new ideas, and process evaluation are paramount to coalition building. It can be challenging to include everyone's feedback in a coalition, so ensuring to evaluate and track the process of community mobilization will provide a way for everyone's voice to be heard.

Create coalition-developed mission, vision, and bylaws. A co-created mission statement helps to include everyone in the process of community mobilization, provides an ongoing purpose for the group, inspires people to keep participating in the process, and provides a sustainable goal. The mission statement also paves the way for a coalition-created vision statement. A vision statement provides inspiration by bringing to light what outcomes are possible as a result of coalition building. Bylaws help steer the coalition in the right direction and provide an objective way to ensure that the coalition is successful. Structure and organization of the coalition are critical for sustainability. Bylaws also provide expectations for members of a community coalition.

CONCLUSION

It is time for us as clinicians to recognize that the queer community deserves our support and responsibility. We have an opportunity to facilitate change and lessen hate, shame, and fear, perhaps like never before. Informed and compassionate community mental health approaches will help. It's time to create a safer and more inclusive world for the next generation.

REFERENCES

American Association of Sex Educators, Counselors and Therapists. (2012). Medical schools devote just five hours to LGBT issues. *Contemporary Sexuality*, *46*, pp. 1, 6.

American Psychiatric Association. (2000). "Therapies focused on attempts to change sexual orientation (reparative or conversion therapies: Position Statement." Retrieved from http://www.psychiatry.org/practice/professional-interests/diversityomna/diversity -resources/apa-position-statements-related-to-diversity

Allegretto, S., & Arthur, M. (2001). An empirical analysis of homosexual/heterosexual male earnings differentials: Unmarried and unequal? *Industrial and Labor Relations Review*, 54: 631–646.

Beautrais, A., Bradford, J., Brown, G., Clayton, P., Cochran, S., D'Augelli, A., . . . Turner, M. (2010). Suicide and risk in lesbian, gay, bisexual, and transgender populations: Review and recommendations. *Journal of Homosexuality, 58*, 10–51.

Bell, D., & Binnie, J. (2000). *The sexual citizen: Queer politics and beyond.* Malden, MA: Blackwell.

Brook, D. (2004, March/April). The problem of prison rape. *Legal Affairs: The Magazine at the Intersection of Law and Life.* Retrieved from http://www.legalaffairs.org/issues /March-April-2004/feature_brook_marapr04.msp

Brown, M., & Rounsley, C. (1996). *True selves: Understanding transsexualism; for families, friends, coworkers, and helping professionals.* San Francisco, CA: Jossey-Bass.

Bukstein, O., Friedman, M., Gold, M., King, K., Marshal, M., Miles, J., Morse, J., & Stall, R. (April, 2008). Sexual orientation and adolescent substance use: A meta-analysis and methodological review. *Addiction, 103*, 546–556.

Butterworth, M., & Diamond, M. (2008, March 29). Questioning gender and sexual identity: Dynamic links over time. *Sex Roles, 59*, 365–376.

Cass, V. C. (1979). Homosexual identity formation: A theoretical model. *Journal of Homosexuality, 4*, 219–235.

Center of Excellence for Transgender Health. (April, 2011). Primary care protocol for transgender patient care. Department of Family and Community Medicine, University of California, San Francisco. Retrieved from http://transhealth.ucsf.edu /trans?page=protocol-screening#S9X

Centers for Disease Control and Prevention. (2009, April 7). Obama administration announces new campaign to refocus national attention in the HIV crisis in the United States: First national CDC HIV/AIDS communication campaign in more than a decade. Retrieved from http://www.cdc.gov/nchhstp/newsroom/AAAPress Release.html

Centers for Disease Control and Prevention. (2011). Fact sheet: HIV and AIDS among gay and bisexual men. Retrieved from http://www.cdc.gov/nchhstp/newsroom/docs /fastfacts-msm-final508comp.pdf

Clark, L., Desai, M., Rabinovitz, S., & Schneir, A. (2010). No way home: Understanding the needs and experiences of homeless youth in Hollywood. Hollywood Homeless Youth Partnership. Retrieved from http://www.hhyp.org/downloads/HHYP_TCE_ Report_11-17-10.pdf

Crepaz, N., Finlayson, T., Herbst, J., Jacobs, E., McKleroy, V., & Neumann, M. (2008). Estimating HIV prevalence and risk behaviors of transgender persons in the United States: A systematic review. *AIDS Behavioral Health, 12*, 1–17.

D'Augelli, A. (2006). Developmental and contextual factors and mental health among lesbian, gay and bisexual youth. In A. Omoto & H. Kurtzman (Eds.), *Sexual orientation and mental health: Examining identity and development in lesbian, gay and bisexual people* (pp. 37–53). Washington, DC: American Psychological Association.

D'Augelli, A., & Grossman, A. (October, 2007). Transgender youth and life-threatening behaviors. *Suicide and Life-Threatening Behavior, 37*, 527–537.

Diaz, R., Huebner, D., Ryan, C., & Sanchez, J. (2009, January 1). Family rejection as a predictor of negative health outcomes in White and Latino lesbian, gay, and bisexual young adults. *Official Journal of the American Academy of Pediatrics, 123*, 346–352.

Dragowski, E., Sandigorsky, A., & Scharrón-del Rio, M. (2011). Childhood gender identity . . . disorder? Developmental, cultural, and diagnostic concerns. *Journal of Counseling and Development, 89*, 360–367.

Eisenberg, M., & Resnick, M. (2006). Suicidality among gay, lesbian and bisexual youth: The role of protective factors. *Journal of Adolescent Health, 39*, 662–668.

Gearhart, J., & Reiner, W. (January 22, 2004). Discordant sexual identity in some genetic males with cloacal exstrophy assigned to female sex at birth. *The New England Journal of Medicine, 350*, 333–341. Retrieved from http://www.nejm.org/doi/full/10.1056/NEJMoa022236?hits=20&andorexactfulltext=and&searchid=1081207688152_68&excludeflag=TWEEK_element&author2=gearhart%2C+j&author1=reiner%2C+w&tmonth=Apr&sortspec=Score+desc+PUBDATE_SORTDATE+desc&fmonth=Apr&andorexacttitleabs=and&FIRSTINDEX=0&fyear=1994&journalcode=nejm&searchtitle=Authors&tyear=2004&sendit=GO&search_tab=authors&

Grant, J., Harrison, J., Herman, J., Keisling, M., Mottet, L., & Tanis, J. (2009, November). Preliminary findings: The national transgender discrimination survey. The National Center for Transgender Equality and the National Gay and Lesbian Task Force. Retrieved from http://transequality.org/Resources/Trans_Discrim_Survey.pdf

Guardian and Transgender Law Center. (2006). Good jobs now! A snapshot of the economic health of San Francisco's transgender communities. Retrieved from http://transgenderlawcenter.org/pdf/Good%20Jobs%20NOW%20report.pdf

Hammer, H., Finkelhor, D., & Sedlack, A. (2002). *Runaway/throwaway children*. National estimates and characteristics. Washington, DC: U.S. Department of Justice, Office of Juvenile Justice and Delinquency Prevention. Retrieved from http://www.ojjdp.ncjrs.org

Hartzell, E., Frazer, M., Wertz, K., & Davis, M. (2009). *The state of transgender California: Results from the 2008 California transgender economic health survey*. San Francisco, CA: Transgender Law Center.

Horton, M. (2008, September). The cost of transgender health benefits, out and equal workplace summit. Retrieved from http://www.tgender.net/taw/thb/THBCost-OE2008.pdf

Hyatt, S. (2011). Struggling to survive: Lesbian, gay, bisexual, transgender, and queer/questioning homeless youth on the streets of California. California Homeless Youth Project. Retrieved from http://cahomelessyouth.library.ca.gov/docs/pdf/StrugglingToSurviveFinal.pdf

Intersex Society of North America. (2008). What is intersex? Retrieved from http://www.isna.org/faq/what_is_intersex

Jenness, V., Matsuda, K., Maxson, C., & Summer, J. (April, 2007). *Violence in California correctional facilities: An empirical examination of sexual assault*. Retrieved from http://ucicorrections.seweb.uci.edu/pdf/PREA_Presentation_PREA_Report_UCI_Jenness_et_al.pdf

Just Detention International. (2009). Fact sheet: LGBTQ detainees chief targets for sexual abuse in detention. Retrieved from http://justdetention.org/en/factsheets/JD_Fact _Sheet_LGBTQ_vD.pdf

Kort, J. (2008). *Gay affirmative therapy for the straight clinician.* New York, NY: Norton.

Krehely, J. (2009, December 21). *How to close the LGBT health disparities gap.* Center for American Progress. Retrieved from http://www.americanprogress.org/issues/2009 /12/pdf/lgbt_health_disparities.pdf

Maccio, E. (2011, July). Self-reported sexual orientation and identity before and after sexual reorientation therapy. *Journal of Gay & Lesbian Mental Health, 15,* 242–259.

Mallory, C., & Sears, B. (2011, July). Documented evidence of employment discrimination and its effects on LGBT people. The Williams Institute. Retrieved from http:// williamsinstitute.law.ucla.edu/wp-content/uploads/Sears-Mallory-Discrimination -July-2011.pdf

McIntosh, J. L. (2002). U.S.A. suicide statistics for the year 1999: Overheads and a presentation guide. Washington, D.C.: American Association of Suicidology.

National Center for Lesbian Rights. (2006). Rights of transgender prisoners. Retrieved from http://www.nclrights.org/site/DocServer/RightsofTransgenderPrisoners.pdf?doc ID =6381

National Coalition of Anti-Violence Programs. (2010). Hate violence against lesbian, gay, bisexual, transgender, queer and HIV-affected communities in the United States. Retrieved from http://www.avp.org/documents/NCAVPHateViolenceReport2011 Finaledjlfinaledits.pdf

Preston, J. (2001). The importance of telling out stories. In B. Berzon (Ed.), *Positively gay: New approaches to gay and lesbian life* (3rd ed.). Berkeley, CA: Celestial Arts.

Shaffer, D. (2009). Social and personality development (6th ed.). Belmont, CA: Wadsworth/ Cengage Learning.

Whitbeck, L., Chen, X., Hoyt, D., Tyler, K., & Johnson, K. (2004). Mental disorder, subsistence strategies, and victimization among gay, lesbian, and bisexual homeless and runaway adolescents. *Journal of Sex Research, 41,* 329–342.

Wilson-Stronks, A. (2009). A call to action for healthcare professionals to advance health equity for the lesbian, gay, bisexual and transgender community. Human Rights Campaign. Retrieved from http://www.hrc.org/files/assets/resources/health_callto action_HealthcareEqualityIndex_2011.pdf

World Professional Association for Transgender Health. (2011). Standards of care for the health of transsexual, transgender, and gender nonconforming people. Retrieved from http://www.wpath.org/documents/Standards%20of%20Care%20V7%20-%20 2011%20WPATH.pdf

Chapter 5

Mental Health in Schools: Opportunities and Challenges

Linda Taylor and Howard S. Adelman

Mental health concerns must be addressed if schools are to function satisfactorily and students are to succeed at school. It has long been acknowledged that a variety of psychosocial and health problems affect student learning and performance in profound ways. School policy makers have a lengthy history of trying to assist teachers in dealing with a variety of problems that interfere with schooling. Prominent examples of efforts to assist are seen in the range of counseling, psychological, and social service programs schools provide (Adelman & Taylor, 2010). In addition to interventions by school support staff, there has been renewed emphasis in recent years on increasing linkages between schools and community service agencies. This "school-linked services" agenda has added impetus to advocacy for mental health in schools.

Although many societal considerations are involved, for the most part, the rationale for strengthening mental health in schools stresses one or both of the following points:

1. Schools need to address psychosocial and mental and physical health concerns to enable effective school performance by some (often many) students.

2. Schools can provide good access to students (and their families) who require mental health services.

Implied in both these points is the hope of enhancing the nature and scope of mental health interventions to fill gaps, enhance effectiveness, address problems early, reduce stigma, and fully imbue clinical and service efforts with public health, general education, and equity orientations (Adelman & Taylor, 2006a). Point 1 reflects the perspective and agenda of student support professionals and some leaders for school improvement, and also provides a supportive rationale for those wanting schools to play a greater role related to addressing young people's health concerns. Point 2 typically reflects the perspective and agenda of agencies and advocates whose mission is to improve mental health services.

In most places, mental health in schools still gets defined mainly as mental illness, and the form of intervention tends to be case-oriented and clinical. This provides services for only a relatively few of the many students experiencing behavior, learning, and emotional problems. It is fortunate that school personnel and/or colocated and linked community service providers are able to provide individual and small group counseling/therapy for some children and adolescents who need it. It is tragic, however, that not enough of these clinical services are equitably available and accessible. It is poignantly evident that the number of students in need far outstrips the possibility of providing more than a small percentage with clinical services even if this were the best way to address the wide range of concerns. Moreover, an overemphasis on clinical services tends to work against developing programs to prevent problems and promote social and emotional health (Adelman & Taylor 2006b; Kutash, Duchnowski, & Lynn, 2006).

A FULL CONTINUUM APPROACH

Schools need and provide a unique opportunity to develop a comprehensive system for addressing mental health and psychosocial concerns. Such a system is built around a full continuum of interventions. The continuum is conceived as an integrated set of subsystems for

- promoting healthy development and preventing problems,
- intervening early to address problems as soon after onset as is feasible, and
- assisting those with chronic and severe problems.

The continuum encompasses approaches for enabling academic, social, emotional, and physical development and addressing learning, behavior, and emotional problems. It does so in ways that yield safe and caring schools. Such a range of interventions is intended to meet the needs of all students and, properly implemented, should significantly reduce the number of students requiring individual assistance.

Promoting Positive Mental Health and Preventing Problems

Interventions to promote mental health encompass not only strengthening individuals but also enhancing nurturing and supportive conditions at school, at home, and in the neighborhood. All this includes a particular emphasis on increasing opportunities for personal development and empowerment by promoting conditions that foster and strengthen positive attitudes and behaviors (e.g., enhancing motivation and capability to pursue positive goals, resist negative influences, and overcome barriers). It also includes efforts to maintain and enhance physical health and safety and inoculate against problems (e.g., providing positive and negative information, skill instruction, and fostering attitudes that build resistance and resilience).

Although schools alone are not solely responsible, they do play a significant role, albeit sometimes not a positive one, in social and emotional development. School improvement plans need to specify ways for schools to (a) directly facilitate social and emotional (as well as physical) development and (b) minimize threats to positive development. In doing such planning, appreciation of differences in levels of development and developmental demands at different ages is fundamental, as is personalized implementation to account for individual differences. From a mental health perspective, helpful guidelines are found in research clarifying normal trends for school-age youngsters as they strive to feel competent, self-determining, and connected with significant others (Deci & Moller, 2005). Further, measurement of such feelings can provide indicators of the impact of a school on mental health (Center for Mental Health in Schools, 2011a). Positive findings are expected to correlate with school engagement and academic progress. Negative findings are expected to correlate with student anxiety, fear, anger, alienation, a sense of losing control, a sense of impotence, hopelessness, and powerlessness. In turn, these negative thoughts, feelings, and attitudes can lead to externalizing (aggressive, "acting out") or internalizing (withdrawal, self-punishing, delusional) behaviors. Promoting mental health has definite payoffs both for academic performance and reducing problems at schools. Furthermore, promoting healthy development, well-being, and a value-based life are important ends unto themselves (Adelman & Taylor 2008a).

A number of specific concerns related to schoolwide mental health prevention include substance abuse, suicide, bullying, and violence. Another important topic for prevention in schools is dropout rates. There has been a great deal of investment in evaluation of effective prevention programs (see the U.S. Department of Education's *What Works Clearinghouse* at http://ies.ed.gov/ncee/wwc; see also Terzian, Hamilton, & Ling, 2011).

Intervening as Soon as a Problem Is Noted

School personnel identify many mental health problems each day and seek assistance when it is available. Some identified students are best served by helping to ensure that appropriate interventions are implemented to minimize the need for referral. For example, problems that are mild to moderate often can be addressed through participation in programs that do not require special referral for admission. Examples are regular curriculum programs designed to foster positive mental health and socioemotional functioning; social, recreational, and other enrichment activities; and self-help and mutual support programs. Because anyone can apply directly, such interventions can be described as *open-enrollment* programs.

Other students require immediate referral. The process of connecting the student with appropriate help can be viewed as encompassing four facets:

1. Screening/assessment
2. Client consultation and referral
3. Triage
4. Monitoring/managing care (Adelman & Taylor, 2010)

Many schools do this work through a team (e.g., student assessment team). Given that there are never enough resources to serve those who need individual services, it is inevitable that the processing of such students will involve a form of triage (or gatekeeping) at some point. When referrals are made to on-site resources, it falls to the school to decide which students need immediate attention and which can be put on a waiting list. Schools can enhance access to external referral resources by cultivating school–community collaboration.

In general, when someone becomes concerned about a student's problems, the main consideration is ensuring the student is connected directly with someone who can help. This involves more than simply referring the student or parents to a resource. Efforts to connect students with effective help are significant interventions in and of themselves. Such an intervention begins with a consultation session involving the concerned parties (student, family, teacher, other school staff). Using all the information that has been gathered, the focus is on exploring what seems to be wrong and what to do about it. The aim is to detail the steps involved in connecting with potential assistance.

From the time a student is first identified as having a problem, someone must be assigned to monitor and manage the case. Monitoring continues until the student's intervention needs are addressed. Care management is basic to ensuring coordination among all involved (e.g., other services and programs including the efforts of the classroom teacher and those at home). The process encompasses a constant focus on evaluating intervention appropriateness and effectiveness.

Providing Support for Chronic and Serious Problems

According to a recent report, approximately 11% of children in the United States are diagnosed with emotional, behavioral, or developmental conditions, and a large number do not get the mental health services they need (U.S. Department of Health and Human Services, 2010). In schools, the federal special education act mandates that schools create an *Individualized Education Plan* (IEP) for students who meet criteria for diagnosis related to physical, learning, and emotional disabilities. The intent in formulating such plans is to assist diagnosed students in an inclusive school environment so they are not isolated or excluded from regular students and important educational opportunities (e.g., situations that do not restrict and disrupt their development).

Special education stresses a continuum of interventions, with an emphasis on using the least disruptive intervention necessary to meet a student's needs. In the past, this often meant pulling the student from regular classrooms for certain instructional periods to receive more personalized instruction in a *resource room* with special education staff. For those needing more intensive help, full-time special education classes were commonly used. These classrooms might be in the regular public school or a special school in the district. If appropriate facilities were not available, the student might be funded to attend a private special education school (a nonpublic school).

Over the past few years, evaluation of special education outcomes has resulted in significant changes related to special education (Bryant, Deutsch, Smith, & Bryant, 2007). One fundamental change was the mandate for *inclusion*, which aims to keep special education students in regular classrooms by bringing in such resources as a resource teacher, a special education aid, and special equipment and supplies. Although the process of identifying students with special education needs is carefully delineated, the extensive misdiagnoses of learning disabilities and attention-deficit/hyperactivity disorder have generated a federal policy introducing *Response to Intervention* (RtI) as a method for minimizing premature testing, mislabeling, and consumption of sparse special education resources.

Recognition of the reality that students with chronic and severe problems often are involved with out-of-school interventions has led to efforts to connect all the activity into a system of care, sometimes referred to as a wraparound approach. Hodges, Ferreira, Israel, and Mazza (2007) stressed that such a system is an adaptive network of structures, processes, and relationships reflecting system of care values and principles that is designed to provide children and youth and their families with access to necessary services and supports across administrative and funding jurisdictions. Efforts to promote school and community coordination of interventions vary. A recent statewide example is seen in a Louisiana initiative to ensure that four child-serving agencies (i.e., education, children and family services, health, and juvenile justice) work together to better support youth with significant behavioral health needs).

The Continuum and Response to Intervention

As noted, RtI is a recent federal policy focus delineating a method for schools in responding to problems as soon as they are noted. This approach is being operationalized across the country with a significant push from the federal government. Properly conceived and implemented, the strategy is expected to improve the learning opportunities for many and reduce the number inappropriately diagnosed with learning disabilities and behavioral disorders. The approach stresses a continuum of three tiers but does so primarily in terms of intensity of instruction (Center for Mental Health in Schools, 2011b). The method overlaps some ideas for what have been called prereferral interventions but is intended to be more systematically implemented. The aim is also to improve assessment for determining whether more intensive and perhaps specialized assistance and diagnosis are required (Brown-Chidsey & Steege, 2010).

RtI calls for making changes in the classroom designed to improve a student's learning and behavior as soon as problems are noted and using student's response to such modifications as information for making further changes if needed. The process continues until it is evident that it cannot be resolved through classroom changes alone. Through this sequential approach, students who have not responded sufficiently to the regular classroom interventions would next receive supportive assistance designed to help them remain in the regular program, and only when all this is found insufficient would there be a referral for special education assessment. (If the problem proves to be severe and disruptive, an alternative setting may be necessary on a temporary basis to provide more intensive and specialized assessments and assistance.)

Basic to making the strategy effective is truly personalized instruction and appropriate special assistance that can be used as necessary. Think in terms of a two-step process. Step 1 involves *personalizing instruction*. The intent is to ensure a student *perceives* instructional processes, content, and outcomes as a good match with his or her interests and capabilities. The first emphasis is on *motivation*. Thus, Step 1a stresses use of motivation-oriented strategies to (re)engage the student in classroom instruction. This step draws on the broad science-base related to human motivation, with special attention paid to research on intrinsic motivation and psychological reactance. The aim is to enhance student perceptions of significant options and involvement in decision making. The next concern is *developmental capabilities*. Thus:

Step 1 stresses use of teaching strategies that account for current knowledge and skills. In this respect, the emphasis on tutoring (designated as supplemental services in Title I) can be useful if the student perceives the tutoring as a good fit for learning. Then, if necessary, the focus expands to encompass **Step 2** *special assistance*. The emphasis is on special strategies to address any major barriers to learning and teaching. The process stresses the intervention principle of using the least intervention necessary for addressing needs. There will, of course, be students for whom all this is insufficient. In such cases, some other forms of supportive assistance must be added to the mix inside and, as necessary, outside the classroom. Referral for special education assessment only comes after all this is found inadequate.

A core difficulty in using RtI strategically involves mobilizing unmotivated students (particularly those who have become actively disengaged from classroom instruction). If motivational considerations are not effectively addressed, there is no way to validly assess whether a student has a true disability or disorder. If RtI is treated simply as a matter of providing more and better instruction, it is unlikely to be effective for a great many students. However, if the strategies are understood broadly and as part and parcel of a comprehensive system of classroom and schoolwide learning supports, schools will be in a position not only to address problems effectively early after their onset but to prevent many from occurring. We stress that instruction must be supported by schoolwide interventions (e.g., related to providing supports for transitions, responding to and preventing crises, enhancing connections with the home, and more). Response to intervention needs to be part of a comprehensive system designed to reduce learning, behavior, and emotional problems, promote social/emotional development, and effectively reengage students in classroom learning. This will not only reduce the numbers who are inappropriately referred for special education or specialized services, it will also enhance attendance, reduce misbehavior, close the achievement gap, and enhance graduation rates.

A Note about Evidence-Based Interventions

In recent years, schools have been challenged to adopt practices that are evidence-based (Bandy & Moore, 2011). Increasingly, terms such as *science-based* or *empirically supported* are assigned to almost any intervention identified as having research data generated in ways that meet scientific standards and that demonstrates a level of *efficacy* deemed worthy of application (Raines, 2008). A somewhat higher standard is used for the subgroup of practices referred to as evidence-based *treatments*. This designation is usually reserved for interventions tested in more than one rigorous study (multiple case studies, randomized control trials) and consistently found better than a placebo or no treatment.

Currently, most evidence-based practices are discrete interventions designed to meet specified needs. A few are complex sets of interventions intended to meet multifaceted needs, and these usually are referred to as programs. Most evidence-based practices are applied using a detailed guide or manual and are time limited. No one argues against using the best science available to improve professional expertise. However, the evidence-based practices movement is reshaping public policy in ways that have raised concerns. A central concern is that practices developed under highly controlled laboratory conditions are being pushed prematurely into widespread application based on unwarranted assumptions. This concern is especially salient when the evidence-base comes from short-term studies and has not included samples representing major subgroups with whom the practice is to be used.

Until researchers demonstrate a prototype is effective under real-world conditions (e.g., schools and classrooms), it can only be considered a promising and not a proven practice. Even then it must be determined whether it is one of the best options as well as a cost-effective practice. With respect to the designation of *best*, it is well to remember that best simply denotes that a practice is better than whatever else is currently available. How good it actually is depends on complex analyses related to costs and benefits.

As the evidence-based movement has gained momentum, an increasing concern is that certain interventions are officially prescribed and others are proscribed by policy makers and funders. This breeds fear that only those practitioners who adhere to official lists will be sanctioned and rewarded. In addition, we have heard widespread concerns raised about "flavor of the month" initiatives being introduced by schools, districts, and states. Although all are well intentioned, the tendency is to introduce them in an ad hoc and piecemeal manner and as add-ons. It is commonplace for those staffing the various efforts to function in relative isolation of each other and other stakeholders, with a great deal of the work oriented to discrete problems and with an overreliance on specialized services for individuals and small groups. This contributes to widespread fragmentation, counterproductive competition, and wasteful redundancy (Adelman & Taylor, 2008b).

Schools confronted with a large number of students experiencing barriers to learning pay dearly for the current state of affairs. Although specific evidence-based practices might be helpful, a few more services or programs will not equip most schools to ensure that all youngsters have an equal opportunity to succeed at school. For schools, the need is not just to add evidence-based practices; it is to do so in ways that contribute to development of a comprehensive system for addressing barriers to learning and teaching.

EMBEDDING MENTAL HEALTH INTO SCHOOL IMPROVEMENT POLICY AND PRACTICE

Earlier in this chapter, we highlighted the continuum of interventions relevant to mental health in schools. Operationalizing the continuum calls for organizing programs and services coherently at every level.

The Continuum Has Content

To enhance efforts across the continuum, pioneering work is underway to coalesce programs and services into a multifaceted and cohesive set of content arenas (Center for Mental Health in Schools, 2011c). In doing so, they have moved from a laundry list to a defined and organized way of capturing the essence of basic intervention domains. The prototype defines the following six content arenas as follows:

1. In the classroom: focuses on how the teacher and support staff affect student engagement and address students who are having difficulty with tasks. Specific emphasis is given to the following:

- Interventions to enhance engagement and minimize reducing engagement
- Interventions to reengage disconnected students
- Modifying instruction to fit those who are having difficulty
- Bringing support staff and volunteers into the classroom to work with the teacher in addressing engagement and instructional fit concerns

2. Transition support focuses on supports for the many transitions that occur daily and throughout the school year. For example, starting a new school is a critical transition period; so is changing schools. New personnel also need supports. In addressing newcomer transitions, for instance, schools need to have a well-designed and implemented welcoming program and mechanisms for ongoing social support (especially staff development) so that teachers, support staff, and other stakeholders can learn how to establish

- Welcoming procedures
- Social support networks
- Proactive transition supports for family members, new staff, and any other newcomers
- Training and resources to the members of the office staff so they can create a welcoming and supportive atmosphere to everyone who enters the school

3. Crisis prevention and response focuses on identifying what can be prevented and taking effective action, establishing appropriate schoolwide prevention strategies, and developing and implementing a well-designed system for crisis response and follow-up. From a psychological perspective, basic concerns are the degree to which experiences related to school

- Enhance or threaten students' feelings of safety
- Minimize threats to and maximize students' feelings of competence, self-determination, and connectedness with significant others (e.g., relationships between staff and students and among students)
- Minimize overreliance on extrinsic reinforcers to enforce rules and control behavior or generate psychological reactance

4. In home involvement/engagement the stress is on home rather than parents to account for the variety of caretakers who schools may need to consider (including grandparents, siblings, foster caretakers). Although the value of home support for student schooling is well established, variations in caretaker motivation and ability to participate at school require a continuum of supports and outreach to any who are not able or motivated to positively support a child's success at school. Examples include interventions to

- Address specific support and learning needs of the family
- Enhance personalized communications with the home
- Outreach positively to caretakers who have not shown the motivation and/or ability to connect with the school

- Involve all families in student decision making
- Provide effective programs to enhance home support for learning and development

5. Community outreach for involvement/engagement—focuses on recruiting and collaborating with a wide range of community resources (e.g., public and private agencies, colleges, local residents, artists and cultural institutions, businesses, service and volunteer organizations). Special attention is given to
   - Establishing mechanisms for outreach and collaboration
   - Building capacity for integrating volunteers into the school
   - Weaving together school and community resources

6. Specialized assistance for a student and family focuses on ensuring special needs are addressed appropriately and effectively. Special attention is given to ensuring there are systemic and effective processes for
   - Referral and triage
   - Providing extra support as soon as a need is recognized and in the best manner
   - Monitoring and managing special assistance
   - Evaluating outcomes

A Special Note about Involving Families in School Mental Health

When youngsters are referred for counseling, parent follow-through is estimated at less than 50%, and premature termination occurs in 40% to 60% of child cases (Kazdin, Holland, & Crowley, 1997). Clearly, not all parents feel that such counseling is worth pursuing. Even if they do enroll their child, dropping out in short order is likely if the family experiences the process as burdensome, unpleasant, or of little value. Conversely, children seem to do better when parents perceive few negatives related to the intervention and its potential outcomes (Kazdin & Wassell, 1999).

In addition to reducing dropouts, there are many reasons to involve parents. For example, it seems essential to do so when they are the cause of or an ongoing contributor to a youngster's problems. Moreover, in more cases than not, we want the family's cooperation in facilitating, nurturing, and supporting desired changes in the youngster. Equally important, what parents learn in the process may generalize to other venues, such as home involvement in school and parent advocacy (Taylor & Adelman, 2001).

Focusing on Managing Behavior Problems as More Than Social Control

Good classroom teaching is the ability to create an environment that first can mobilize the learner to pursue the curriculum and then can maintain that mobilization, while effectively facilitating learning. Misbehavior disrupts this. In some forms, such as bullying and intimidating others, it is hurtful, and observing such behavior may disinhibit others. Because of this, discipline and classroom management are daily topics at every school.

Concern about responding to behavior problems and promoting social and emotional learning are related and are embedded into the six content arenas described in the previous section. How these concerns are addressed is critical to the type of school and classroom climate that emerges and to student engagement and reengagement in classroom learning. As such, they need to be fully integrated into all agendas for mental health in schools.

In an extensive review of the literature, Fredricks, Blumenfeld, and Paris (2004) concluded that the disengagement of many students is associated with behavior and learning problems and eventual dropout. The degree of concern about student engagement varies depending on school population. In schools that are the greatest focus of public criticism, teachers are confronted with the challenge of finding ways to reengage students who have become disengaged and are often resistant to broadband (nonpersonalized) teaching approaches. To the dismay of most teachers, however, strategies for reengaging students in learning are rarely a prominent part of preservice or in-service preparation and seldom are the focus of interventions pursued by professionals whose role is to support teachers and students (National Research Council and the Institute of Medicine, 2004). As a result, they learn more about *socialization* and *social control* as classroom management strategies than about how to engage and reengage students in classroom learning, which is the key to enhancing and sustaining good behavior.

When a student misbehaves, a natural reaction is to want that youngster to experience and other students to see the consequences of misbehaving. One hope is that public awareness of consequences will deter subsequent problems. As a result, a considerable amount of time at schools is devoted to discipline and classroom management. An often-stated assumption is that stopping a student's misbehavior will make her or him amenable to teaching. In a few cases, this may be so. However, the assumption ignores all the research that has led to understanding *psychological reactance* and the need for individuals to maintain and restore a sense of self-determination (Deci & Moller, 2005). Moreover, it belies two painful realities: the number of students who continue to manifest poor academic achievement and the staggering dropout rate in too many schools.

Unfortunately, in their efforts to deal with deviant and devious behavior and to create safe environments, too many schools overrely on negative consequences and plan only for social control. Such practices model behavior that can foster rather than counter the development of negative values and often produce other forms of undesired behavior. Moreover, the tactics often make schools look and feel more like prisons than community treasures. In schools, short of suspending a student, punishment essentially takes the form of a decision to do something that the student does not want done. In addition, a demand for future compliance usually is made, along with threats of harsher punishment if compliance is not forthcoming. The discipline may be administered in ways that suggest the student is seen as an undesirable person. As students get older, suspension increasingly comes into play. Indeed, suspension remains one of the most common disciplinary responses for the transgressions of secondary students.

As with many emergency procedures, the social control benefits of using punishment often are offset by negative consequences. These include increased negative attitudes toward school and school personnel. These attitudes often lead to more behavior problems, antisocial acts, and various mental health problems. Because disciplinary procedures are also associated with dropping out of school, it is not surprising that some concerned professionals refer to extreme disciplinary practices as push-out strategies. In general, specific discipline practices should be developed with the aim of leaving no child behind. That is, stopping misbehavior must be accomplished in ways that maximize the likelihood that teachers engage or reengage the student in instruction and positive learning. The growing emphasis on positive approaches to reducing misbehavior and enhancing support for positive behavior in and out of the classroom is a step in the right direction. So is the emphasis in school guidelines stressing that discipline should be reasonable, fair, and nondenigrating (i.e., should be experienced by recipients as legitimate reactions that neither denigrate one's sense of worth nor reduce one's sense of autonomy). Introduction of strategies such as Positive Behavioral Interventions and Supports (PBIS) represent a step in moving away from the overemphasis on punishment.

In general, it is increasingly recognized that social control strategies are insufficient in preventing future misbehavior. Schools need to address the roots of misbehavior, especially underlying motivational bases, and move beyond overreliance on behavior modification. This calls for an expanded view of engagement and human motivation and of facilitating social and emotional development. Such thinking is essential to improving (a) efforts to prevent and anticipate misbehavior and (b) actions taken during and after misbehavior, with fundamental consideration given to concerns about the impact on engagement in classroom learning.

Responding to behavior problems and promoting social and emotional development and learning can and should be done in the context of a comprehensive system designed to address barriers to learning and teaching and reengaging disconnected students. An agenda for mental health in schools must be embedded in such a system.

Embedding Case-Oriented into a Resource-Oriented Operational Infrastructure

Most schools have teams that focus on individual students identified as having problems. Among the many terms used for these teams are *student support team* and *student assistance team*. Teams focus on such functions as referral, triage, and care monitoring or management. In embedding mental health into school improvement policy and practice, case-oriented teams need to be part of an operational infrastructure that is resource-oriented and not marginalized (Adelman & Taylor, 2008a, 2008b, 2010). Such an infrastructure assumes responsibility for guiding how resources are deployed and redeployed in developing a comprehensive system for addressing barriers to learning and teaching. A key mechanism is a resource-oriented team. In various places across the country, these teams are called *learning supports resource teams*.

Whatever it is called, a resource-oriented team focuses specifically on ensuring appropriate use of existing resources and enhancing efforts to address barriers to learning and teaching. Such a team works with a school's administrators to expand on-site leadership for comprehensively addressing these matters. In doing so, it ensures all such activity is coordinated and increasingly integrated to develop a comprehensive system of student and learning supports. Properly constituted and operated, the mechanism can reduce marginalization and fragmentation and enhance cost-efficacy. For this to happen, it must be fully integrated as a primary component of school improvement planning. More specifically, the team's work provides ways to

- Make prioritized decisions about resource allocation
- Maximize systematic and integrated planning, maintenance, and evaluation of learning supports (enabling) activity
- Outreach to create formal working relationships with community resources to bring some to a school and establish special linkages with others
- Upgrade and modernize the enabling or learning supports component to reflect the best intervention thinking and use of technology

Examples of the team's major functions are as follows:

- Aggregating data across students and from teachers to analyze school needs
- Mapping resources in school and community
- Analyzing resources
- Identifying the most pressing program development needs at the school
- Coordinating and integrating school resources and connecting with community resources, establishing priorities for strengthening programs and developing new ones
- Planning and facilitating ways to strengthen and develop new programs and systems
- Recommending how resources should be deployed and redeployed
- Developing strategies for enhancing resources
- Social "marketing"

Connecting school resource-oriented mechanisms across a cluster of schools (e.g., a feeder pattern) and at the district level provide oversight, leadership, resource development, ongoing support, and economies of scale. At each system level, the tasks require that staff adopt some new roles and functions and that parents, students, and other representatives from the community enhance their involvement. They also call for redeployment of existing resources as well as finding new ones.

CONCLUSION

Current approaches to mental health in schools promote an orientation that overemphasizes individually prescribed treatment services to the detriment of prevention programs, exacerbates the marginalization and fragmentation of interventions, and undervalues the human and social capital indigenous to every neighborhood. School improvement policy must be expanded to support development of the type of comprehensive, multifaceted, and cohesive approach that can effectively address barriers to learning and teaching. To do less is to make values such as *We want all children to succeed* and *No child left behind* simply rhetorical statements. Needed is a fundamental, systemic transformation in the ways schools, families, and communities address major barriers to learning and teaching. Such a transformation is essential to enhancing achievement for all, closing the achievement gap, reducing dropouts, and increasing the opportunity for schools to be valued as treasures in their neighborhood.

REFERENCES

Adelman, H. S., & Taylor, L. (2006a). *The school leader's guide to student learning supports: New directions for addressing barriers to learning.* Thousand Oaks, CA: Corwin Press.

Adelman, H. S., & Taylor, L. (2006b). *The implementation guide to student learning supports in the classroom and schoolwide: New directions for addressing barriers to learning.* Thousand Oaks, CA: Corwin Press.

Adelman, H. S., & Taylor, L. (2008a). Best practices in the use of resource teams to enhance learning supports. In A. Thomas & J. Grimes (Eds.). *Best practices in school psychology.* Bethesda, MD: National Association of Psychologists.

Adelman, H. S., & Taylor, L. (2008b). School-wide approaches to addressing barriers to learning and teaching. In B. Doll & J. Cummings (Eds.), *Transforming school mental health services: Population-based approaches to promoting the competency and wellness of children.* Thousand Oaks, CA: Corwin Press.

Adelman, H. S., & Taylor, L. (2010). *Mental health in schools: Engaging learners, prevention problems, and improving schools.* Thousand Oaks, CA: Corwin Press.

Bandy, T., & Moore, K. (2011). What works for promoting and enhancing positive social skills: Lessons from experimental evaluations of programs and interventions. *Child Trends Fact Sheet.* Retrieved from http://www.childtrends.org/Files/Child_Trends_2011_03_02_RB_WWSocialSkills.pdf

Brown-Chidsey, R., & Steege, M. (2010). *Response to intervention: Principles and strategies for effective practice* (2nd ed.). New York, NY: Guildford Press.

Bryant, D., Deutsch, D., Smith, D., & Bryant, B. (2007). *Teaching students with special needs in inclusive classrooms.* New York, NY: Allyn & Bacon.

Center for Mental Health in Schools. (2011a). *About short-term outcome indicators for school use and the need for an expanded policy framework.* Los Angeles, CA: Center for Mental Health in Schools, University of California at Los Angeles. Retrieved from http://smhp.psych.ucla.edu/pdfdocs/outind.pdf

Center for Mental Health in Schools. (2011b). *Moving beyond the three tier intervention pyramid toward a comprehensive framework for student and learning supports.* Los Angeles, CA: Center for Mental Health in Schools, University of California at Los Angeles. Retrieved from http://smhp.psych.ucla.edu/pdfdocs/briefs/threetier.pdf

Center for Mental Health in Schools. (2011c). *Where's it happening? Examples of new directions for student support & lessons learned.* Los Angeles, CA: Center for Mental Health in Schools, University of California at Los Angeles. Retrieved from http://smhp.psych.ucla.edu/summit2002/nind7.htm

Deci, E. L., & Moller, A. C. (2005). The concept of competence: A starting place for understanding intrinsic motivation and self-determined extrinsic motivation. In A. J. Elliot & C. J. Dweck (Eds.), *Handbook of competence and motivation* (pp. 579–597). New York, NY: Guilford Press.

Fredricks, J. A., Blumenfeld, P. C., & Paris, A. H. (2004). School engagement: Potential of the concept, state of the evidence. *Review of Educational Research, 74,* 59–109.

Hodges, S., Ferreira, K., Israel, N., & Mazza, J. (2007). *Lessons from successful systems [of Care].* Tampa: University of South Florida. Retrieved from http://rtckids.fmhi.usf.edu/rtcpubs/study02/IssueBrief1Definition.pdf

Kazdin, A., Holland, L., & Crowley, M. (1997). Family experience of barriers to treatment and premature termination for child therapy. *Journal of Consulting and Clinical Psychology, 65,* 453–463.

Kazdin, A., & Wassell, G. (1999). Predictors of barriers to treatment and therapeutic change in outpatient therapy for antisocial children and their families. *Mental Health Service Research, 2,* 27–40.

Kutash, K., Duchnowski, A., & Lynn, N. (2006). *School-based mental health: An empirical guide for decision makers.* Tampa: University of South Florida.

National Research Council and the Institute of Medicine. (2004). *Engaging schools: Fostering high school students' motivation to learn.* Washington, DC: National Academies Press.

Raines, J. (2008). *Evidence-based practice in school mental health.* New York, NY: Oxford University Press.

Taylor, L., & Adelman, H. S. (2001). Enlisting appropriate parental cooperation and involvement in children's mental health treatment. In E. R. Welfel & R. E. Ingersoll (Eds.), *The mental health desk reference.* New York, NY: Wiley.

Terzian, M., Hamilton, K., & Ling, T. (2011). What works for acting-out (externalizing) behavior: Lessons from experimental evaluations of social interventions. *Child Trends Fact Sheet.* Retrieved from http://www.childtrends.org/Files//Child_Trends-2011_03_03_RB_WWExternalizing.pdf

U.S. Department of Health and Human Services, Health Resources and Services Administration, Maternal and Child Health Bureau. (2010). The mental and emotional well-being of children: A portrait of states and the nation 2007. Rockville, MD: U.S. Department of Health and Human Services. Retrieved from http://mchb.hrsa.gov /nsch/07emohealth/moreinfo/pdf/nsch07titlecitetoc.pdf

Case Study

School-Based Services

Niki Berkowitz

While working at a community-based mental health agency, part of my job was to see students in the special education department at one of the largest high schools in San Francisco, one day per week. Despite being one of the highest performing schools in the city, the special education department was located in the temporary classroom trailers at the edge of campus. Most of the students in the program were minority students from low-income neighborhoods throughout the city. In another trailer, alongside the special education classrooms, was the Wellness Center. The Wellness Initiative (http://www.sfwellness.org) is a partnership between the San Francisco Department of Children, Youth and Their Families (DCYF), the San Francisco Department of Public Health/Community Behavioral Health Services (DPH/CBHS), and the San Francisco Unified School District (SFUSD). The mission of the Wellness Centers is to improve the health, well-being, and educational outcomes of San Francisco's high school students by providing comprehensive, school-based student health programming focused on prevention and early intervention in areas critical to student wellness. I worked for a nonprofit agency that had a partnership contract with the school to provide individual and group therapy to students primarily in the special day classes (SDC) and provide consultation to the staff. Referrals came from either the special education teachers or the Wellness Center staff.

Providing school-based services can be challenging for various reasons, such as the collaboration between multiple systems including school, family, client, and any other providers. Schools try to provide a space for therapy, but it is not always a quiet, private, calming, or clean space. Another challenge lies in the fact that as an expressive arts therapist working with youth, I am used to having a variety of tools at my disposal, including games and art supplies; it is difficult to carry around all the necessary tools.

Confidentiality is another challenge that arises when providing school-based treatment. School staff members are in contact with the student almost daily and hold a great deal of information. Staff members create a subsystem whose members work together, for better or worse. Gossip can occur among staff members. Even when the gossip comes from a place of concern, it is important for a therapist, who becomes part of this subsystem, to remember to respect and hold the clients' confidentiality. As with any case, the following case exemplifies this delicate balance.

LANISE

Through my work with this school, I met Lanise. She was a 15-year-old African American girl who was a high school sophomore. Lanise spent a great deal of time in the Wellness Center. She was bright, charismatic, outgoing, friendly, and thoughtful. Lanise also struggled with a short attention span, poor attendance, frequent tardiness, difficulty following adults' directions (including not coming home on time, or not at all), irritability, low frustration tolerance, and aggression toward students and staff, primarily verbal, with occasional physical altercations as well. Since elementary school, she was placed in SDC because of behavioral issues and a mild auditory processing disorder.

Lanise lived with her father and her 12-year-old brother. She was exposed in utero to crack cocaine and alcohol. Her mother was present, on and off, during the first years of her life before moving to another state 7 or 8 years earlier. Her mother had sporadic contact with her children and their father. Lanise's father had a full-time job working for the city. He used marijuana regularly and had little external support from friends or family, yet he did his best to parent his children. Both children had behavioral issues, and he struggled with discipline, boundaries, consequences, and rewards. Lanise was rarely held accountable.

Both children had been involved with a busy independent community center for several years. They attended after school programs and summer camps and had case managers. The center's staff had a relationship with her father and helped diffuse conflict between Lanise and her father as needed. Case managers opened their homes to Lanise to provide an alternative to staying on the streets when she refused to go home. This is a very nontraditional intervention.

Lanise received individual therapy during elementary and middle school for her behavior and at one time took attention-deficit/hyperactivity disorder medication. As a result of her family issues, in particular the abandonment by her mother, as well as abandonment by numerous therapists, she had trust issues that affected her ability to connect with me. She also exhibited fluctuating moods and could become easily triggered. As a result of all of these factors, Lanise tested me a great deal as our therapeutic relationship formed. Some weeks she was resistant to meeting altogether. Other sessions she could not tolerate the enclosed office. On a couple of occasions, the content of the session was too evocative, and she left the session prematurely.

As an expressive arts therapist, I have worked in a variety of settings with youth and their families including schools, homes, agencies, and other locations within the community. I believe it is important to be flexible; this was certainly the case with Lanise. Rarely could she simply engage in a talk therapy session. Sometimes she enjoyed art therapy activities, other times she played board games with me.

*Sometimes we met in the room in the Wellness Center, and other weeks we estab-
lished a preset system in which Lanise would indicate her choice of where our therapy
session would take place—on a walk, on campus, on the track, sitting on the stands,
for example.*

*Consistency was crucial for our developing relationship, especially given her trust
issues. Consistency of appointment date and time was important, but more than
that was follow through. Lanise tested me to see if I would keep my word. This is
important in any therapeutic relationship, but even more so for a youth with such a
background. It was crucial for me to keep my promises, which included showing up
when I said I would; following through with her father, her case manager, her teachers, and administrators; or bringing an activity or game as planned.*

*Overall we developed a strong rapport. I was deeply struck by her strong personal-
ity, resilience, assertiveness, confidence, ability to be vulnerable and honest, and her
sense of leadership and genuine concern for others. Through all the ways she tested
me, we developed a fairly strong connection, and Lanise slowly began to drop her
defenses.*

The goals of the treatment plan included the following:

- *Learning to identify and express her thoughts and feelings in an age-appropriate
  way*
- *Developing and applying self-soothing skills to address her anger*
- *Decreasing the frequency of conflicts with peers and family members*
- *Identifying when she is frustrated so she can reach out to a trusted adult to dif-
  fuse situations before sharp escalation of behavioral reactivity occurred*
- *Improving relationships with parents through increased communication*
- *Increasing the frequency that she followed adults' directions*

*Lanise had an active social life and was personable. She had many friends; her
socializing interfered with her academic life when she was at school. She was roman-
tically involved with an older girl, but their relationship was conflicted, full of drama
and frequent arguments. She was fairly open to discussing her sexual identity in
treatment. Lanise was confident and did not appear to be deeply affected by her
father's confusion about her sexuality or others' judgments.*

*After several months of treatment, conflict increased with her father and brother,
and her school truancies increased. When she was at school, she did not always want
to meet, especially in the treatment room. She was often volatile. After consulting
with Lanise and her case manager, we decided to meet at the community center. This
setting did not work either, because this environment was socially stimulating, and
the space offered little privacy.*

*I shifted the treatment to provide family therapy in her home. It was crucial to work
with the family to create some structure, rules, and accountability while improving
their dyadic relationship and communication. Lanise could not always tolerate full
family sessions and resisted being held accountable or willing to accept any guidelines*

for her behavior. Both father and daughter became frustrated easily. During a few sessions, we were able to make some headway and create some homeostasis. This resulted in improved attendance at school and in the after-school program.

Our treatment shifted again when her mother moved back to the city, unannounced. She was trying to repair her relationship with her children as a friend, not a parent. For a brief time, Lanise's behavior maintained an even level as she navigated moving freely between her father's home, where she had lived all her life, and her mother's friend's apartment. In time, she began splitting: Mother became "all good," and father "all bad." This was a confusing time for her.

A homeostasis such as this rarely lasts. Her anger toward her mother's abandonment resurfaced, but Lanise directed her anger toward her father. Conflict between them escalated. One night, after coming home late, an argument resulted with her father hitting Lanise. The police were called, her father was arrested, and Lanise went to her case manager's home. Her father was released the following day. Child Protective Services (CPS) consulted with Lanise, her parents, and her case manager. It was decided that Lanise and her brother would live with her mother. CPS closed the case soon after.

During this time, Lanise was rarely in school, and when she was, she was rarely in class. Based on the rules of the San Francisco Unified School District, school administrators wrote multiple letters to her family to address her poor attendance. This eventually resulted in a Student Attendance Review Board hearing. I was still actively involved in Lanise's case, although my contact with her was inconsistent at best. I attended the hearing with her case manager, the school principal, Lanise, and her mother.

A SYSTEMIC VIEW

This case exemplifies how providing school-based services occurs within multiple systems. As her therapist, I was not only in a relationship with my client, I was also constantly negotiating the school system, including teachers, administration, and the school district; her family and extended family systems (including the community center staff); and then CPS. The challenge of working with so many systems and her parents' inconsistent involvement made it difficult as well. The community center staff and I were left working harder than the family.

My supervisor reflected on how hard I was working, particularly given how much case management I was providing during the last couple of months of treatment and my challenges in seeing her for regular therapy. For the most part, supervision provided a place for me to share my reactions, including frustration, and discuss various tactics to approach the case.

Lanise's case also illustrates the challenges of working in a school-based setting. I did have a release to share information with all parties regarding her case, and I wanted to gain information as needed from school staff, yet did not always need to share with them Lanise's or her family's private details. This can be challenging to balance, depending on the individuals involved. There were incidents when a school staff member became frustrated that I did not share all details, but for the most part, they were fairly respectful and did not push for information or speak publicly about her. Early in work at this school, I explained to teachers that I would not discuss cases with students present, even if we whispered.

I speculate that her trauma history, home life, and exposure to drugs in utero affected her ability to learn and to tolerate the academic environment. Her school was also fairly big and did not have a great deal of structure; the students had freedom including the ability to leave campus for lunch. As much as Lanise fought overtly against structure, internally she craved it. After many meetings with all the members of the greater systems, including Lanise, it was decided that she would do better in a Continuation High School. Lanise initially resisted the change, her typical response to the many changes she had experienced throughout her life.

My numerous attempts to engage Lanise at her new school, the community center, and on her mother's phone were unsuccessful. Eventually, I had to close the case. My program had rules about how long I could keep a case open that was inactive. In many ways, I was disappointed, as I felt a strong connection to her and truly believed in her potential. I think my countertransference was triggered in that I did not want to fail. Nor did I want to be another adult who simply walked away. Fortunately, Lanise was a youth who had people on her side who supported and believed in her, unlike many of the other youth with whom I work. I also was not able to have any formal termination with her. We spoke on the phone once, at the community center, and I sent her a card. I highlighted all of her many strengths and normalized some of her challenges to focus, study, and grow given the chaos in her life. I wished her well and reflected on some of the hopes and dreams she had shared with me.

Many months after I closed her case, her case manager shared a positive update. She was working at the community center and living with her father. About a year ago, I ran into her on the bus. Now 19 years old, she approached me through a sea of people and we had a very good interaction. She was living with her father again, working, had a long-term boyfriend, and was completing her GED. Her brother, who was 17 years old, had a baby with his girlfriend.

There will always be certain clients who affect you deeply. Sometimes because of the positive clinical work you did or the strong clinical relationship, other times because of the challenges you had in your work with them. In my work with Lanise, I was affected by the complexity of the case, but more importantly by her strong, charismatic, and resilient spirit. I am forever grateful for the opportunity to have worked with Lanise and for what I learned from her. I was reminded how important it is to meet a client where she is at, while paying attention to the process as opposed to the content or the emotional turns of an adolescent navigating inner and external conflict and chaos. Even though she tested me and pushed me away at times, I was reminded to trust my clinical judgment and our relationship.

Chapter 6

Unleashing Creativity in Veterans

Beryl Brenner

The brain, in all of its glory, interprets what it sees. It lights up, and a work of art is conceived. It renders instruction to the hands so that they may fashion such work. As it assimilates the work that is being developed, the analytical progression unfolds until that splendid moment when it is finally deemed to be complete. Creativity is a breathtaking ability for those innovative, imaginative, resourceful souls who are blessed to have the gift of producing art. What a great gift it is! Where does the brain get its flash of inspiration? How does the magic begin? Why do styles of painting suddenly appear in various settings? Why do other artists buck all trends and defy classification?

OVERVIEW OF THE WORK

The information I am writing about is the result of nearly three and a half decades of working with current and former members of the military and the arts in a variety of programs. Services of this nature are provided by the Veteran's Administration, which offers art therapy at 15 U.S. medical centers. These services fall under the umbrella of Recreational Therapy Services, which include art, music, drama and dance (McElveen, 2007). Other groups and creative experiences are offered in community-based clinics and in workshops designed specifically for the veteran community. For the most part, the vast majority of participants in these programs are not professional artists. They had had either limited or no exposure to the arts. They were accustomed neither to creating artwork nor analyzing it. In general, they did not even know how to appreciate making or viewing it. They certainly did not understand anything about what their artwork revealed about themselves before this exposure. They could not possibly have imagined that the artworks they were creating would help them to have a greater sense of self-understanding and heightened self-esteem. This work would reveal their distinctive essence. It would break down defenses and it would build knowledge. In fact, it would be like nothing they had ever seen or done before.

Throughout the course of doing this work, I met with groups of people who came from a wide variety of backgrounds, but they were all connected by the fact that they were veterans. The natural connection among veterans created a strong comfort zone even for those who were somewhat fragile. In essence, they felt that they were among their own kind of people, and as such, they could be themselves. Likewise, it could be said that even for those who were not fragile, the company of their peer group helped them to relax because the group was familiar to them.

Veteran Culture

At this point in time, I would like to write a few words about various subgroups as well as the specifics of what could be deemed a veteran's way of life. "The culture of combat veterans is informed by a shared experience, often traumatic and rooted in the work of soldiers" (Hobbs, 2008, p. 337). Subgroups of people are well known to have their own specific customs. They may be connected by nationality, religions, race, genders, sexual preferences, professions, hobbies, families, or an extensive variety of other associations that foster various connections within a group. These connections might include political perspectives, adherence to various moral philosophies, musical preferences, viewpoints about family life and the responsibilities associated with it, culinary choices, decisions about where to live, attitudes about money, thoughts about the nature of working, as well as a wide variety of methods of thinking about other topics.

Despite these extensive commonalities, it is worth noting that within specific subgroups, people are ultimately human beings and as such are profoundly individualistic. Each person has his or her own personality and preferences. Ultimately, this is the strange dichotomy of the situation. Groups of people are very much the same and simultaneously very different. In short, they are uniquely identifiable, even when this does not appear to be obvious to the world at large. This individualism is what aids the creative process as well as the life process in general.

This is particularly true of veterans. Veterans have a distinctive culture. Indeed, they are a singular subgroup. While they are on active duty, they are required to wear the same uniform that others within their rank and branch of service wear. Upon discharge from the military, many I have encountered retain this "sense of fashion" and continue to wear army fatigue pants, jackets that identify the places that they have served in, or hats that signify with which branch of service they were affiliated. Of course, veterans popularized the notion of having a permanent tattoo placed on one's body as a bold reminder of their time in service.

While they are in the military and stationed at a specific base, they have access to many of the functional resources that they will need to survive. These include a military chapel for spiritual guidance, a PX for shopping, a clinic for medical assistance, restaurants for eating, military housing, a tailor shop that maintains uniforms, a community service center geared toward helping veterans and their families adjust to military demands, recreational facilities, a youth center, a day-care center where their children can mix with other veteran dependants, and a variety of additional resources. All in all, the installation provides the structural foundation for veteran culture. This familiar environment can be appealing for a young soldier who is far from home for the first time in his or her life. Indeed, it is self-contained and instantly recognizable as American.

Even after retiring from the military, it is not uncommon to see retirees using the same amenities that they used while in the service. In recognition of the veteran's service, the subculture provides a rich cadre of governmental and private support that includes medical, educational, and financial benefits. During the course of utilizing these services, veterans invariably will encounter other veterans who are also seeking them. In short, like all other groups of people, veterans often feel most comfortable among other veterans. There is a feeling that it is this group of people that will best understand them and their unusual profession.

In addition to military culture, trauma is also "part of what underlies the shared system of beliefs among those who have served in the military . . . veterans are at much greater risk for certain health conditions, such as PTSD [posttraumatic stress disorder], than the general population due to the nature of their military work" (Hobbs, 2008, pp. 338–340).

Approaching Veterans as Individuals

As I have previously noted, regardless of the social order that they find themselves in, people are, in varying degrees, individualistic by nature. Although the military seeks to create a climate of cohesiveness within its particular domain, there is still room for individualized thinking. It is recognized that the encouragement of this attribute is highly beneficial to the organization.

Of course, every human being would like to have the opportunity to live freely, communicate openly, and be listened to. They want their distinctiveness to be respected. For people who are part of a veteran culture that fosters unity through consistency and obedience, the challenge becomes both educational and creative. After a person has made the commitment to comply with all of the demands and practices of an orthodox system, the crucial question for them is how to tap into the part of their psyche that is not conformist. This is an extremely challenging proposition. After all, it can become quite easy to become lethargic about such matters when many of life's decisions are being made for you. However, deep within the resources of the human spirit, the desire for individualism is compelling. By its very nature, individualism is the lifeblood of the creative process.

Matching Traits between Veterans and Artists

Unless they have actually been a part of it, most people do not understand veteran culture. So many myths and misinterpretations persist. Despite the countless things people have said about soldiers in Vietnam during the war and the veterans after it, the sad truth is that many of these people never actually personally knew one. Vietnam veterans have a slogan that states, "If you weren't there, shut up!" It is only natural that the American veteran would become one of the most probable constituencies for learning and embracing the opportunity to create original art; after all, who can best interpret their own story than the veterans themselves?

Astonishingly, the single most prominent trait that artists and veterans share is discipline. Discipline is widely thought of as synonymous with the military, and this presupposition is true. One cannot run an effective military operation without it. The mission would never be accomplished. Discipline and the military are practically synonymous. What fewer people realize is that discipline is an indispensable quality for the artist. They think of artists as free spirits lacking in discipline. Nothing could be farther from the truth. Oddly enough, it is only through rigorous discipline that an artist can break through and experience the necessary freedom to create. Like the artist, the veteran is able to accomplish the mission through the most rigorous discipline. Because discipline is so ingrained within the culture, I always found it was easy to promote creative experiences with the veterans whom I served.

Another thing that veterans and artists have in common is that they are highly adaptive. Military folks are required to live in places that are foreign and unfamiliar. They may be unused to the weather, the language, the culture, and the customs in general, but they have to relocate to any place that they are told to go to. They are a part of an organization that demands they follow the orders of superior officers with whom they may disagree. Artists must also be willing to be highly adaptive. When their work doesn't sell, they often have to adjust to the most extreme criticism and poverty if they wish to remain in the profession of their choice and training. They learn early in the game that they had better adapt or they will not survive.

There are other significant similarities. Artists are risk takers by nature. Just like their veteran counterparts, they courageously dare to enter a profession that is associated with economic struggles, ruthless competitors, and difficult challenges. Both groups are well aware of the risks, yet they nonetheless choose to enter these professions. Veterans and artists are people who must stay focused to get the job done. Veterans in combat situations know full well that if they fail to observe even the smallest details, it could cost them their lives or the lives of their fellow soldiers. Artists know that they are engaged in one of the world's most subjective professions. As a result, the work that they produce has to make sense on a visual level and a conceptual one as well. Both groups are known for their sense of pride. Veterans are proud of the unique role that they and they alone play in society. They know that it is special and that it is different. After all, who else will perform this role? Artists are proud of the fact that they are the standard bearers for all that is "cool" in the world. They design the new products, and they play a major role in shaping the cultural agenda of the society. Lastly, both veterans and artists are nurturers by nature. It takes a really special person to sign up for a job that puts their own safety at risk so that they may protect other people, most of whom they do not even know. Artists are nurturers as well. They are well known for their generosity toward the poor and the downtrodden. They are constantly being asked to donate their work to worthy causes, and these noble efforts raise a great deal of money for various charities. Also, they nurture inventiveness, the twin sibling of freedom. Inventiveness has a precarious quality to it. Without it we would stand still, frozen in time, and never move forward.

BENEFITS THAT PRODUCING ARTWORK PROVIDES TO VETERANS

The actual benefits that learning to produce and comprehend artwork provides veterans are numerous and varied. Good art demonstrates the visual presentation of an idea, a concept, or an emotion. It has the capacity to be a truly honest process of communicating. As is often said, "pictures don't lie." With veterans, the journey to deeper self-expression through artwork can help participants to unlock their creative potential. It gives them an intensely profound understanding about who they are as human beings. I have found that most often, veterans with whom I have worked did not realize how great this potential was. For most, it proved to be a powerful undeveloped resource. It lies hidden within human beings, but when it is carefully and gingerly retrieved, it is like a faucet that has been stuck for years. Once it is opened, it becomes fairly difficult to shut it down because blocked emotions have been released. Consequently, I would never engage in this process if it would be more damaging than helpful. It is extremely delicate and should be viewed as such. It requires a great deal of patience and trust. After all, the point of honest communication is that it should help people rather than hurt them. If it appears that the individual will be more damaged by the process, then there is absolutely no point in doing it. When secrets come to light, it is wise to be prepared for anything.

Combat experiences are surely the most difficult ones to articulate. Clearly, they do not have any equivalent in the world. By their very nature, they are often associated with trauma, depression, horror, and violence. All too often, those who experience war cannot speak about it, so they suffer silently for many years. On the other hand, drawing the experiences can frequently be perceived as a much more benign method of disclosure. Although research is limited, "a number of small studies of art therapy for veterans with Post Traumatic Stress Disorder have yielded promising results," finding art therapy to be the component among 15 standard components that produced "the greatest benefits for veterans with the most severe PTSD symptoms" (Collie, Backos, Malchiodi, & Spiegel, 2006 p. 159). Throughout the course of my career, I have seen drawings with countless tiny airplanes dropping tiny bombs as well as tiny figures shooting weapons or having weapons shoot at them. When I have discussed this with the artists who created the drawings, they were much more comfortable discussing the incidents portrayed after the drawings were completed rather than before. Whether it was the fact that the incident that was exposed was done so through simplistic drawing techniques or whether it was the fact that the hidden trauma had finally seen the light of day, simply getting things out into the open proved to be remedial for the person that created the image. In the vast majority of cases, a verbal dialogue was established as a result of this experience.

The same process was highly effective for victims of military sexual trauma. By its very nature, the military is associated with strength. The whole idea of being a victim can carry so much shame with it. It often ignites the idea that one was unable to defend oneself, so it dismantles one's entire concept of who they are as human beings. At times, long after the attack the effects linger in the form of guardedness, depression, excessive anger, suicidal ideation, low self-esteem, and hopelessness. Somehow, when this is portrayed through tiny figures, victims are better able to confront their fears and discuss what actually happened.

The mechanism of art therapy works as a means to reconnect "implicit and declarative memories," which help to resolve "memory fragmentation" and can supplement memory retrieval and the integration of traumatic memories when words alone fail. These benefits include: (Collie et al., 2006, p. 160)

- Reconsolidation of memories
- Progressive exposure to traumatic material
- Externalization of traumatic events toward emotional distance
- Reduction of arousal
- Reactivation of positive emotion
- Enhancement of self-efficacy
- Improved self-esteem

This process is also valuable when it is applied to veterans who have histories of substance abuse. Interestingly enough, the experience of existing within an environment entrenched in hard-core drug use can often be as traumatizing as a war zone. Violence is prevalent and frightening for the individuals who have this problem. I have known many veterans who have drawn some harrowing images of experiences they had in dangerous neighborhoods rather than combat images when they were asked to draw pictures of their painful ordeals. One can only imagine how horrifying the experiences of drug culture are if they supersede the traumatic experiences of combat as nightmares. In essence, these images could be considered secondary traumas.

I have previously mentioned that veterans are nurturers by nature. They often view themselves as protectors. One of the most interesting things I have observed was the drawings of substance abusers. Despite having been immersed in the dysfunction of drug-infested neighborhoods and living as an addict, the veteran often portrays himself as a superhero who will try to save the community. There is a sense of disgust over this dysfunction because unlike other drug addicts who never served, veterans have a background of discipline and exposure to an organization that promotes honorable behavior. Many of the drawings show the veterans as action figures dressed up as superheroes who wear little capes. This indicates that they are there to save the community. Within the drawings they remove their self-images from the chaos by flying above the mayhem in which the other figures are engaged. Indeed, this perspective indicates that veteran substance abusers live lives filled with denial about the fact that they are part of the bedlam within the drug culture.

As I have previously noted, veterans are, of course, individuals and human beings. This means that not all of what they draw will be about things that happened in military situations. Many of the veterans with substance abuse histories relate to their drug experiences as the most horrifying trauma that they could express, and many others consider their personal lives to be the most distressing part of their lives. I have looked at countless drawings of appalling love relationships, dreadful parents from families of origin, rude children, terrible siblings, ghastly friends, and dreadful bosses. None of these relationships could be perceived as good ones. Oftentimes, even for combat veterans, these are the issues that trouble them most.

Not all of the artwork that my clients have created over the years has been depressing. There are many other ways of learning about art and many other reasons for doing it. For example, it is rather obvious that if someone is suffering from posttraumatic stress disorder and feels sad all time, the objective is to cheer up that person. The production of artwork or the viewing of artwork can serve this purpose. Cheerful themes can help to improve people's moods. Research has theorized that art therapy is not only a distraction from posttraumatic stress, but that it "helped vets deal with traumatic memories at their own pace" (Hontz, 2006).

In addition to exploring cheerful themes and modulating pacing, the group process helps reduce isolation among participants. Isolation is often a chronic problem for those who are depressed. They do not have the ordinary social skills that are necessary for one to enter easily into new and vibrant relationships. The group makes this process easier. It brings together people who have a veteran heritage in common, and it gives them a purpose—the appreciation and production of art. Veteran culture is well known to promote camaraderie. Dialogue ensues between the members, and they bounce ideas off of each other in a comfortable manner. One Canadian researcher found Veteran's Group particularly helpful and noted that "through the process of creating and discussing art with peers, participants were able to open up and express important thoughts and emotions in an atmosphere of mutual support" (Desjardins, 2001).

The group becomes a natural breeding ground of intellectual and creative stimulation. How important is this? It is very important. The process helps reduce boredom and lack of structure, two of depression's greatest friends. It creates an atmosphere of engagement, and the individuals who are involved become much more interesting human beings as a result.

Producing artwork helps to raise their self-esteem and make them feel good about themselves. It is tangible and can be displayed, admired, or given as a gift to a loved one. It is real and a by-product of one's talent. It gives the veteran who produces it a real sense of accomplishment.

The group's atmosphere is critical. I am fond of playing music while the veterans are working. This helps to enliven the atmosphere within the art studio where they are working. When one is engaged in an inventive process, they have to feel comfortable enough to let their guard down so that the creativity can flow. Having a specific art room helps to define the process as well as the group. In short, it gives them an "identity" in the same way that a sports team has an identity. We know that people are profoundly loyal to sports teams from their specific hometowns. This sense of collaborative identity works in the same way. They feel a connection to the art group because it is their own. In fact, they are the ones who are involved with the innovative work that makes the group special and interconnected.

SPECIFIC PROJECTS

When I meet a veteran for the first time, my favorite initial art assignment is to have him or her draw a self-portrait. Over the years, I have seen thousands of these. This is the perfect introductory assignment because the artists are telling the world exactly how they see themselves. This is a critical piece of the progression because it is specifically generated from the mind of the artist, and we immediately learn a great deal about the person who drew it. If the portrait is large, we can often tell that the individual has an inflated sense of self. If the portrait is small, the reverse may well be true, and low self-esteem is an issue. If the ears are exaggerated than this person is probably a good listener. If the eyes are large and open, this person is probably an observant individual who notices everything. If the face is shown on its side and only reveals half of the person's features we may well be dealing with someone who generally tells us only half of the story. If parts of the face are not closed off and defined, it is most likely that we have encountered a person who has difficulty with boundary issues. The position that the image occupies on the page is important as well. If the portrait is located on the left side of the page, the individual may well be preoccupied with the past and the right side would indicate a preoccupation with the future. If the portrait is squarely located in the center, than chances are the person is living in the present. Of course, the person in the portrait may be smiling and this would generally imply happiness. A frown would be indicative of sadness. Eyebrows crouched toward the center of the face on an angle would suggest anger, and worry lines above the eyebrows would imply that the individual is an anxious person. There are times when I have seen an excessive amount of facial hair, particularly around the mouth, and this would indicate that the individual is trying to cover things up. On the contrary, an open mouth that shows many teeth would suggest the person is not as guarded and is willing to engage freely.

Wow! All of this visual, self-divulging information comes from individuals who entered the room less than 15 or 20 minutes earlier who had never done anything like this before. They probably have not drawn anything since childhood and don't have the slightest understanding about how artwork can be examined or used. They are then given an opportunity to discuss the work. Because the process is so unfamiliar, this is usually brief. Immediately afterward, the rest of the group is asked to make some observations, and initially this is somewhat brief as well because they are not really familiar with the process. It is at this point that I make some of the observations that I delineated in the preceding paragraph. In the vast majority of cases, these observations are accurate descriptions of how the artist views himself or herself. I base this statement on the concurrence of the person that has drawn the picture.

It is in this manner that the method of working is introduced. Knowledge of how it works is relayed, and the group members begin to get to know a great deal about themselves and each other in a relatively short period of time. Generally, they enjoy the process because it is somewhat like a treasure hunt where the artist provides clues. Despite all of the personal information being revealed, a feeling of comfort permeates the room because on the surface, the procedure is so benign. In an effort to heighten visual awareness, I try to point out the things that the group members' body language can tell us about how they are receiving the information. If a person has his arms folded across his chest, the group discusses the fact that this is a barrier and he is resistant. If a person has her pointer finger pressed against her temple, she is pointing to the brain area and is trying to process what is going on within the group. Interestingly enough, what is going on in the drawings is also going on with many of the people in the group. Smiles reveal delight, and frowns reveal sadness.

There is more. At another session, I might ask the participants to draw pictures of their families. Just like their self-portraits, this exercise gives the artist and the community a world of information. Although it has not been specified, some people will draw their family of origin, and some will draw the family they have created through marriage. Some will draw both groups on the same page. If the family of origin presents the artist with unhappy memories, then the artist may be reluctant to explore these events. The same thing can be said of the person who is married and has children but chooses to draw his family of origin rather than his current family. He may feel a greater connection to his original family. He may have an unhappy marriage or difficulties with his children. Those participants that draw both usually have families with greater linkage. The size of the other family members may vary in relationship to their importance to the artist. The largest sibling is not always the oldest one but rather the more important one. This is also true of the placement on the page and who is placed next to whom. Sometimes various family members stand alone on the page and do not intermingle with the rest of the group. Of course, the artist perceives these folks as outsiders. Sometimes it is the artists themselves who stand alone. It is useful to note that sometimes the married couples stand together, and sometimes they are apart. This proximity or lack thereof may be reflective of the state of their marital relationship. Once again, the facial expressions of each family member reveal how the artists perceived them.

One of the recurring assignments that I was fond of requesting from the veteran artists that I encountered was to draw a picture of how they would best like to spend the last day of their lives. I gave this assignment to countless veterans from various ethnic backgrounds as well as various generations. Some were combat veterans, and some were peacetime veterans. The vast majority of the veterans who produced the drawings that I requested invariably came up with some adaptation of the same theme. If they knew that it was the last of their life, they would like to spend it with their families. Usually this event occurred around a dinner table. Essentially, they wished to connect with their relatives and settle any unfinished business that they may have with them. Of course, once the drawings were completed and the veterans discussed the people in the drawings, the advice of the group was to seek out those people with whom the veteran had conflicts and to attempt to resolve these issues.

Other effective assignments might include drawing dreams as windows to the subconscious, constructing miniature altars as a way of learning about the veterans spiritual perspectives, designing personalized Valentine's cards to a person who is considered to be beloved as a means of exploring healthy relationships, creating masks that reveal rather than hide the inner self, or drawing self-images of what the artist looks like when he or she is angry as a segue into the topic of anger.

As I mentioned, the idea of incorporating a bit of cheer in the process is an effective way of working. After all, making art should not be punishment. In December, the holidays present a plethora of creative opportunities that are both challenging and fun. I have asked veterans to design miniature Christmas trees that reflect who they are as people and unique wreaths with themes that defy conventional motifs. Wildly original ornaments, unique hall decorations, and innovative centerpieces have all served as glowing testaments to the artist's imagination. So have highly unusual Chanukah menorahs and Kwanza mats. American veteran culture is one of the most ethnically diverse ones in the world.

One of my favorite assignments is a challenge I have routinely given to my homeless clients. I ask them that if money were no object, what kind of home would they live in, and they proceed to design these homes. The results have been spectacular. People who have lived in homeless shelters and park benches have designed grand palaces with bowling alleys, penthouses, swimming pools, horse stables, and elaborate gardens demonstrating levels of grandiosity that would rival that of royalty. Others designed bunkers that had been painted black with no windows. Of course, these folks were depressed, isolationists. Some designed homes with windows and doors wide open, and these folks were welcoming human connections. Some designed bright, colorful homes that showcased the colorfulness of their ethnic backgrounds. Others have designed the humble place where they grew up, and when they discussed the project, they invariably indicated "for me, it's home!" Each project disclosed an abundance of information about the person who created it.

Another enjoyable challenge that I have presented to clients is simultaneously joyful yet profoundly self-reflective: designing an autobiographical comic book. The purpose of the comic book was to give the participant the opportunity to assess his or her life history. Because comic books are often thought of as comedic, this method of self-exploration was perceived to be benign and nonthreatening. The best way to stimulate creativity and honest communication is to make the artist feel comfortable. Invariably the work that is produced is so much more meaningful. It's always great to see depressed people use their imaginations to develop innovative ways in which they can produce humorous art. Watching them smile and laugh as they produced the work was like watching roses bloom.

I found that specific themes that are relevant to the clients were wonderful to work with because they help to keep the groups focused. One of the most interesting and jovial assignments that I have given to the clients is to have them design an actual game that focuses on the theme. I usually allow them to pick a significant personal theme such as living with sobriety, enhancing social skills, recreation enrichment, or health improvement. The challenge of designing an attractive board game can be fascinating both from an artistic perspective and an educational one. It can be used to present the client with the opportunity to explore various problems or issues by playing out different scenarios within the game. When self-improvement manages to incorporate play, it tends to be more pleasurable. Of course, the artists take great pride in their accomplishments during these sessions.

Up until this point, we have been focusing on artwork that is often produced as an introspective piece of work that explores the artists' veteran experiences as well as their personal ones. Sometimes this information is analyzed and focused on, and at other times it is more beneficial just to "have fun" with art and utilize it as a means of stress reduction.

An example of a different type of veteran artwork is functional artwork. I have vivid memories of several young active duty clients of mine who designed the most beautiful cribs for their brand new babies in the wood shop at the base. For these particular gentlemen, their whole world revolved around the birth of their children. I have run groups for veterans where they have explored the topic of "time" and they designed their own clocks. They have produced fancy heirloom scrapbooks with family photographs as well as unusual t-shirts that tell the world something about who they are. They have designed jewelry pieces that are adorned with custom-made symbolism as well as custom-made picture frames for special people that they know.

Interesting Materials

Exposing the members of the art group to a wide variety of interesting materials can provide them with additional stimuli for creating their artwork. At times, our groups even used food as an art material, and the clients designed culinary platters of fruits or chocolates that were almost too beautiful to eat. I have been working with glass, both stained and fused, for decades and love exposing the veterans to what is generally a new and exciting material for them. When working with glass, one of the common assignments that I present them with is to convey a fragile part of their identity through the use of glass as an arts material. Often it is challenging for veterans to admit that they have a fragile side because the whole culture is associated with strength. Clay, photography, wax, feathers, stencils, exotic papers, markers, charcoal, paint, plastics, leather, stone, metal, printmaking supplies, batik, mosaics, and fiber are some of the other materials that the veterans that I have worked with over the years have enjoyed.

Off-Site Experiences

Going off site to see artworks in museums and galleries can be a glorious experience. Sometimes a change of scenery helps to get people out of their doldrums as they are exposed to new and exciting things that they have never seen before. I have had the good fortune to work in a community where there is access to many cultural attractions, and this has enabled me to present the veterans with these opportunities for many years. However, any community has access to some art within its vicinity, even if it is in the form of folk artists in small towns. These experiences hone the artistic analytical skills group members have developed during the course of their own work. My clients have actually visited other arts facilities where they have created works. This has helped to expose them to novel materials, different art instructors, and new artists outside of our group. If people truly understand art, then they understand that it is a growth process, so these outings present veterans with new opportunities for expansion and development. So many veterans I have met have traveled all over the world, and regardless of their education levels, they are inclined to be open to new experiences.

In addition to the established museums, galleries, and arts centers to which I have exposed the clients, I have tried to make them more conscious of "all things visual" in general. During the holiday season in December, New York City, where I live, experiences a dramatic and breathtaking artistic transformation. The sheer level of aesthetic vitality and stimulation is astonishing. Large sections of the town are beautifully decorated. On many occasions, I have methodically explored this fascinating environment with the clients. When December passes, we are fortunate enough to have access to striking and picturesque settings within our area. I like to encourage our group to speak about how beautiful environments have the capacity to improve one's mood. This reaction is usually a subliminal one in human beings, and often we do not really have an understanding of it. Once we delve into this concept and bring the notion to the surface, the idea of surrounding oneself with an attractive environment to improve one's mood becomes a simple and handy coping skill for those folks who never previously thought about this. Likewise, connecting with the beauty of nature provides a peaceful respite from the stresses of everyday life. Even the most urban areas have access to some natural settings, such as city parks or nearby suburban and rural communities. Many of the clients I have served have enjoyed bringing a sketchbook along when visiting such places.

Different Forms of Creative Expression

Up to this point, I have written about using the visual arts as a means of helping veterans improve their lives. Over the years, I have attempted to familiarize them with other types of creative experiences as well. I presented the groups with a variety of topics that lent themselves to creative writing, such as money management, increasing happiness, taking personal inventory and reducing boredom. On some occasions they wrote essays, and on others they wrote poems. I have conducted many groups in which musical lyrics were analyzed. Topics such as obsession, love relationships, and forgiveness were explored. I engaged the veterans in a variety of role-playing drama exercises and found that these were particularly helpful for substance abusers because they presented real-life scenarios. At times, the acting was so dramatic that it felt quite real. Periodically, I would run a group on movement or dance in the interests of alternative self-expression. It helps to be open-minded in deciding the proper approach for the goals that you wish to achieve.

GROUP DYNAMICS

At this point, I would like to shed some light on group dynamics. Structure is important because it clarifies things. Normally, the group meets at a certain place and a certain time. If it benefits the group, this might be varied on certain occasions. Generally, there are various limitations within the group such as the prohibition of using unsafe art materials. Other groups may have a limited amount of acceptable absences. The goals of the group should be clear and concise so that the participants understand them and can work toward achieving them.

The vast majority of groups have group leaders. Leadership styles vary considerably from person to person. Inevitably, the group leader sets the tone for the whole process. Strong leadership is an asset, but the leader should not be a dictator. Such behavior inhibits free and open discourse and is counterproductive.

Invariably, some of the members of the group will bond with each other. At other times, it will be noticeable that some members tend to separate from the mainstream. Although this is a natural development within group dynamics, the flow of the group is largely enhanced when the members get along with each other and show mutual respect. Creativity is delicate and responsive to external stimuli, both negative and positive.

Lastly, the best groups are those in which every member has a voice and feels valued. One of the great things about art groups is that an actual assignment is given to all of the participants so everyone is automatically involved. The challenge comes when the artwork is being discussed. The more outgoing people tend to dominate the conversation. The goal of the process is to give everyone a voice and let those voices all be heard. This is critical because if all the members of the group feel validated in this manner, they will tend to be much more invested in the process. Generally, the groups will be more interesting and effective. The positive energy is contagious.

PART ARTIST, PART HISTORIAN

Veteran artists are often aware that they are part artist and part historian. Their artwork may keep a record of or provide evidence of the veteran perspective. The images portrayed in these works may be images of their private military experiences or references to other soldier's portraits, tanks, weapons, barracks, installations, uniforms, and military campaigns. Some historians are good artists. They may record people, places, and events through painting, drawing, sculpture, photography, and a wide variety of additional arts media. Because they are communicating their concepts in a visual language their work has the capacity to enlighten us in a profoundly different, yet simultaneously illuminating fashion. These artists are uniquely qualified to present a pictorial documentation of the military experience.

Or not.

Sometimes these veteran artists are like any other artist in the world. They are historians that present us with a visual map of what has occurred in their own personal world. Thank goodness that they are allowed to do so. There is a veteran saying that goes something like this: "Freedom, brought to you by the United States veteran." May it always be so.

REFERENCES

Collie, K., Backos, A., Malchiodi, C., & Spiegel, D. (2006). Art therapy for combat-related PTSD: Recommendations for research and practice. *Art Therapy: Journal of the American Art Therapy Association, 24,* 157–164.

Desjardins, S. (2001, April 18). Make art not war. *Concordia University*. Retrieved from http://www.concordia.ca/now/what-we-do/research/20110418/make-art-not-war.php

Hobbs, K. (2008). Reflections on the culture of veterans. *AAOHN Journal, 56*, 337–341. Retrieved from ProQuest Health and Medical Complete (Document ID: 1546366 701)

Hontz, J. (2006, March 20). The healing canvas. *Los Angeles Times*. Retrieved from http://articles.latimes.com/2006/mar/20/health/he-art20

McElveen, R. (2007, September/October). Using art as therapy. *U.S. Department of Veterans Affairs: Vanguard*, 18–21.

Chapter 7

Mental Health Services in the Juvenile Justice System

Emily B. Gerber, Jennifer Leland, and Karina Wong

> In jail and on probation, I hated it the whole time. But with my charges
> getting dismissed, I can look back and see that I'm better off. Proba-
> tion got me to some folks, like my mentor, who see some good in me
> and set me on a different path. Now I use my head instead of thinking
> with my fists all the time.
>   —Youth, San Francisco Wellness Court Graduation

An estimated 1,504,100 youth (approximately 8% of youth ages 12–18) are
involved in the U.S. juvenile justice system (Puzzanchera & Kang, 2012). A majority are male (72%), White (63%), and young (52% are age 15 and under). Most
crimes committed by these youth are not violent offenses (Puzzanchera & Kang,
2011), and many are in secure confinement for reasons other than their offense(s).
These reasons can include a lack of family support, residential instability, cost
and availability of supervision, and appropriate and effective community treatment resources (Butts & Evans, 2011). Although they are not the majority of the
juvenile justice population, youth of color are overrepresented, especially in urban
areas, for many of the reasons already mentioned (for more on disproportionate
minority contact, see Kempf-Leonard, 2007; Piquero, 2008). Although the federal

government plays a role primarily as a funder, juvenile justice is largely a state and local responsibility. In the United States, there are 51 separate systems and an uncounted number of tribal youth courts (National Research Council, 2001).

Youth with mental health disorders are at increased risk for engaging in behaviors that bring them into contact with the juvenile justice system. Significant risks for juvenile justice involvement include substance abuse history, disruptive disorder, cocaine use, being sexually active, and having a history of aggressive behavior (Cropsey, Weaver, & Dupre, 2008). Youth who enter detention are usually admitted not because of the nature of their crime but because of their behavior at the time of the arrest (Grisso, 2008). Because many childhood mental disorders involve impaired emotion regulation and difficulty with impulse control, these adolescents are more likely to exhibit aggressive behaviors and appear unmanageable at the time of arrest, contributing to their disproportionate numbers in this population.

An estimated 70% of children and youth involved in the juvenile justice system have one or more mental health disorders in stark contrast to 20% of youth in the general population (Shufelt & Cocozza, 2006). Although most are not in immediate need of treatment (Grisso, 2008), more than a quarter of juvenile justice–involved youth experience disorders so acute that their functioning is significantly impaired. Some of these youth receive mental health services for the first time while in juvenile hall, and others may have been bouncing in and out of the behavioral health system for years (Cauffman, Scholle, Mulvey, & Kelleher, 2005; Kates, Gerber, & Casey-Cannon, 2012). Why these problems are so widespread in this group of youth is still the subject of much inquiry. In our work, we have found that the vast majority of youth in juvenile detention who have co-occurring mental health disorders are "multisystem" youth with past or current services through child welfare, special education, probation, or a combination of these. The reasons given for these high rates of disorder are numerous and complex. They include challenges such as poverty, racism, ineffective services, neighborhood and domestic violence and crime, unstable or unavailable caregivers, school disengagement (e.g., "the school-to-prison pipeline"; Hatt, 2011), and stigma and the tendency to view behavioral problems as unrelated to mental illness (Watson, Kelly, & Vidalon, 2009). Although most children and youth, even those exposed to continuous trauma are resilient, for some, any one of these problems are enough to make the climb toward adulthood a difficult and uncertain terrain. While waiting for appropriate services in the community, youth with mental health disorders experience a longer length of stay than those without disorders, which creates a higher cost for those caring for these youth (Cohen & Pfeiffer, 2010).

Increased media scrutiny of this crisis (Moore, 2009) as well as greater recognition on the part of both systems of the scope of the problem have resulted in new models for collaboration, such as the sequential intercept model (Munetz & Griffin, 2006) and the comprehensive model (Skowyra & Cocozza, 2006). These models offer a framework that maps a continuum of critical intervention points (from initial contact with police, to judicial processing, to disposition, to reentry) to keep people with serious mental illness from penetrating deeper into the criminal or juvenile justice systems. New assessment tools and procedures have been developed and tested (Grisso, 2005) with growing knowledge about "what works and for whom," and as a result, an increased reliance on evidence-based practices (such as multisystemic therapy) has improved mental health responses to the needs of these youth and their families (Trupin, 2007). Following trends in adult criminal justice, Juvenile Justice Mental Health Court is another emerging strategy. As of 2007, at least18 juvenile mental health courts were operating as a way to monitor and structure cross-agency strategies to reduce recidivism and increase access to community treatment in lieu of traditional court processing (Council of State Governments Justice Center, 2008).

Systems vary considerably in how and at what point they identify problems, make decisions about case plans, and the quality and quantity of services that are provided inside the walls of "detention settings" and in the community. Clinicians' roles vary considerably depending on the type and extent of services offered by the system or location. Positions can be with the juvenile probation department, the county mental health system, or with an outside contractor who works with youth in the system. In part, because of deficiencies in or lack of community mental health services, some systems have focused on developing their own comprehensive detention-based treatment programs, and others offer little or no services internally. Others provide emergency care only to the most acutely ill and reduce confinement of others in favor of community treatment alternatives. Clinicians may provide treatment or be contacted to conduct criminogenic risk assessments with the Youth Assessment and Screening Instrument, which assesses risk, needs, and protective factors and helps develop case plans for youth (Orbis Partners, 2007; for more information on standardized assessment in juvenile justice, see Bailey, Doreleijers, & Tarbuck, 2006). Clinicians may also be part of a team offering a continuum of care from detention-to-reentry services that uses standardized assessment and evidence-based treatment (see Washington State's Family Integrated Transitions program for an example of this comprehensive and evidence-based approach: http://www.wsipp.wa.gov).

Most youth present with a mix of complex past and current symptoms and rarely have just one diagnosis. In fact, a majority of youth (57%) have more than one disorder (see Figure 7.1; Shufelt & Cocozza, 2006), which can complicate treatment planning. The most common mental health disorders for juvenile involved youth are disruptive, substance use, mood, anxiety, and posttraumatic stress disorder (Shufelt & Cocozza, 2006; Teplin, Abram, McClelland, Dulcan, & Mericle, 2002) with rates differing by gender (see Figure 7.2).

Given the high prevalence rates and comorbidity across a range of disorders, clinicians need to be familiar with the signs and symptoms of these disorders to understand the complex interplay of adolescent development and mental illness and to learn how to prioritize treatment need. For example, impulsivity could be

Figure 7.1.
Number of diagnoses among youth in the juvenile justice system (based on Shufelt & Cocozza, 2006).

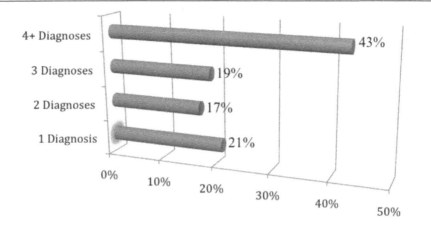

Figure 7.2.
Prevalence rate of behavioral health disorders among males and females in the juvenile justice system (based on Shufelt & Cocozza, 2006).

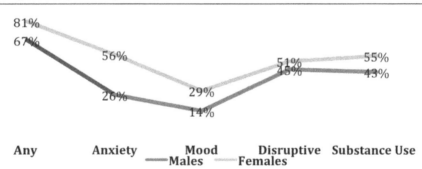

a sign of immaturity that will eventually be outgrown, a symptom of trauma, a symptom of attention-deficit/hyperactivity disorder, or all three (Costello, Copeland, & Angold, 2011).

Despite the promise of emerging strategies, numerous studies from juvenile justice systems in counties around the country have found consistent failures to identify detained youth that have mental health disorders and to systematically plan and to connect those youth with treatment to address their needs (Hazen, Hough, Landsverk, & Wood, 2004). For example, a recent study in a Chicago detention facility found that only 15.4% of youth who met criteria for a mental disorder received treatment while in the center and only 8.1% received treatment in the community (Teplin, Abram, McClelland, Washburn, & Pikus, 2005).

The variety of responses to the problem of mental illness in the juvenile justice system may be dizzying, but there is one consistent factor across all: The juvenile court has the final say about dispositional alternatives, for example, whether a youth receives treatment as a detention alternative, returns home with probation supervision, or is sent to an out-of-home, secure placement. Typically, the primary consideration in this decision is criminogenic risk, that is, whether a youth can safely return home with community-based services and is likely to desist from delinquent behavior. Clinicians learn to negotiate the tension between rehabilitation and punishment that has existed in the juvenile court since its inception.

A BRIEF HISTORY AND ROLE OF THE JUVENILE COURT

> The child who must be brought into court should, of course, be made to know that he is face to face with the power of the state, but he should at the same time, and more emphatically, be made to feel that he is the object of its care and solicitude. (Mack, 1909, p. 120)

The first juvenile courts emerged at the turn of the 19th century. In many ways, the clinician's role in the current system is consistent with the original intentions of Judge Julian Mack, a founder of the first juvenile court in Cook County, Illinois. The core principle was that delinquent youth were immature, should not be punished as adults, and should instead receive treatment and monitoring as a response to their infractions. This approach has held sway despite a rise in juvenile serious crime over the past two decades and a push for "adult time for adult crime." The early juvenile courts were based on doctrine of *parenspatriae*, a Latin term referring to "parent of the nation," giving the state the power to serve as the guardian (or parent) of those with legal disabilities, including juveniles. From this parental role, juvenile courts seek to offer a collaborative, informal approach that focuses on rehabilitation rather than punishment.

On the basis of the premise that adolescents differ developmentally from adults and therefore require differential treatment, the early juvenile courts in the *parenspatriae* role sought to be informal and nonadversarial, creating a system that treated cases as civil action as opposed to "criminal." This also means that in juvenile court, there is no finding of "guilt," no "conviction," and no "sentence." Trials are referred to as hearings and "sentencing" refers mostly to diversion programs, supervision, or community placements. In some cases, juveniles are sentenced to residential treatment programs or nonsecure facilities that provide greater supervision than a youth might receive in a community or home environment, often referred to as "home detention." In line with this differing language of the juvenile court, the roles of the stakeholders are also distinguished from their adult system counterparts.

The primary stakeholders in the juvenile justice system include judges, the district attorney, public and private attorneys, police officers, probation officers, and increasing numbers of social workers, clinicians, case managers, and mentors who comprise both county and nonprofit programs that constitute "alternatives to detention" and aim to rehabilitate delinquent youth in the least restrictive environment deemed appropriate. In general, police officers make the initial arrest of a youth; it is their job to protect the public and enforce the law. The district attorney (DA) is a lawyer who represents the "people" and has the responsibility to prove that a crime was committed, prove the case "beyond a reasonable doubt," and advocate for appropriate "sentencing." The lawyers (some public defenders and others private attorneys) represent youth who are facing charges, and it is their role to defend youth against allegations or charges brought against them by police and the DA. Juvenile court judges make the final decisions in a juvenile case, deciding both the culpability of youth in the charges brought against them and the response the system will take to rehabilitate youth and prevent future delinquency. There is no jury in juvenile court. The judge does not declare youth "guilty" or "not guilty" but rather decides whether the charges have been proven to be true or "sustained" or "not sustained," that is, not proven true. This marked departure from confinement and punishment toward rehabilitation has been the subject of much debate since the inception of the juvenile courts (Scott & Steinberg, 2008). The notion of whether juvenile courts have been successful in their efforts to "reparent" or "rehabilitate" young offenders continues to inspire rich debates that often challenge and reform this rather new concept behind a separate system for juveniles in the criminal justice systems.

Clinicians working in the juvenile justice system should be prepared for understanding and managing conflicting views about what causes delinquent behaviors. In a sense, this is another version of one of the oldest debates in psychology: Is it nature or nurture that has the most impact on development? Although science has firmly established that genetic effects on delinquency are moderated by life experiences (Guo, Roettger, & Cai, 2008), this debate is still very much alive in the juvenile justice system and can influence how youth are perceived and the dispositions and services they receive (Lopez-Williams, Vander Stoep, Kuo, & Stewart, 2006). At one end of this continuum is the belief that youth who engage in delinquent behaviors are "born bad" and must be punished. At the other end is the belief that youth are victims of poor environment and need corrective interventions.

Regardless of how this argument plays out and the resulting legal disposition (probation vs. placement), the clinician's role is to keep the focus squarely on identifying and addressing the specific needs of youth and their families or caregivers in the settings where they will be receiving services. To do this, the first task of working with youth in the juvenile justice system is to understand the many tensions that exist within this collaborative approach toward rehabilitation. The multiple stakeholders that inhabit the system, each tasked with their own roles and responsibilities, can create a rich "checks and balances" approach to the idea behind promoting rehabilitation of the juvenile delinquent while simultaneously protecting public safety. This increased understanding enhances the ability to bridge differences in the service of creating a case plan that includes appropriate and effective services for youth.

PARTNERING WITH THE PROBATION OFFICER

> Ms. Waller. She cares about me. My PO knows I'm a good kid. She came to my house just to talk me outta doing something stupid one day. She really cares.
>
> —San Francisco Youth

From their origins as "child savers" in the 19th century (Glowacki & Hendry, 2004), probation officers are now seen primarily as the hand of law enforcement and less as the social workers originally imagined by the reformists. The probation officer, or "PO," plays multiple roles within the juvenile system from investigating the initial law violations, developing plans to successfully monitor and rehabilitate youth while under the custody of the juvenile courts and arresting youth when these terms have been violated or revoked by the court. More than any other role in the system, it has been influenced heavily by politics and changing attitudes toward youth crime. In recent times, caseloads for many jurisdictions have increased so much that many cases are "banked," meaning that a computer will alert the assigned PO that a youth has committed another crime, and this response to the computer-generated message will be the primary action in the case (DeMichele, 2007). Where caseloads are more manageable, POs conduct home checks, attend school meetings and graduations, and develop a more genuine relationship with youth. In recent years, these gaps created in the role of the PO have been filled instead by nonprofit program staff, case managers, clinicians, and mentors who must now partner with probation officers to ensure safety and supervision in addition to holding this transformational relationship with youth.

Successful and effective partnerships with the PO, although sometimes challenging, are often the most influential and predictive indicator of successful engagement in services and completion of probation. POs and clinicians often approach youth work from different assumptions (Butts, Bazemore, & Meroe, 2010), and they are motivated by different responsibilities. At the most extreme, POs view youth as "villains," and clinicians view youth as "victims." These lenses are shaped by the different roles played. POs must ensure youth are complying with court orders, while clinicians are often focused on engaging youth in treatment and less so on monitoring their compliance. Understanding the differing perspective and role of the PO can assist clinicians in understanding how best to integrate diverse approaches, use youth as a resource, and create effective juvenile justice–mental health collaborations to best serve youth who often need both approaches for successful transformation.

CLINICAL PRACTICE IN FORENSIC SETTINGS: THE BASICS

> Hey, I've got this kid in my office and he's acting kinda funny. Can you come eyeball him?
>
> —San Francisco Probation Officer

Clinicians can play a variety of roles within forensic settings—case managers, individual and family therapists, clinical case managers, social workers, and forensic assessment specialists. Clinicians who work within juvenile justice are often perceived by other stakeholders to be "mental health specialists" who work within a system that does not identify as such and are often called on to intervene when juvenile justice staff request assistance in crisis situations. Often probation officers are unfamiliar with the language of behavioral health and request assistance in understanding and translating psychological evaluations into case planning. In addition to providing direct treatment, clinicians function as clinical consultants to the stakeholders in the juvenile justice system. For example, clinicians may be asked to conduct additional assessment on youth facing arson charges or identify appropriate sanctions for youth with phobias, traumatic stress, or psychotic symptoms that can often be exacerbated in an adversarial courtroom setting.

Unlike traditional mental health settings, clinicians are expected to work collaboratively with POs and other stakeholders when establishing treatment goals. Treatment goals often address mental health needs identified in assessments as well as supervision needs identified by the court. Goal setting prioritizes safety, symptom reduction, and improved functioning in key domains such as home, school, and community settings. Probation officers, clinicians, and other stakeholders (such as the public defender) may often differ on which goal is most important. Codevelopment of a coordinated, realistic plan of care requires working together and negotiating these differences. Effective implementation of a treatment plan requires that the team be aware of the same information and make collaborative decisions based on actual needs rather than bias or strategy. For example, a gang-involved youth with a plan that requires clinic-based services may face threats to his safety as he makes his way to and from treatment. As a clinician, one must individualize treatment plans to address not only identified behavioral health needs but other factors (such as location, accessibility, or cultural/linguistic issues) that could have an impact on the youth and family's engagement in services. Most important, the plan needs be doable. Often probation plans are packed with services that can feel overwhelming and unrealistic to youth and families. While creating a plan packed with structured activities may seem in the best interest of the youth, for many it can lead to resistance and treatment failure.

Clinicians should be aware of the dynamics that can lead to heightened resistance in forensic settings. Often services may be mandated by a judge as an alternative to detention, which can feel more like a punishment than a service. Or probation officers may cultivate the perception that services are mandated even if they are not. Typically, engaging any adolescent in treatment can be tough and even more difficult with system-involved youth (Abram, Paskar, Washburn, Teplin, & Al, 2008). Many have had prior experiences with services that have failed them in some way. In addition, juvenile court is responsible for monitoring treatment engagement and may sanction youth who are noncompliant with services. In response, clinicians may feel the pull to protect "the alliance" and not disclose critical information about lack of engagement or stalled progress to protect youth from possible detention. Reporting and disclosing clinical information can often bring tension to the therapeutic relationship that will be important for clinicians to navigate effectively. This should be a familiar tension because it often emerges when working with adolescents and their families. The system version of triangulation or "splitting" often backfires and youth feel betrayed when probation officers discover "hidden" information (such as a missed curfew or a failed drug test). On the other hand, when probation officers and clinicians act in concert clear incentives for adherence to treatment goals or consequences for risky behaviors can result in an effective behavior modification plan for treatment progress. In short, clinicians working within the juvenile justice system must balance their alliance with youth and families with the collaborative and institutional structure of the juvenile system.

CRISIS AND OPPORTUNITY: READINESS FOR CHANGE AND TREATMENT ENGAGEMENT

Although a difficult experience for youth and families, contact with the juvenile justice system can often become a powerful turning point and a path toward restoring hope for families that often have been struggling in isolation before the first contact with police. Juvenile justice systems can offer youth access to a broad range of meaningful "sanctions" for offenders. These often include supervision and supportive services including behavioral health services that are otherwise unavailable to youth who have no involvement with the system.

Effective systems focus on "leveraging the crisis" so that while the youth is in custody, the probation department can identify needs and create a plan for release that will most effectively target the unique needs and strengths of the youth and family. Upon entering the system and during periods of detention, youth are often motivated for change, and it is an ideal time to offer interventions that not only curb delinquency but can also have a significant positive impact on youth in all areas of their lives—increasing school performance, employment skills, and community involvement and getting access and treatment for mental and physical health problems. Youth who do not have helpful or consistent family support are at risk of violence and prolonged involvement in the court system (Garbarino & Ganzell, 2000).

If the initial crisis (contact with juvenile court) can lead to transformational opportunities, courts must maximize these opportunities to engage with caregivers and empower families in similar transformational ways that can restore caregiver roles and connection. There is enormous potential for harm and healing and often there are enormous obstacles and challenges to partnering with families in the juvenile court system. Engaging families is not always easy but is crucial to sustained successful outcomes in the daily lives of youth. Institutional racism, language and cultural barriers, feelings of shame, helplessness, and implications of generational incarceration often conspire to keep families from participating in the court system and in their child's rehabilitation.

The current focus on returning youth to their home environment or "least restrictive" environment and the overwhelming majority of youth serving "home detentions" puts additional pressure on caregivers to provide institutional-level, round-the-clock supervision. For caregivers, often single working mothers, these mandates can be overwhelming and sometimes impossible. When most successful, the courts and clinicians working with juveniles have found additional resources to shore up families in crisis and to increase family engagement with the courts.

Clinicians can offer both practical and supportive services to families throughout their contact with the juvenile justice system. They often transport and accompany families to court. Where family therapy is a mandated part of treatment, clinicians can offer home-based sessions or after-hours appointments. Many programs, including wraparound programs, have added "Parent Partners" to behavioral health support teams, advocates for caregivers who are often intimidated by the many institutions in which they find their families—special education, mental health, juvenile justice. A family therapist in a multisystemic program, for example, may purchase gas cards or grocery cards to reward parents for reaching family goals—for youth reducing truancy or runaway behaviors or for parents' increased ability to set limits. A clinical case manager may link a caregiver to his or her own mental health therapist so that they can better tolerate the stressors of a child with oppositional-defiant disorder or substance abuse issues.

Ingredients for an Effective Plan

Community transition planning ("step-down"), including the coordination and provision of community services, is a critical component of a successful return to the community for youth and is associated with lower rates of recidivism during the first year after discharge (Trupin, Turner, Stewart, & Wood, 2004). To counteract the gender and racial biases that can influence who receives what services (Wasserman et al., 2008), plans should be based on standardized assessment(s) that identifies and prioritizes critical needs. When all stakeholders rely on evidence rather than opinion, a transparent and rational plan with clear benchmarks for progress can be developed. Crucial to the success of any plan is the identification of youth strengths and talents. Although youth may appear angry, defiant, and rejecting of help, this is typically armor worn to protect them from more disappointment, hurt, and the potential risks they face as they return to the community. By focusing on "badges of ability" as well as areas of need, you are opening the door to hope and increasing opportunities for validation rather than the cycle of failure often experienced by these youth (Crenshaw & Garbarino, 2007; Hardy & Laszloffy, 2005). A strengths-based approach will increase the odds of youth engagement in and the success of their treatment.

Aftercare Treatment Settings and Modalities

Treatment can be provided in detention or residential settings ("out-of-home placements") or in the community. Ideally, youth with acute behavioral health needs and high criminogenic risks should receive treatment in a structured residential setting; however, these facilities have been in sharp decline due the tightening of state budgets and an ideological shift driven by the System of Care movement to treat youth in the "least restrictive settings" (Geller & Biebel, 2006; Hodges, Ferreira, Israel, & Mazza, 2010). As a result, critical gaps now exist at the higher tiers of care and juvenile justice has relied more on intensive community-based services provided at home, in schools, or in other community settings. Aftercare treatment of youth with significant behavioral health needs and risks, in the community, has made probation–behavioral health partnership and the use of proven practices even more critical.

Although most youth are released soon after arriving at juvenile hall, for those who do spend any length of time in detention or other residential settings, aftercare is a critical point for planning and step down for youth as they return to the community. Youth can step down from very structured short- or longer-term detention or from residential placement settings. Effective reentry and aftercare requires the collaboration and support from the juvenile justice system as a whole—the court, prosecution, law enforcement, corrections, probation, education, and social services—to accomplish the goal of preventing juveniles from reoffending and returning to the system. It utilizes supervision to reduce juveniles' opportunity and ability for committing crimes and interventions to help them change their behavior. Depending on their age and circumstances, some youth may need to negotiate how to rejoin their families, start a new school, or function as an independent adult. All aftercare planning should begin several months before release. Clinicians play an important role in anticipating and helping youth overcome various personal and environmental obstacles that can potentially threaten their success in the community (Ashford, Sales, & Lecroy, 2001). Additionally, by using standardized assessment and identifying treatment goals, clinicians can help keep plans doable and focused on critical needs.

Clinicians must be mindful of environmental factors that may impact youth on return to their homes. Some of these factors may include family conflicts, unstable or unsafe living arrangements, and the presence of gangs. It is common for justice-involved youth to have prior exposure to maltreatment and violence in and out of the home (Ford, Chapman, Hawke, & Albert, 2007). Those who have experienced abuse or neglect (or both) are at higher risk for criminality and arrests. Youth are going back to a home or community and need treatment that helps them develop skills to cope with the same pressures and temptations (Bouffard & Bergseth, 2008) that existed before detention. Sometimes, alternative living situations may be necessary. Younger youth may need placement with extended family or other responsible adults, whereas older youth may benefit from independent living.

Over the past decade, advances in proven and effective therapies have emerged and helped the field better identify and respond to the mental health needs of youth (Trupin, 2007). When implemented with fidelity, many of these evidence-based practices have been shown to improve outcomes for juvenile justice-involved youth (see Table 7.1). A key common element across these interventions is a practical focus on building skills and strengthening the informal supports around youth and families. However, two of the most popular interventions for youth in the juvenile justice system, wraparound and case management, have yet to establish indisputable evidence of effectiveness (Bruns, Suter, & Leverentz-Brady, 2008; Suter & Bruns, 2009). Both practices have been plagued by vague definition and inconsistent standards. Efforts have been underway (for example, see the National Wraparound Initiative at http://www.nwi.pdx.edu) to better define and operationalize their components and have resulted in improved models and practice (Bruns et al., 2008; Suter & Bruns, 2009). As currently defined, wraparound is an individualized, team-based service planning and care coordination process for youth with complex behavioral health needs.

Case management is also a common intervention for youth in multiple systems, but there is wide variability in its implementation (Bruns & Walker, 2010; Walker & Bruns, 2008). A case manager serves as the glue that holds the plan together through coordination and communication with all stakeholders. The core functions of a case manager include assessment, psychoeducation, service planning, implementation and coordination, monitoring and evaluation of progress, and advocacy. A case manager may also provide clinical services, as well as manage funding related to care, outreach and education to the community.

AGING OUT OF THE JUVENILE SYSTEM

Transitioning into adulthood can be difficult to manage for most youth, but it is especially so for those in the juvenile justice system. Youth generally age out when they reach the age of majority (age 18 or 19) while detained, on probation, in out-of-home care, or receiving services through the juvenile justice system. Youth will no longer be "chased" by case managers or probation officers. Many may still lack the skills necessary to function successfully as independent adults. Academic and cognitive deficits, as well as hazardous living conditions and placements, can

Table 7.1.
A Sample of Evidence-Based Practices for Juvenile Justice Involved Youth

Psychosocial[a]	Home and Community-Based[b]	Medication[c]
Cognitive behavioral	Brief strategic family therapy	**Attention-deficit/ hyperactivity disorder**
CBT for psychosis	Functional family therapy	Ritalin, Focalin, Adderall, Strattera
Trauma-focused CBT	Multidimensional treatment foster care	**Mood disorders**
Aggression replacement training	Multisystemic therapy	Celexa, Lexapro, Paxil, Prozac, Zoloft
Mindfulness		**Psychotic disorders**
Dialectical behavior therapy		Abilify, Clozaril, Haldol, Risperdal, Seroquel, Zyprexa
Seeking Safety		
Motivational		
Family check-up		
MET-CBT-5		

[a] CBT = cognitive-behavioral therapy; MET-CBT = motivational enhancement–cognitive behavioral therapy.
[b] See Substance Abuse and Mental Health Services Administration National Registry for Evidence-based Programs http://nrepp.samhsa.gov.
[c] http://www.aboutourkids.org/articles/guide_psychiatric_medications_children_adolescents.

greatly affect their development and transition to adulthood (Moffit, Avshalom, Harrington, & Milne, 2002). As young adults, they will find that fewer services are available and more competition for those services that do exist. Your critical role with transitional age youth (TAY) will be to help them take responsibility for their lives by pursuing the services and supports that will help them maintain their health and reach their goals.

Many youth continue to struggle with mental health issues as they transition into adulthood. Some have had various combinations of behavioral, thought, and mood disorders throughout their childhood, and some may experience their first symptoms during this transition period (Lyons & Melton, 2005). Several studies have shown that mental health conditions stabilize from childhood to early adulthood, whereas others have indicated that early behavioral and emotional issues can predict chronic severe mental health issues.

As a result, these youth and their families need to learn and acquire specific skills, and they need the social and economic support that will allow them to better cope with their serious, often debilitating, illness. As noted earlier, eligibility for services for adults often differs from those for children. Children who had been receiving benefits for developmental disorders may no longer be eligible for services as adults (Baltodano, Mathur, & Rutherford, 2005). On the other hand, mental health issues that are encountered in adulthood (e.g., schizophrenia) may allow youth suddenly to become eligible for services and federally funded programs such as Supplemental Security Income (SSI).

With the number of issues and the lack of skills to handle adult responsibilities, it is no wonder that this vulnerable population is known to have more difficulties with securing employment and housing. Many of these youth have less education and lower academic success. This, along with their involvement with crime and the justice system, appears to decrease their later employment prospects and financial stability. With little time spent preparing for employment while in detention or placed out of home, they tend to be at a disadvantage in finding a job (Nellis & Wayman, 2009) and are at greater risk for homelessness (Desai, Lam, & Rosenheck, 2000).

Despite all these challenges, having the appropriate supports from caring people and communities and appropriate services can greatly reduce recidivism and increase the success of juvenile justice involved youth as they enter adulthood. If clients leave the system with a greater sense of their abilities, have received appropriate and effective treatment, and reengaged in education or employment, they are much more likely to succeed and have healthy and productive lives (Chung, Mulvey, & Steinberg, 2011).

CONCLUSION

We have found that providing mental health services in the juvenile justice system is enormously challenging but very rewarding work. Racing against the odds and the clock, clinicians work to instill hope, reduce symptoms, and mobilize change to prevent children and youth from penetrating more deeply into the juvenile or adult criminal justice system. Doing so requires a varied set of clinical skills and interventions at multiple levels of complex systems (e.g., the family, probation community mental health, and child welfare). On any given day, clinicians face outcomes that are unexpected, demoralizing, or uplifting.

Clinicians identify complex needs, have the skill to triage the ones that are most acute, and take action to address them. Although knowing the evidence for which interventions work best is important (e.g., aggression replacement training for oppositional-defiant disorder), more practically, clinicians must be familiar with what services and expertise actually exist within local mental health systems, and how to creatively match what's available to achieve interim goals (e.g., CBT to reduce stress) and desired outcomes (e.g., prosocial responses to threats).

Clinicians must be able to rapidly shift roles (e.g., therapist with youth and families, psychoeducation with probation officers, and progress reporting to judges) and lens (e.g., legal vs. mental health) to understand and unify the differing perspectives of system stakeholders. Getting stakeholders on the same page is critical to a rational planning and decision-making process.

Initially a paradox for most clinicians, collaboration with probation officers can feel like "ratting" on clients. Resisting the urge to "protect" youth by minimizing setbacks and openly acknowledging steps forward and back will lead to more effective collaboration and better outcomes. This unique partnership of supervision and treatment offers structure, limit setting, coaching, and nurturing—the basic building blocks youths require to develop into healthy and productive adults.

Most important, keep in mind that the most resistant youth and families have the deepest injuries but often possess the greatest strengths. When these "hidden treasures" are uncovered and recognized, they are powerful incentives for transformation and recovery.

REFERENCES

Abram, K. M., Paskar, L. D., Washburn, J. J., Teplin, L. A., & Al, A. E. T. (2008). Perceived barriers to mental health services among youths in detention. *Journal of the American Academy of Child and Adolescent Psychiatry, 47*, 301–308.

Ashford, J. B., Sales, B. D., & Lecroy, C. W. (2001). Aftercare and recidivism prevention. In B. Ashford, W. H. Reid, J. B. Ashford, & B. D. Sales (Eds.), *Treating adult and juvenile offenders with special needs*. Washington, DC: American Psychological Association, 373–400.

Bailey, S., Doreleijers, T., & Tarbuck, P. (2006). Recent developments in mental health screening and assessment in juvenile justice systems. *Child and Adolescent Psychiatric Clinics of North America, 15*, 391–406.

Baltodano, H. M., Mathur, S. R., & Rutherford, R. B. (2005). Transition of incarcerated youth with disabilities across systems and into adulthood. *Special Education, 13*, 103–124.

Bouffard, J. A., & Bergseth, K. J. (2008). The impact of reentry services on juvenile offenders' recidivism. *Youth Violence and Juvenile Justice, 6*, 295–318.

Bruns, E. J., Suter, J. C., & Leverentz-Brady, K. (2008). Is it wraparound yet? Setting quality standards for implementation of the wraparound process. *The Journal of Behavioral Health Services & Research, 35*, 240–252.

Bruns, E. J., & Walker, J. S. (2010). Defining practice: Flexibility, legitimacy, and the nature of systems of care and wraparound. *Evaluation and Program Planning, 33*, 45–48.

Butts, J. A., Bazemore, G., & Meroe, A. S. (2010). Positive youth justice. *Youth Justice*. Retrieved from http://www.juvjustice.org/media/resources/public/resource_390.pdf

Butts, J. A., & Evans, D. N. (2011). Resolution, reinvestment, and realignment: Three strategies for changing juvenile justice. New York, NY: John Jay College of Criminal Justice. Retrieved from http://www.reclaimingfutures.org/blog/sites/blog.reclaimingfutures.org/files/userfiles/Resolution-Reinvesment-JButts-DEvans-JohnJay-Sept2011.pdf

Cauffman, E., Scholle, S. H., Mulvey, E., & Kelleher, K. J. (2005). Predicting first time involvement in the juvenile justice system among emotionally disturbed youth receiving mental health services. *Psychological Services, 2*, 28–38.

Chung, H. L., Mulvey, E. P., & Steinberg, L. (2011). Understanding the school outcomes of juvenile offenders: An exploration of neighborhood influences and motivational resources. *Journal of Youth and Adolescence, 40*, 1025–1038.

Cohen, E., & Pfeiffer, J. (2010). *Costs of incarcerating youth with mental illness. Methods* (p. 49). Prepared for the Chief Probation Officers of California and the California Mental Health Directors Association. Retrieved from http://67.199.72.34/php /Information/Papers/Costs%20of%20Incarcerating%20Youth%20with%20Men tal%20Illness.pdf

Costello, E. J., Copeland, W., & Angold, A. (2011). Trends in psychopathology across the adolescent years: What changes when children become adolescents, and when adolescents become adults? *Journal of Child Psychology and Psychiatry, and Allied Disciplines, 10,* 1015–1025.

Council of State Governments Justice Center. (2008). Mental health courts: A primer for policymakers and practitioners. Retrieved from www.ojp.usdoj.gov/BJA/pdf/MHC _Primer

Crenshaw, D. A., & Garbarino, J. (2007). The hidden dimensions: Profound sorrow and buried potential in violent youth. *Journal of Humanistic Psychology, 47,* 160–174.

Cropsey, K. L., Weaver, M. F., & Dupre, M. A. (2008). Predictors of involvement in the juvenile justice system among psychiatric hospitalized adolescents. *Addictive Behaviors, 33,* 942–948.

DeMichele, M. T. (2007). Probation and parole's growing caseloads and workload allocation: Strategies for managerial decision-making. Lexington, KY: The American Probation & Parole Association. Retrieved from http://www.appa-net.org/eweb/docs /appa/pubs/SMDM.pdf

Desai, R. A., Lam, J., & Rosenheck, R. A. (2000). Childhood risk factors for criminal justice involvement in a sample of homeless people with serious mental illness. *Journal of Nervous and Mental Disease, 188,* 324–332.

Ford, J. D., Chapman, J. F., Hawke, J., & Albert, D. (2007). Trauma among youth in the juvenile justice system: Critical issues and new directions. NCMHJJ Research and Program Brief. Delmar, NY: National Center for Mental Health and Juvenile Justice.

Garbarino, J., & Ganzell, B. (2000). The human ecology of early risk. In J. P. Shonkoff & S. J. Meisels (Eds.), *Handbook of early childhood intervention* (2nd ed., pp. 76–93). New York, NY: Cambridge University Press.

Geller, J. L., & Biebel, K. (2006). The premature demise of public child and adolescent inpatient psychiatric beds: Part I. Overview and current conditions. *The Psychiatric Quarterly, 77,* 251–271.

Glowacki, P., & Hendry, J. (2004). *Hull-House: Images of America.* Charleston, SC: Arcadia.

Grisso, T. (2005). Why we need mental health screening and assessment in juvenile justice programs. In T. Grisso, G. Vincent, & D. Seagrave (Eds.), *Mental health screening and assessment in juvenile justice* (pp. 3–21). New York, NY: Guilford Press.

Grisso, T. (2008). Adolescent offenders with mental disorders. *The Future of Children, 18,* 143–164. Retrieved from http://www.ncbi.nlm.nih.gov/pubmed/21338001

Guo, G., Roettger, M. E., & Cai, T. (2008). The integration of genetic propensities into social-control models of delinquency and violence among male youths. *American Sociological Review, 73,* 543–568.

Hardy, K. V., & Laszloffy, T. A. (2005). Teens who hurt: Clinical interventions to break the cycle of adolescent violence. New York, NY: Guilford.

Hatt, B. (2011). Still I rise: Youth caught between the worlds of schools and prisons. *The Urban Review, 43,* 476–490. doi:10.1007/s11256-011-0185-y

Hazen, A. L., Hough, R. L., Landsverk, J. A., & Wood, P. A. (2004). Use of mental health services by youths in public sectors of care. *Mental Health Services Research, 6*, 212–226.

Hodges, S., Ferreira, K., Israel, N., & Mazza, J. (2010). Systems of care, featherless bipeds, and the measure of all things. *Evaluation and Program Planning, 33*, 4–10.

Kates, E., Gerber, E. B., & Casey-Cannon, S. (2012). Prior service utilization in detained youth with mental health needs. *Administration and Policy in Mental Health and Mental Health Services Research*. Retrieved from http://www.springerlink.com/con tent/m425lj2357312643. doi: 10.1007/s10488-012-0438-4

Kempf-Leonard, K. (2007). Minority youths and juvenile justice: Disproportionate minority contact after nearly 20 years of reform efforts. *Youth Violence and Juvenile Justice, 5*, 71–87.

Lopez-Williams, A., Vander Stoep, A., Kuo, E., & Stewart, D. (2006). Predictors of mental health service enrollment among juvenile offenders. *Youth Violence and Juvenile Justice, 4*, 266–280.

Lyons, P. M., & Melton, G. B. (2005). Coping with mental health problems in young adulthood: Diversity of need and uniformity of programs. In D. W. Osgood, E. M. Foster, C. Flanagan, G. R. Ruth (Eds.), *On your own without a net: The transition to adulthood for vulnerable populations* (pp. 304–321). Chicago, IL: The University of Chicago Press.

Mack, J. (1909). The juvenile court. *Harvard Law Review, 23*, 104. doi:10.2307/1325042

Moffit, T. E., Avshalom, C., Harrington, H., & Milne, B. J. (2002). Males on the life-course-persistent and adolescence-limited antisocial pathways: Follow-up at age 26 years. *Development and Psychopathology, 14*, 179–207.

Moore, S. (2009). Mentally ill offenders strain juvenile justice system. *The New York Times*. Retrieved from http://www.njjn.org/media/resources/public/resource_1296.pdf

Munetz, M. R., & Griffin, P. A. (2006). Use of the sequential intercept model as an approach to decriminalization of people with serious mental illness. *Psychiatric Services, 57*, 544–549.

National Research Council. (2001). *Juvenile crime, juvenile justice*. Washington, DC: The National Academies Press.

Nellis, A., & Wayman, R. H. (2009). *Back on track: Supporting youth reentry from out-of-home placement to the community*. Washington, DC: Youth Reentry Task Force of the Juvenile Justice and Delinquency Prevention Coalition.

Orbis Partners. (2007, November). Long-term validation of the Youth Assessment and Screening Instrument (YASI) in New York State juvenile probation (p. 86). Submitted to the New York State Division of Probation and Correctional Alternatives. Retrieved from dpca.state.ny.us/pdfs/nyltyasifullreport20feb08.pdf

Piquero, A. R. (2008). Disproportionate minority contact. *The Future of Children, 18*, 59–79.

Puzzanchera, C., & Kang, W. (2012). Easy access to juvenile court statistics: 1985–2009. Retrieved from http://www.ojjdp.gov/ojstatbb/ezajcs/

Scott, E. S., & Steinberg, L. (2008). Adolescent development and the regulation of youth crime. *The Future of Children, 18*, 15–33.

Shufelt, J. L., & Cocozza, J. J. (2006, June). Youth with mental health disorders in the juvenile justice system: Results from a multi-state prevalence study. National Center for Mental Health and Juvenile Justice Research and Program Brief.

Skowyra, K., & Cocozza, J. J. (2006, June). A blueprint for change: Improving the system response to youth with mental health needs involved with the juvenile justice system. Delmar, NY: National Center for Mental Health and Juvenile Justice. Retrieved from http://www.ncmhjj.com/Blueprint/pdfs/ProgramBrief_06_06.pdf

Suter, J. C., & Bruns, E. J. (2009). Effectiveness of the wraparound process for children with emotional and behavioral disorders: A meta-analysis. *Clinical Child and Family Psychology Review, 12,* 336–351.

Teplin, L. A., Abram, K. M., McClelland, G. M., Dulcan, M. K., & Mericle, A. A. (2002). Psychiatric disorders in youth in juvenile detention. *Archives of General Psychiatry, 59,* 1133–1143.

Teplin, L. A., Abram, K. M., McClelland, G. M., Washburn, J. J., & Pikus, A. K. (2005). Detecting mental disorder in juvenile detainees: Who receives services. *American Journal of Public Health, 95,* 1773–1780.

Trupin, E. (2007). Evidence-based treatment for justice-involved youth. In C. L. Kessler & L. J. Kraus (Eds.), *The mental health needs of young offenders: Forging paths toward reintegration and rehabilitation* (pp. 340–367). New York, NY: Cambridge University Press.

Trupin, E. W., Turner, A. P., Stewart, D., & Wood, P. (2004). Transition planning and recidivism among mentally ill juvenile offenders. *Behavioral Sciences & the Law, 22,* 599–610.

Walker, J. S., & Bruns, E. (2008). Phases and activities of the wraparound process: Building agreement about a practice model. *The resource guide to wraparound* (pp. 1579–1585). Portland, OR: National Wraparound Initiative, Research and Training Center for Family Support and Children's Mental Health.

Wasserman, G. A., McReynolds, L. S., Whited, A. L., Keating, J. M., Musabegovic, H., & Huo, Y. (2008). Juvenile probation officers' mental health decision making. *Administration and Policy in Mental Health, 35,* 410–422.

Watson, A. C., Kelly, B. L., & Vidalon, T. M. (2009). Examining the meaning attached to mental illness and mental health services among justice system-involved youth and their parents. *Qualitative Health Research, 19,* 1087–1099.

Case Study

Working with Mandated Juveniles

Catherine Howland

My official position is as a clinical case manager in a program providing intensive home-based supervision and clinical case management to youth who are on probation or are otherwise involved in the Juvenile Justice System in San Francisco. In the agency where I work, each clinical case manager provides a minimum of three face-to-face clinical hours per week per client. These hours include therapy, case management, and supervision services. The supervision services tasks involve compiling monthly records for the client's probation officer (PO) with regard to the client's attendance to, and engagement in, therapy, school, and other program involvement.

Much of my caseload involves working with youth who are court mandated to participate in therapy and have made the choice to meet with me twice a week instead of being placed in custody or sent to a group home. Different from private clients who elect to be in therapy, much of my initial engagement with these clients and their families often involves explaining that the court expects and receives reports about the client's attendance to therapy and case management meetings. Flexibility and follow up are two ideas I had to incorporate into my approach in the treatment of mandated youth. I make client attendance to our appointments as easy as possible by meeting them during the school day on their school campus, or at the Youth Guidance Center following a client's meeting with his or her PO. If a session is missed and I cannot reach the client, I follow up with the caregiver and probation officer if I can't phone the client directly.

Because many of my clients feel resentment, anxiety, or frustration about being forced to meet with someone who is reporting their engagement to the court, once I've initiated contact with a client, I take care to normalize these feelings and to make space for them to be expressed. Conversations about the complexity of the client's court mandate are an ongoing part of the treatment, but treatment often gets off to a better start when these topics are broached in the beginning.

My role in the clients' lives is often practical, action-oriented, short-term, and focused on helping the client meet criteria to get off of probation. Some clients are interested in personal growth and insight and have some curiosity about how they ended up on probation and how they might be able to change to avoid being in this position again. To best engage clients in their treatment, I invite them to come up with their own goals for treatment and empathize with the difficulty of having so many people monitoring his or her actions. I ally myself with the client's perspective and offer empowerment by highlighting how he or she is the only one who can make choices to change his or her current situation.

KYLIE

Kylie, an 18-year-old female Samoan client, had been on probation for 8 months for fighting peers on a city bus. Three months ago, the client had been functioning well on probation, and had been close to getting her high school diploma. All that changed in one night when Kylie was out with friends and a few family members, witnessed the fatal shooting of her cousin. This traumatic event resulted in posttraumatic stress disorder. She stopped attending school, discontinued meeting with her probation officer, and began smoking marijuana heavily. These behaviors indicated some severe impairment in Kylie's recreational, educational, and legal functioning and continued for approximately 1 month. At that time, the client was arrested for failing to meet with the terms of her probation. While in detention, she was assessed for mental health needs. My experience with clients exhibiting classic PTSD symptoms was limited, and I looked at this case as an opportunity to advance my skills.

Kylie had been having nightmares, headaches, intrusive thoughts about the shooting, and irritability upon her arrest. As a result of her assessment, Kylie was referred to Juvenile Justice Center's (JJC) psychiatrist, who had prescribed selective serotonin reuptake inhibitor (SSRI), a pain medication, and a sleep medication to help with her headaches, sleep, and anxiety symptoms. Kylie had been somewhat stabilized by coming back to JJC and seeing the psychiatrist for medication but was having some anxiety about her exit plan. Her court hearing was in 2 days; she believed that she'd be released to live with her mother. She wanted to get her state ID card, graduate high school, get a part-time job, and start community college. Kylie hadn't had any therapy related to the trauma.

When I met with Kylie, she appeared tired, sweet, sincere, and extremely focused on having an exit plan. She had her dark wavy hair piled up in a bun on top of her head, and she wore JJC-issued clothing—a purple sweatshirt, khaki pants, socks, and flimsy sandals. Her face didn't express much emotion, and her fatigue was apparent. We talked about how she wanted to spend her first day out of JJC. She said she knew she wanted to go right to her school campus to make sure she was enrolled in classes. I agreed to meet her on campus as soon as her class ended her first day back to school. We made a plan to have twice weekly meetings on her school campus.

Kylie was released 2 days later to her father, as opposed to her mother. The judge didn't want Kylie living with her mother because her mother lived in the neighborhood where the shooting had taken place. There was some concern about whether

Kylie would be a target because she had witnessed a murder and could likely identify the shooter. When I met with Kylie for our first appointment, she was angry that she'd been placed with her father because he was a much more structured parent than her mother. In addition, her PO forbade her from visiting her mother because of the danger to Kylie being in the neighborhood, and her father agreed. Basically, Kylie went to school and home. Eventually, she found a job in an after-school program, and she was relieved to have some income and another activity to occupy her time. When Kylie was released, she was given a short-term supply of medication, and as her case manager, I linked her immediately with a JJC-affiliated psychiatrist so that her medication would be continued. I then began to formulate the treatment plan.

In Kylie's first few sessions, she indicated that she was still having intrusive thoughts and feeling high levels of irritability, anxiety, and depressive symptoms. I gave Kylie some simple techniques for focusing her attention away from the thoughts, including exercises that involve focusing on sensations in different parts of the body. She said she felt dumb and didn't like trying to relax on purpose. I realized that I was focused on the symptoms and my goal-oriented treatment plan, not on Kylie.

My supervisor reminded me that the healing in therapy comes from the relationship between the client and therapist, not from a black-and-white treatment plan. When I put the PTSD-driven treatment plan aside for a few sessions and invited Kylie to tell me how she was and what she was thinking, what emerged was a young woman who was riddled with grief at having lost her cousin, who was the same age and height and had resembled Kylie. Kylie revealed in these sessions that she was really struggling in her relationship with her father. As she told me little by little about herself, I reflected back to her what she'd said and asked her about some of the feelings I was hearing her tell me about. I normalized her experiences and her perspective. I invited Kylie's father to have some family therapy sessions. Kylie's father expressed that he did not like or agree with mental health therapy and would not be communicating with me about Kylie at all. Any communication he had about her was going to go straight to Kylie's PO. I asked Kylie's PO to advocate for Kylie's father to participate in family therapy but to no avail.

Kylie and I continued to work with her PTSD symptoms. When there was a shooting on a bus in the neighborhood that Kylie heard about, her exaggerated startle response came back, and she almost couldn't take the bus to school. I taught her some meditation techniques, which she hated. She responded positively to some distraction techniques. Kylie felt she could use these by herself no matter where she went, transferring an object from one hand to the other, counting backward silently in her head. We talked about how different animals cope with and handle danger differently: some freeze, some fly, and some fight. Kylie carried so much grief and so much alienation. She felt separate from the world as if no one could understand her. I found stories online of people talking about their grief; I used psychoeducation and taught her about the stages of grief. We talked together about how grief might be different for someone who experienced the trauma and someone who didn't.

Kylie also felt isolated because she had been court ordered to stay away from her neighborhood. She was attending a high school for probation students, and her father didn't allow her to participate in any recreational activities during her free time. Kylie and I worked on having daily plans for Kylie to get through her week, then the month, and toward her graduation goal. A few days before graduation, Kylie came to her session crying and said she hadn't gone home to her father's house the night before. Instead, she spent the night at her mother's house. She said she wanted to quit school and couldn't spend any more time with her father because she felt he was scrutinizing and micromanaging everything she did. Kylie said she wanted to live with her mother, who had a relaxed parenting style.

I accompanied Kylie to advocate for herself with her PO. She requested to stay with her mother for the remaining few days until she could graduate and have her final court date. We both knew it was up to the PO and that he was concerned about safety issues in her mother's neighborhood. The PO told Kylie to stay with her father for the remainder of probation because that was the court order. Kylie was angry and cried and kicked the wall once we left the PO's office. We sat down and planned the next few days. Kylie would go to school, work, and home to her father's house. We worked on how Kylie would get along with her father just enough to reach the end of probation. If she failed to comply with her PO's direction, the consequence would be to be returning to JJC or to adult detention. Kylie made it to the last day of school and passed her classes, earning her high school diploma. She appeared for her final court date and was released from juvenile probation. I told her we could continue with therapy even though her probation had ended. She said she wanted to think about it.

I called Kylie three times over the next month and didn't hear back from her. Her school said that she didn't show up for graduation and her PO didn't hear from her again.

Kylie's treatment lasted 4 months and was effective in that she had fewer symptoms of anxiety related to her trauma, fewer nightmares and sleep disturbances by the end of treatment, and had been released from probation. Her stress and irritability were still high, but she had been able to function enough to meet her probation-related goals. She graduated high school, got her state ID card, was home by curfew every night, except the night she stayed at her mother's house. Much of our work dealt with coping with the anger and frustration of living with her father's rules and trying to understand the reasons behind the rules.

Many, but not all, probation clients only invest into therapy to the extent that it will help them meet the concrete terms of probation, and I suspect this was the case with Kylie. Court-ordered case management and therapy is often pitched to clients in this way to get initial buy-in in the hopes that once treatment begins other related issues can be addressed. Often, however, because these cases last a short period of time and although many goals are often reached, some of the work inevitably feels unfinished.

CONCLUSION

I have experienced this work to be fulfilling in some ways, as many clients respond positively to more monitoring and like Kylie are eventually released from probation. Those clients may not have experienced much monitoring at home growing up, and, when they get it, they suddenly function in ways that aid in their maturation and development into young adults. Sometimes clients get better grades, have new peer relationships, or begin to think more positively about their future. Often they do not, however, and that's when this work can be difficult and challenging. I have had to reframe and adjust expectations for both my clients and myself.

Much of the "therapy" is in taking actions that illustrate to the client that he or she is important and worth showing up for. I've found that being physically present for a client before and after a court date can build a therapeutic alliance with the client and his or her family and, as a result, aid in more honest and useful conversations during other meetings. It can be difficult to attempt to meet with a client who is on probation because, as a beginning therapist, I understand that his or her level of behavior is indicative of a lifetime of experiences that likely cannot be completely addressed in the time we have. I have felt hopelessness when a client was not engaged and ended up in a group home.

Through this work, I've learned that doing my best for a client can mean that I am therapeutically multitasking. I am working to be present for the client; as case manager, empathetic yet firm adult advisor, and therapist. When I am sure I've done all of these things, with the help and experience of my supervisors and colleagues, then I'm sure I've done the client a service. I have to trust that if a client is able and ready to use the resource of therapy, then he or she will. If no concrete result is apparent in their lives, I still hold onto the notion that connecting with others is why I went into this field in the first place. If I can honestly say that I was available for connecting, and I was responsive to my client's needs, whatever the outcome, then no effort was wasted, and I've met my goals for myself.

Chapter 8

Mental Health with Adult Offenders— Not Another Nurse Ratched: Why More Laughter Is Needed in Community Mental Health

Gardner Fair

In 1998, then-U.S. president Bill Clinton led a public discussion on race with a variety of experts on the matter. What resulted was so much stiff and humorless avoidance of the real issue in the name of an enlightened multicultural tolerance that it drew the following critical response from the renowned critical race theorist Michael Eric Dyson:

> What we don't need is the crass and deceitful politics of toleration that masks the sources of real power that conceals the roots of real inequality, that ignores the voices of the most hurt, and that is indifferent to the faces of the most fractured. What we need is *real* conversation, the sort where hidden ambitions are brought to light, where masked motives are clarified to the point of social discomfort. (2004, p. 124)

In solidarity with Dyson's critique, "critical Whiteness studies" has emerged not simply to examine blatant, mean-spirited White supremacy but also to detail the problem with an attitude of well-meaning Whites, variously called "White fright" (Myers, 2003), "White shame" (Thandeka, 2002), "fearful" and "directionless" perspectives (McKinney & Feagin, 2003), "White aversion" (Kovel, 1970), the "good White" (Hage, 2000), "White liberal racism" (Horton & Shimin, 2007), or "micro-aggression" (Sue, 2010). In this chapter, I apply these insights to working as a White professional in a community mental health setting where such White fright (or worse) is especially prevalent—the urban county jail.

Yes, confrontation across racial divisions in a typical urban jail is an unavoidable daily occurrence, yet the typical "color-blind" White professional psychotherapist is ill prepared for this challenge. Scholars such as Michelle Alexander (2010) in *The New Jim Crow: Mass Incarceration in the Age of Colorblindness* detail the social history of this terribly disturbing fact. Here I want to detail its personal side. Even after working as a psychotherapist in the jail setting for many years, the temptation for me as a straight, male, White professional walking down the mainline is still to walk as silently and quickly as possible, stiffly looking straight ahead, purposely ignoring the largely non-White inmates at the bars crammed into the all-surrounding, noisy, smelly, claustrophobic cells. Coldly freezing up like this ill prepares me to meet with my client waiting for me in shackles at the end of the hall. If I don't catch myself, I would end up treating my client much like the stiff and uptight Nurse Ratched in the classic 1975 film *One Flew Over the Cuckoo's Nest*.

To explore this highly contentious issue, I discuss my work with one client in jail by resorting to a drastic cut in time and space. Namely, I find some much-needed temporal and spatial perspective with the specific help of Seshadri-Crooks's (2000) psychoanalytic study of what's funny about George Orwell. Orwell worked from 1924 to 1927 as a British colonial police officer in Burma and faced strikingly similar issues as does a clinician in a U.S. county jail. The way he handled himself, ultimately by quitting his job and becoming a writer devoted to fully disclosing the complexity of the social situation from his openly avowed, flawed standpoint, gives us crucial clues as to how to handle ourselves within a community mental health setting serving variously marginalized and multistressed people. Surprisingly, this trail will lead us to an appreciation of a seasoned clinician's free-flowing verbal wit. Like Winnicott's (1971) notion of clinical playfulness, a certain clinical wit is a crucial, though often overlooked, feature of our work when we are at our best and, as we shall analyze, stands in visceral contrast to the stiff, bad humor and repressed, shut-down demeanor of someone like Nurse Ratched.

WHAT'S FUNNY ABOUT THIS?

At the beginning of his autobiographical story that depicts his police work, "Shooting an Elephant," Orwell describes how he reacts to a problem on the job much as does Nurse Ratched in *One Flew Over the Cuckoo's Nest*—namely, by maintaining a humorless, stiff semblance of dignity and feigned neutrality. Although he is only in his early 20s, Orwell is in charge and anxious to show that he's up to the task. Someone comes to tell him that a normally tame elephant has gone on a rampage, breaking free from its chains and ravaging a local market. Young as he is, Orwell is the imperial policeman on duty and thus looks into this odd report:

> We began questioning the people as to where the elephant had gone and, as usual, failed to get any definite information. That is invariably the case in the East; a story always sounds clear enough at a distance, but the nearer you get to the scene of events the vaguer it becomes. Some of the people said that the elephant had gone in one direction, some said that he had gone in another, some professed not even to have heard of any elephant. I had almost made up my mind that the whole story was a pack of lies. (1981, p. 150)

For any clinician in a community mental health setting, it is crucial to stop at just this point of Orwell's famous essay and consider what is already at stake. Clinicians everywhere but especially in a jail setting are faced with the same question as Orwell: whether to believe what the other is saying.

Let's be truthful: Something funny is always going on. The "secondary gain" of telling lies is painfully obvious in underserved populations of community mental health settings, jail especially. The huge power differentials between clinician and client generate an atmosphere of widespread mistrust and manipulation—on both sides. At the tip of everyone's tongues is a dismissal of the other's story as "a pack of lies."

Consider the case of a 30-year-old Latino jail client I'll call Jose. When assigned to my case load, he had been moved from the regular jail population to what is called "psychiatric housing" because he was unable to get along with his peers on the mainline. He had an oddly pretentious demeanor symbolized by his overly stylized bushy mustache, the way he would pronounce his name with a clearly manufactured French accent, and then the aristocratic way he would walk with his cane. Already vulnerable because he was grossly overweight with an amputated foot, he was increasingly at risk for being beaten up by mainline inmates who had had enough of his fancy pronunciations, big words, and pompous strut. New to us, we as a team of clinicians were trying to figure out what was going on. Some suspected a delusional thought disorder with manic tendencies because he was claiming the most outlandish things—that he was a famous sports reviewer and so on. Some thought he suffered from a schizotypal personality disorder. Other clinicians suspected him of "malingering"—of lying deliberately for secondary gain, acting crazy both to get into the more slack psychiatric housing area and also so that he could get some psychiatric medication to perpetuate his addictive lifestyle through other means. Although he denied having any drug problem, he had been arrested for possession of sedatives, and as the saying in jail goes, he was presumed guilty before being proved innocent. Finally, other clinicians had had enough of worrying about him and just wanted him diagnosed with bipolar disorder and medicated to keep him quiet so that we could focus on more serious clients.

During this staff discussion, some clinicians gave vent to the frustration of sitting with conflicting opinions between us by letting loose ridiculing imitations of Jose. One used a stapler as a mustache and office chair as a cane and hopped around the office wildly caricaturing Jose's accent and physical disability. At the time, I knew something was wrong with this workplace humor but didn't know what to say. I didn't want to be a spoilsport and ruin the fun. I felt that some type of comic relief was helpful to clear our minds and give us some perspective. But looking back now, I am mortified to think I was an audience to this type of joking. If anyone would have seen us, we would have appeared like so many Nurse Ratcheds, stiff and uptight in front of the clients while relaxing behind the safety glass in our private office with our peers, letting off steam, contemptuously snickering at our clients' easily mocked absurdities.

Orwell zones in precisely on this dynamic. With his own mounting sense of frustration at those he interviews, he's ready to write everyone off as a bunch of liars and verge toward typical racist contempt. Giving up a search for the elephant with this conclusion, Orwell would have had a funny study in local practices to tell at his all-White club that evening, drawing ridiculing caricatures of the upset "natives." The colonial masters would break out with hysterical laughter, cut up about the ridiculed colonized subjects. To quote Freud on humor, these Whites would then be sitting back thinking of themselves as the mature adults, humored by the "trivialities and sufferings which seem to the child so big" (1981, p. 266). Retiring to their all-White club (as Orwell describes in *Burmese Days*, his 1934 fictional account of his days in Burma), the Whites would elevate themselves to the gloating position of superior adults in-the-know, humored by the infantilized natives who they take to be worked into a frenzy by a mere hysterical spread of rumors, if not an idiotic pack of exaggerations and lies. "All riled up about an elephant that couldn't ever be found, how typical of those childish idiots!" the Whites would hoot in contemptuous self-satisfaction.

This overtly racist scenario might seem quite distant in time and place from any well-meaning work at a community mental health clinic in this day and age. To understand how the same thing still happens today on a more covert but still very real level, we need to appreciate how insidious and infectious such joking can be. Making fun of Jose's antics was not an isolated incident in any of the community mental health agencies at which I've worked. Retiring to our protected (often all-White) offices, my colleagues and I would vent with each other with sometimes questionable humor. Inevitably, some of my coworkers would "go too far." There would never be any overt racism, but it would be there in code, as in the case of Jose, where only his physical disability was overtly mocked—a common ploy as wonderfully explored by Tobin Siebers (2010, pp. 21–56). These clinicians were often reprimanded by their supervisors for their "unprofessionalism." Yet even though these reprimands were given and even though various agency-wide diversity trainings were provided to alter the culture of the workplace, the joking would continue. The humor was simply too infectious, meeting some subterrane-ous need, so that it could never be completely eradicated.

The lesson: Professionalism taken to an obsessive attention to rigidly policed language is not the solution to questionable joking in the workplace. The solu-tion is not to eliminate all joking—that would merely return us to the humorless, uptight, overcontrolled position of Nurse Ratched. What is needed is not less jok-ing but more joking—that is, less crude and self-serving snickering behind doors and more artful and fully disarmed open joking. In my experience, the best super-visors as well as the best therapists are most effective not because of any serious theory they know or precise technical interventions they perform but a certain clinical wit they possess that is much more personal yet still able to be artfully cul-tivated and passed on (or "transferred" in the case of a training analysis). Simply put, I could only make use of a supervisor's theories or techniques to the degree that the supervisor helped me on this more personal level. The best of my super-visors helped me develop in this way through their incredible wit that artfully touched something personal in me without triggering any pseudo-independent defensiveness on the one hand or regressive dependence on the other.

This is the clue I follow to take up in earnest in what Dyson calls a "*real* conver-sation" about underlying power structures and hidden motives and ambitions. The path will rest on the claim that our unconscious is inherently liberating and actu-ally quite funny when fully embraced. This position was explored, of course, by Freud. Paralleling his 1900 work on dreams (2010) and his 1901 study of slips of the tongue (2008), Freud sought to popularize his analysis of the unconscious through a study of an equally everyday but seemingly irrational phenomenon, laughter, in *Jokes and Their Relationship to the Unconscious* (1960). In this study, he carefully reviewed the scholarly literature on the topic and then proposed his own distinc-tion among humor, comedy, and wit, focusing most of his study on wit (which he further subdivides into being either tendentious or nontendentious jokes). In a later 1928 essay, "On Humour," he expanded on this division by associating it to his tripartite division of the psyche, linking humor with the superego, and by exten-sion, comedy with the ego, and wit with the id, as displayed in Table 8.1.

To see how to distinguish repressive from liberating laughter, and thus the help-ful place for laughter in our workplace as psychotherapists in community mental health settings, I explore these three columns in Table 8.1 one at a time, attentive to both the social and psychic processes involved, as I draw further parallels between Orwell's essay and my work with Jose.

BAD VERSUS GOOD HUMOR

Let us begin with the question of humor and what constitutes "bad" versus "good" humor. Freud gives the example of a criminal being led to the gallows on a Monday declaring, "Well, this is a fine beginning to the week!" (1963, p. 263).

Table 8.1.
What's Funny?

	Humor	Comedy	Witty jokes—tendentious vs. innocent
"Social process" (1905)	One person	At least two people	At least three people
Primary psychic agency (1928)	Superego's contribution to the comic	Comic comparisons of egos to alter-egos	Id's contribution to the comic
Applied to community mental health settings	?	?	?

That's how impervious this person is to what he sees as the puny reality around him. In reality, he's about to be put to death, but his humor only acknowledges his imminent hanging as might another person discuss the weather.

Attentive to what he calls in his 1905 work the "social process," Freud is careful to point out in his later 1928 essay on humor that there need be only one person involved for the effect of this humorous comment to take effect (1963, p. 263). Funny as it might be for others to hear the criminal's shockingly dismissive comment, what is ultimately funny doesn't depend on any listener. The humor lies precisely in the criminal's brazen disregard of the audience and, more generally, the reality of the situation—that he or she is about to die. This brash disregard of reality clues Freud into the psychic source of humor. It is to be located in a certain self-aggrandizement of the ego that is elevated to the status of the superego:

> This ego is not a simple entity; it harbours within it, as its innermost core, a special agency: the super-ego. . . . We obtain a dynamic explanation of the humourous attitude, therefore, if we conclude that it consists in the subject's removing the accent from his own ego and transferring it on to his super-ego. To the super-ego, thus inflated, the ego can appear tiny and all its interests trivial. (1963, pp. 266–267)

Humor, in this sense of superegoic enjoyment, is potentially much more sinister than either comedy or wit. Why sinister? In its worst manifestation at a workplace, a certain cynical culture can develop that is immune from any management or supervisory intervention, buoyed as this workplace culture is by its pervasive bad humor.

Consider in this light Stephen Karpman's (2007) "drama triangle" with its three points of "victim," "persecutor," and "rescuer." A clinician might begin working in a community mental health setting out of an admirable identification with these clients, understanding them as "victims" persecuted by this or that oppressive system. Positioned as a "rescuer," the clinician hopes to help his or her clients thus positioned as "victims" against various "persecutors." Yet as Karpman's model helps us conceptualize, the roles can quickly change, such as when clinicians experiences repeated rejections by those they had hoped to help. They now feel like the victim, persecuted by the client who has rejected and abused their goodwill. Yet another change in dramatic positions happens when the thus wounded clinician swings into the role of persecutor, mocking their clients in the safety of their office. Such is the stuff of what's been called "burnout," "compassion fatigue," "learned helplessness," "vicarious traumatization," "identification with the aggressor"—or what I'm calling most simply a *bad sense of humor*.

By contrast, what would be a good sense of humor in a community mental health setting? The answer lies with a certain playful befriending of our superego. When clinicians hit their stride, this is exactly what happens. They might be just as pressured as other clinicians by a stressed out administration that forces them to hold an absurdly large caseload. They might experience just as many rejections and attacks by chronically underserved and endlessly needy and understandably irritable and mistrustful clients. They might be under just as much financial stress and other real-life worries as others. But there is a certain good humor to these seasoned clinicians that is truly impervious to such realities. And here's the point: impervious to the realities that might threaten their ego thus reduced to puny proportions by their superego, these clinicians are then able to be sublimely open and masterfully attentive to the realities of their client.

This good humor is apparent from the start, as when these clinicians meet their client for the first time. They carry within them a certain mastery of their trade, an inner sense of confidence. These seasoned clinicians are ready for anything within the safety of a solid frame that they have learned to clearly and firmly set for the meeting. More than any intellectual theory or practical intervention, it is this good humor that sets them apart from their burnt-out, cynical colleagues. It allows them to meet their client where they are at, with true, freed-up spontaneity.

At least this echoes much of the accepted wisdom that can be found in various management, human relations, and positive psychology textbooks. Drawing from this research to write his classic on the topic, Stephen Covey in *Seven Habits of Highly Effective People* stressed the importance of nurturing an "abundance mentality" (2004, p. 219). According to Covey, this optimistic sense of abundance is what is lacking in a workplace's culture of reactive complaint and cynicism. In the face of the chronically underfunded and understaffed community health settings where scarcity continually runs amok, the seasoned clinician develops an inner sense of abundance and thus superegoic largess and generosity, meeting all clients where they are at despite all the surrounding pressures.

But just a minute. Let's not take ourselves too seriously! Just what is this optimistic sense of abundance? It's tempting to consider it in the lofty terms of various cardinal virtues including those of hope, love, faith, and charity, but following the trail of Freud on what makes us laugh, we need to look beyond any pompous mastery of these classical virtues and their masterful moralisms. Instead, we need to consider something less pretentious, something beyond any superegoic enjoyment, something "good" rather than "bad."

COMEDY: FUNNY VERSUS UNFUNNY FLOPS

The young Orwell is caught in his own lie of the colonial master when suddenly, just when he's about to contemptuously reject the talk about the elephant as a "pack of lies," he hears a woman shooing away children. Going to investigate, he finds a dead body. A local man was freshly crushed to death by the elephant, with the disturbing detail that the elephant had scraped the man's skin clear off his back. Any potentially humorous moment that would mock the "natives" with comical caricatures within the safety of some all-White colonial club is now lost. Once the elephant of colonial resistance is awoken, so to speak, colonial masters will indeed lose the skins off their backs. Racist laughter is thus suddenly disrupted by a tragic encounter with death that, literally, stops Orwell dead in his tracks.

Isn't this also the case within community mental health work where clinicians, however burnt out or otherwise self-absorbed, are routinely shocked back into reality through a client's unexpected suicidal gesture, if not death? In my own work, I think of the many times my sense of clinical mastery has been proven wrong by unexpectedly encountering a report of domestic violence, child abuse, suicidal gesture, or drug overdose that I completely didn't anticipate or adequately address with my client.

Most vividly, I think of the time when I worked in a residential hotel for the mentally ill and held an elderly schizophrenic woman suffering from a heart attack while anxiously waiting for the ambulance, holding her as she softly withdrew into herself and died. A few minutes later, a policeman belatedly showed up, clearly skeptical of an emergency call from this location. He authoritatively moved me aside so that he could, from a safe distance, give a rough baton poke to the now dead body of this poor, elderly woman. He wanted to make sure she wasn't putting on an act before the paramedics touched her. Her adult son arrived just as the paramedics roughly flopped his mother to the hard floor and stripped her chest bare to apply the defibrillator. The son and I caught each other's gaze at that exact moment, and I will never be able to forget the sight of absolute horror on his face that I felt perfectly mirrored my own total shock at what was happening.

Anyone working in the public sector, such as a police officer, paramedic, social worker, doctor, nurse, or psychotherapist, is bound to run into these terribly traumatic encounters over time. Our work is so serious, the crises we face on a daily basis so extreme, with life often literally on the line; we have such scarce resources to do our job properly. Yet we are human and need some distance and break, if not release or enjoyment, in what we do. How can we avoid collapsing over time into callous bad humor about our work? How can we avoid developing a sick sense of bad humor or at least welcome some comic relief?

Comic moments return in Orwell's essay, but ones that have been radically reversed. Instead of the comedy centering on caricatures of the colonized locals, the gaze is reversed, and the master colonialist is himself caricatured and lampooned. This reversal of the comic object is one clue to follow, but as we'll see, it is not the most important. Other more telling clues appear when we return to Freud with the help of Jacques Lacan, whose radical brand of psychoanalysis especially lends itself to critical social analysis.

With comedy, at issue for Freud is less the superego than the ego. More precisely, in question is the comparison of one ego to another. So the social relation now involves less a superegoic one than two egos in a dyadic, mirror relation to one another—for example, one ego witnessing another ego slipping on a banana peel.

Note how important it is that the other ego who slips on a banana peel doesn't get hurt. This distances comedy from cruelty, but it still relies on a logic of comparison—what Lacanians such as Seshadri-Crooks (2000) consider an imaginary, narcissistic relationship. In this logic, my ego mimetically identifies with another, such as a well-respected citizen full of pompous self-dignity walking down the street. But wait! Suddenly this icon of respectability slips on a banana peel! For a short, dreadful moment, I anticipate his pain of falling flat on his face. But look at that: He has fallen but is not hurt and is already back on his feet striking an even more exaggerated, self-dignified expression to cover over what just happened. I have all this pent-up feeling of pity, concern, and anguish that quickly welled up in me. Thanks to the fact that no real harm has happened to the good gentleman, I can release this abundant excess of affect without guilt or fear of harm through a good chuckle. It is as if I tell myself, "We are all too human after all! Life goes on as a comedy of errors! Isn't that a joy!" The superiority here is not that of the superego but in the felt community with our base humanity. This survives and in fact thrives in abundance, superior to all the false pretense and self-dignity we stiffly wear like some precariously positioned top hat that is continually flying off our heads at the slightest puff of wind.

Now back to Orwell. With the sight of the trampled and skinned corpse, Orwell realizes that the "natives" were telling the truth after all and that they cannot simply be hystericized as childlike simpletons prone to exaggerations and lies about some fictional elephant. To be sure, Orwell could have continued his obsessive-styled, overcontrolled research into the situation, now examining the corpse from the same contemptuous, safe distance as before. But Orwell sees the corpse as telling a truth about himself. Rather than isolating himself from it in an aloof or rigid manner of a master colonialist, Orwell identifies with the corpse stripped as he's been of the very skin off his back by the elephant's stomping.

This eerie, anxiety-ridden identification with the skinned corpse opens the way for several other shifting identifications: first with the massive local crowd that gathers around Orwell as he faces off with the elephant; and second with the elephant itself in its various manifestations, from the elephant ravaging the local townsfolk to the lonely elephant in the field leered at by the crowd, and finally to the shot elephant who "was dying, very slowly and in great agony, but in some world remote from me where not even a bullet could damage him further." In opening up to these fluid identifications, Orwell becomes hystericized. Rather than retreating into more ego defenses typical of an obsessive, Orwell becomes open to a labile mood of shifting identifications characteristic of hysteria. Another might have coldly dismissed the gathering mob and its rapidly spreading rumors and gossip, but Orwell comes under the spell of the mob and is himself infected with its hysterical mood.

And what does hysteria have to teach us? That the master, such as Orwell himself in this scene of shooting an elephant, is decidedly not the master of the situation. Indeed, Orwell describes the image of the colonial master as a "hollow, posing dummy" (p. 152). To quote his famous line:

> Here was I, the white man with his gun, standing in front of the unarmed native crowd—seemingly the leading actor of the piece; but in reality I was only an absurd puppet pushed to and fro by the will of those yellow faces behind. (p. 152)

This is what the hysteric forces out of the master: the knowledge that the master is castrated, as Lacan (2007) explored in *Seminar XVII*. On the surface, the hysteric would like nothing better than to put all trust in the master. Feeling so alienated, the subject appeals to the master. But the result is always the same: Left over in this interaction will always be a knowledge that the supposed master wants nothing to do with—namely, the knowledge that their mastery is limited; that the master is as riddled with as much insecurity and incompetence as any so-called hysterical subject.

How does this hysterical sense of fun that mocks any pretense to mastery not descend into a workplace culture of gallous humor, morbid cynicism, and a defeatist, collapsed narcissism? In the face of the terrible, systematic brutality that anyone who works long enough in a community mental health clinic will experience, how can a person avoid becoming humorless? How can they hold onto a good sense of humor, Covey's "abundance mentality," absent any superegoic claim to mastery?

The surprising answer to be found from the better scholars on the comic, especially from Alenka Zupancic (2008) and her wonderful *The Odd One In*, is that the liberating side of comedy is not the fact that Orwell makes himself the butt of the joke, making fun of himself rather than laughing at another's expense. To laugh at oneself rather than at another is not what is subversive about Orwell's essay or about comedy in general. To show this, consider Zupancic's example of false comedy and its relationship to mastery: then-U.S. President Bush's mocking himself during a press conference. What is so disturbing about Bush's enjoyment here, embodied in his famous smirk? To quote Zupancic, what is so wrong about "President Bush and his media strategy of mocking his own presidential self, which of course aims precisely at portraying the inflexible war President as 'the guy next door,' as a fallible individual who is aware of his faults and imperfections" (p. 33)? The problem is that the joke doesn't go far enough. Once again, we need more rather than less joking. Bush is using self-effacing jokes precisely to save his face. His jokes are conservative in the exact sense that they conserve his ego then aggrandized to the level of superegoic enjoyment. The telltale sign that Bush's attempt at comedy rings false in this way is his signature smirk, which sticks out as irrepressible material evidence that something remains unsaid by Bush, that he is coveting some enjoyment that he refuses to openly share and put in circulation beyond his own control and mastery. The heart of good comedy, by contrast, is that the enjoyment is all brought to the surface by the comedy, openly propelling it forward toward more and more comic enjoyment, leaving nothing sacred untouched, especially any claim to mastery.

And this is the heart of good therapy as well. Consider again the case of Jose. The joking with my clinical team at its worst veered toward a self-serving consolidation of the power differentials, including but not limited to the differences between the following caricatures: the "insane" Jose and the "normal" mainline client, the "manipulating" Jose and the "unimpressed" staff, the "overinvolved, naive" peer counselors and the "properly trained" psychotherapists, the "green" interns and the "tested" licensed psychotherapist, and the "overly maternal" psychotherapists and the "objective, paternal" psychiatrists. Here is no shortage of hidden agendas and power differentials for a conservative consolidation of one's own ego position in competitive contrast to another's! Here is a situation rife with tensions, misunderstandings, and stock comic characters that could rival TV workplace sit-coms such as *Scrubs*, *The Office*, or *Parks and Recreation*. OK, but how could all this be helpfully brought to the surface with Jose?

During the time I worked with Jose, there was a lice outbreak in his cell block. As is customary in these situations in jail, all the inmates shaved their heads in hopes of mastering this infestation. But Jose refused to even trim, much less shave off his truly huge, bushy mustache or thick head of hair. When I would meet with him, I could actually see the lice crawling on it. He stubbornly refused to let go of his passionate attachment to his look, and it was quite difficult to get him to talk about why he was so attached to it.

To the degree that I withdrew in a mix of pity and disgust, taking refuge in my and my coworkers' class and race superiority, looking down at him as might a parent look down on a helplessly messy child, for example, the more he would have responded in kind, looking down on us contemptuously as "simply not getting it" while idealizing any staff that he imagined did get why his "signature mustache" was so important to him. Conversely, the more I tried to look past and ignore the lice (that were literally right in front of our noses!) and the more I tried to simply bond with him one-on-one, person-to-person, ignoring not just the lice but also the blatant power differentials between us, the more he would, as it were, preen his mustache in delight but still refuse treatment for lice.

There certainly was something funny going on here, but what was it? The situation was comic, or really, tragic. What was I not getting? What angle was I missing? Funny as any sit-com might be, this situation wasn't, at all.

THE JOKE: CONTEMPTUOUS OR LOUSY?

We are just scratching the surface of what's funny (puns intended!) and how the cultivation of this aesthetic sensibility can help in community mental health settings. Just as a good joke keeps things simple and short, let us keep tickling the surface and finally conclude with a direct reference to Kalpana Sheshadri-Crooks's (2000) *Desiring Whiteness: A Lacanian Analysis of Race.*

In her wonderful study, Sheshadri-Crooks contends that, within the conditions of colonialism, our sense of "humor" and the "comic" works overtime to contain what a "joke" any colonial empire really is. Racist stereotypes, in the form of parody, caricature, and slapstick, for example, entertain and cultivate a White person's sense of self as wholesome and safely aloof from the racialized and mocked other. Despite this "good humored" sense of White superiority and its "comic," cartoonlike view of others, there hovers in every colonial interaction a contemptuous "joke" waiting to be cracked by the oppressed "other" that would reveal the absurdly precarious position of White colonialists.

Orwell's observations point us in just this direction, away from the narcissistic nature of conservative, self-serving humor and comedy toward the overt social context of a joke. He draws our attention to how haunted every colonizer is at the thought of being laughed at, which is to say, at the thought of being found out to be nothing but a joke.

To use a Lacanian distinction, the joke waiting to be cracked in Orwell's essay involves less the image of the colonizer as a comic fool and more the social-symbolic structure of colonization itself. At issue is less an image, whether complimentary or caricatured, and more the way any image in this colonial context is structurally framed. The result: The frame—not just an image within the frame—is suddenly made visible allowing for a much more real discussion of the issues. And at the heart of any witty joke is just this: a sudden reframe. Locked into one way of looking at a situation, you are suddenly shown a completely different way of seeing.

Consider the social context of our clients in a typical community mental health setting and how much they are always already "framed" by the situation—as Jose certainly was. Typically, our clients are acutely aware of the huge power differentials between a clinician and them that is far beyond the usual asymmetric relationship between the listening therapist and self-disclosing client in a private office. How can a clinician avoid assuming and maybe even abusing this power differential? How can one invite a radical reframe of their rigidly framed client?

The answer for our purposes lies in being able to count to three. So far, we've only really counted to two. We've discussed the superegoic one of humor and then the dyadic two of comic comparisons. Let's now count with Freud up to three and appreciate something about jokes.

According to Freud, a joke involves, at its minimum, three intersubjective positions: (a) those joked about, the comical material or content; (b) the joke teller who does the hard work of telling the joke but as a rule isn't allowed to laugh at his or her own jokes; and (c) at even a further remove from those joked about, the audience who is left to freely judge whether the joke is funny. An important feature of this audience positioned as judge is just this: their freedom to enjoy. This has to be a true freedom, and ultimately, one without "tendentiousness." In Freud's words, for a joke to work, the audience needs "some degree of benevolence or a kind of neutrality, an absence of any factor that could provoke feelings opposed to the purpose of the joke" (1960, p. 145).

Consider in this light my work with Jose. Put simply, his core issue was his alienation from his peers and the world at large. Jose's refusal of treatment for basic medical conditions such as lice was based on this alienation and only fed into further alienation. The same self-fulfilling dynamic had led 2 years previously to the needless loss of an infected leg due to his refusing medical treatment for diabetes. As he would eventually figure out with me, this situation kept repeating itself over and over again, going back to his childhood. He had grown up in an upper-class White neighborhood as a single child with two professional parents who had distanced themselves long ago from their families still living in Mexico. When Jose was 7, his father caught his mother cheating on him, murdered her, and killed himself. Jose was put in foster care, never feeling like he fit in with his underclass peers while also feeling radically rejected by the White upper-class upbringing of his youth.

Of course, there's much more to Jose's story, and that's the point. To the degree that I just focused on Jose through what Neil Altman (1995) in *The Analyst in the Inner City* called the medical model's "one-person model," I would have fed into the power differentials and hidden agendas of the jail and our agency setting in particular, leaving Jose just as alienated as before, if not more so. I would have been no better than President Bush who tried to joke about himself while further consolidating power differentials, as betrayed by his telltale smirk that contemptuously showed how much enjoyment of the situation he was still coveting for himself.

Yet to the degree that I just focused on Jose and myself (Altman's two-person model) and claimed with Bush's presidential predecessor, Clinton, that "I feel your pain," my treatment would have failed just as miserably. I might have temporarily bonded with Jose on a personal level and helped him feel less alienated and then more open to the treatment of lice, for example. But the joke would have been on us in two possible ways. First, the joke could have been on me to the degree that I simply caved into his own contemptuous smirk as he preened his licentious mustache and gloated about how idiotic other staff were in comparison to me who really got it, disavowing the obvious fact that Jose would mock me just as contemptuously while dyadically bonding with another behind my back. Second, though, the joke would have been on Jose if he came around, cut off or at least trimmed his mustache, and actually began to trust me. Sooner or later after our treatment ended, he would have run into another alienating dynamic for which our work would have ill prepared him, and as a result, he would have felt as betrayed and alienated as ever.

To get someplace with Jose, I had to be attentive to a third position that extended beyond any tendentious "got you!" joking, whether sexual, aggressive, cynical, or otherwise (as listed out by Freud in his still helpful review of jokes). I had to be ready to openly discuss, and in this sense outwardly enjoy (without any leftover gloating smirk or self-satisfied pity), the rather comical limits of our mental health agency and its internal divisions that were vulnerable to certain irrational blind spots and stubborn attachments, not to mention our own assortment of truly comical characters, including myself. The more I began to flow with his contemptuous talk about this in a truly nondefensive, curious, free manner (there's the challenge!), the more he began to let go of his own defensive contemptuousness and open up about his story, including why his mustache in particular was so important to him. Working thus, he eventually accepted treatment for lice. The contempt (or what Freud calls more generally "tendentiousness") on both our sides, in bits and pieces began to be replaced by an increasingly open, witty flow of conversation where Jose's story finally began to get told and heard in its right light.

This is how Freud understood the essence of a joke being "the contribution of the unconscious to the comic." This is also how I understand what object relations psychoanalysts call the "Third" that is the space jointly created between therapist and client. At the beginning of therapy, it is marked by intense discomfort. In different ways, both therapist and client fear being infected and eaten up by it. But the more therapy progresses, the more this in-between space transforms from a threatening, strange space to one that invites the perspective of a benevolent stranger, as it were, who will see things in the proper light. The space then becomes populated by a spontaneous, free association akin to Freud's third position in a joke: an audience benevolently predisposed to some enjoyment without tendentiously taking any one side over another.

So why did Jose not want to treat his mustache for lice by shaving it off, as is usually done in jail? He wasn't delusional, nor was he malingering as some clinicians thought. His story of being a sports reviewer was in fact true, although he greatly exaggerated his success. He wanted to keep his mustache because it was a trademark of his, featured on his blog. True, he finally admitted, he had few if any actual readers of his blog, but he ignored this as irrelevant, focused as he was on an ever-growing future fan base about which he daily fantasized. Because he in fact had no audience to talk this out with, he had little perspective about it. It wasn't until I finally "got it" by making room for a truly "benevolently neutral" audience that he was able, in bits and pieces, to be less consumed and more artfully deft in pursuing his dream of lifting himself above his circumstances, a dream that was, until then, quite literally eating him alive.

Since Nurse Ratched's day of overcrowded state asylums, much has changed. Chronically underfunded and overcrowded as community mental health clinics are, there is some open discussion of a client's "external locus of control" and the importance of helping them shift to an "internal locus of control," "buying in" to the work that often is forced upon them, especially in a place like jail. There is a new wave of counseling approaches epitomized in client-centered, motivational interviewing, solution-focused therapy, and narrative therapy that make clients the expert of what they want and value. And, of course, all clinicians are now required to take classes in cultural competency. All these are crucial changes. But what Seshadri-Crooks wrote about colonialism remains true in today's community mental health settings despite these crucial reforms. On the tips of many clients' tongues is a tendentious, cynical joke waiting to be cracked about the power differentials between clinician and client. This is a joke that, if openly rolled with in a nontendentious manner, opens up Dyson's "*real* conversation, the sort where hidden ambitions are brought to light, where masked motives are clarified to the point of social discomfort." Although various theoretical developments and practical interventions encourage a clinician to enter into such a real conversation, another crucial area to be worked through is the seemingly nonsensical and unimportant aesthetic question of what makes us laugh and enjoy.

Get it?

REFERENCES

Alexander, Michelle. (2010). *The new Jim Crow: Mass incarceration in the age of colorblindness*. Ann Arbor: The University of Michigan Press.

Altman, Neil. (1995). *The analyst in the inner city*. Hillsdale, NJ: The Analytic Press.

Covey, Stephen. (2004). *Seven habits of highly effective people*. New York, NY: Free Press.

Delgado, R., & Stefanic, J. (Eds.). (1997). *Critical Whiteness studies*. Philadelphia: Temple University Press.

Dyson, E. M. (2004). Giving Whiteness a Black eye. In *The Eric Michael Dyson Reader*. New York, NY: Basic Civitas Books.

Freud, S. (1900). *Die Traumdeutung [The interpretation of dreams]*. Leipzig and Vienna: Franz Deuticke.

Freud, S. (1960). *Jokes and their relation to the unconscious*. New York, NY: Norton.

Freud, S. (1963). Humour. In *Character and culture* (pp. 263–269). New York, NY: Macmillan.

Freud, Sigmund. (2008). *Psychopathologies of everyday life*. New York, NY: A.A. Brill.

Freud, Sigmund. (2010). *Interpretation of dreams*. Philadelphia, PA: Basic Books.

Hage, G. (2000). *White nation: Fantasies of White supremacy in a multicultural society*. New York, NY: Routledge.

Horton, R., & Shimin, R. (2007). Retrieved from Untraining.org.

Karpman, S. (2007). "The drama triangle." Retrieved from http://www.karpmandramatri angle.com.

Kovel, J. (1970). *White racism: A psychohistory*. New York, NY: Columbia University Press.

Lacan, J. (2007). *The seminars of Jacques Lacan: The other side of psychoanalysis (Vol. XVII)*. New York, NY: Norton.

McKinney, K., & Feagin, J. (2003). Diverse perspectives on doing antiracism: The younger generation. In A. Doane & E. Bonilla-Silva (Eds.), *White out: The continuing significance of racism* (pp. 233–251). New York, NY: Routledge.

Myers, K. (2003). White fright: Reproducing White supremacy through casual discourse. In A. Doane & E. Bonilla-Silva (Eds.), *White out: The continuing significance of racism* (pp. 129–144). New York, NY: Routledge.

Orwell, G. (1934). *Burmese days*. New York, NY: Harcourt, Brace.

Orwell, G. (1981). *George Orwell: A collection of essays*. New York, NY: Harcourt, Brace.

Seshadri-Crooks, K. (2000). *Desiring Whiteness: A Lacanian analysis of race*. New York, NY: Routledge.

Siebers, T. (2010). Disability aesthetics. Ann Arbor: The University of Michigan Press.

Sue, D. S. (2010). *Microaggressions in everyday life: Race, gender, and sexual orientation*. Hoboken, NJ: Wiley.

Thandeka. (2002) *Learning to be White*. New York, NY: Continuum.

Winnicott, D. W. (1971). *Playing and reality*. London, England: Tavistock.

Zupancic, A. (2008). *The odd one in: On comedy*. Cambridge: Massachusetts Institute of Technology.

Case Study

The Second Cosmogony: The Image World in an Expressive Arts Prison Program

Steve Podry

I would like to dedicate this study to my students whose work appears in the following pages and to all the students who have participated in our program over the years. Your courage and your vulnerability have taught me how to be a human being. Thank you. Students' initials are used throughout to protect their privacy.

The biological and political history of man is an elaborate repetition of the same thing. But the history of the mind offers a different picture. Here the miracle of reflecting consciousness intervenes—the second cosmogony. The importance of consciousness is so great that one cannot help suspecting the element of meaning to be concealed somewhere within all the monstrous, apparently senseless biological turmoil. (Jung, 1965, p. 339)

Expressive arts therapy rests on the premise that imagination is the healer, that encouraging the soul to speak in its own way transforms darkness into light, the hidden and concealed into the open, and thus provides insight and release. (Levine, 1992, p. 96)

The practice of holding human beings in captivity dates back to the beginning of written history. Our various motivations for caging each other range from vengeance to healing, from punishment to rehabilitation, from sacrificing individuals for the sake of a common good to sacrificing individuals for the sake of the powerful. This case study explores the world of poetic and artistic images made by those for whom prison is a poison that may, or may not, heal.

Black darkness eating me
alive
gold light shining to save
the better me inside
        —S.H.

My students are inmate mothers living with their babies. Creative work emerging through the frame of our arts-based literacy and parenting program affords a double opportunity: Without having to pass through gates, fences, or protocol, we can visit these women through their images, so that in some small yet not insignificant way, perhaps, they may visit us.

The faces of you—creating smiles
Arousing questions with curiosity
Formulated into one human soul
Whispers of knowledge
Indelible strength
Your imagination unfolds
Paths cross
Unforeseen friendships
        —V.B.

Paolo Knill's "crystallization theory" highlights the unusually transformative power of an "environment saturated with artistic imagination" (Knill, Barba, & Fuchs, 1995, p. 31). We work to create that kind of environment in the LEAP program. Walking down the hall of the school basement, you'll see the officer at his desk on the right and several giant group paintings on your left. Just past the officer's desk the LEAP classroom door hosts a sign made by students with wildly hand-colored letters that spell out "EDUCATION IS AN UNDERGROUND RAILROAD." What it doesn't quite say, perhaps, is that in LEAP imaginal education is an under-underground railroad. As you open the LEAP door, more colors and images will draw you in. One student wrote in her journal:

I'm really amazed about the pictures on the wall. To me it's like the pictures have life in them. It's like when I'm down and look up in the sky and see a colorful rainbow, it puts a smile on my face.
        —Q.S.

And there's the image of the room itself: brown metal shelves of books, beige cabinets with more books, art supplies, five black computers side by side on wood-colored computer desks, and just over a short divide crowned by a flipchart of animals of all kinds, two djembe drums hold court high on a red-orange tabletop against the blue and white wall where more art lives above books and green plants. There is another table beneath the basement windows, and on the adjacent wall more bookshelves, more group murals and seven or eight chairs surrounding a 6 x 9 "Persian" rug from Sears:

> The carpet is very intriguing, it
> appears to have been around for
> quite some time. It has a beautiful
> pattern that makes me think of
> palaces, riches, and royalty. The
> designs are exquisite, well-defined,
> and it feels like the carpet is
> whispering ancient secrets to me.
> —C.L.

Another large group painting dominates the wall, and if you look closely, to the left of that you'll see a poem the artists wrote when confronted with their own creation:

> Paint all different shapes, colors, styles,
> just paint everywhere!
>
> I see the light surrounded by darkness.
> The light is driving me towards the middle of the hole.
>
> These are some crazy looking colors that make my eyes hurt
> and give me a headache and make me dizzy.
>
> I see a mess with hearts in it that's making me craaaaazy!
> —S.A., Q.S., T.B., N.L.

The incarcerated women in the LEAP program were pregnant when they were arrested. They wanted to keep their babies with them, so they applied and were accepted to the Nursery, a special housing unit apart from "general population" but not isolated from them. In fact, women from general population work as teacher aides in LEAP and as caregivers in the Infant Development Center next to LEAP, where the babies stay while mothers attend their programs. Like the Nursery mothers, these inmate-staff also receive art supplies and arts-based workshops from LEAP, so the artistic spirit is constantly "billowing forth" from our "underground" classroom.

People may wonder why babies are living in prison. Some feel this opportunity goes against the principles of "justice," if not common sense. But LEAP and the Nursery program add to prison's punitive mandate a further level of intention: to foster a *nurturing and sustainable bond between mother and child, for the immediate well-being of both, and as the foundation for a nurturing and sustainable future.*

The babies are allowed to stay in the prison until they are 12 to 18 months old. Nursery mothers typically have sentences short enough to allow them to leave with their babies, or else soon thereafter, and reunite with their family, continuing the new ways of living, thinking, feeling, relating, and creating that have hopefully taken root through the communal life of the Nursery and the artistic "soul-friendly" environment of LEAP. Our arts-based parenting, educational, therapeutic, and mentoring components increase the odds that mothers with babies will transform their incarceration into a meaningful rite of passage. As one mother said near the end of her stay, "After bonding with all the babies and other mothers and writing poetry and drawing, you can't go back to your old life because you know these other possibilities."

These possibilities aren't so clear when an inmate first arrives, however.

> *I am there which is here feeling nothing with no one.*
>   *—L.A.*

The anguish of loss and separation wrought by a world of consequences-become-real means for many an initial sense of personal extinction:

> *I have become no one, with nothing to say.*
>   *—L.A.*

It can be both bewildering and exciting, at this point, to be handed a box of art supplies and invited to participate in the LEAP program's afternoon classes—or required *to participate in a 9-week parenting curriculum that includes "Parenting through Art & Play" and other classes utilizing the arts.*

> *I see the light surrounded by darkness.*
> *The light is driving me towards the middle of the hole.*
>   *—T.B.*

> *When the eyes get used to the dark, a new world appears, and it is primarily a world of images and interrelationships. Even on the darkest prison day, an artistic environment of aesthetic encouragement makes the emergence of images not only possible, but likely. When one of my students lost her entire file on the computer, a frustrating and maddening event most of us know well, I wondered if she might respond with a poem. Although computer glitches are not the worst anguish on Earth, here is a good example of how the shock of pain and frustration can shut us down with a resounding* No! *to some teacher's mad poetic suggestion, while the surrounding atmosphere of artistic culture somehow carries a momentum in the magical direction of an eventual* yes-from-within, *and she finds herself writing a poem.*

LOSING IT
it wasn't meant to be I guess
sometimes starting over is best and
that's what I need to do so I can see
things from a different perspective

empty heart
a blank page
I'm in deep thought
grasping
seeking a foundation
bad luck charm!
I can't do this anymore
let it go
I was doing so good
I just wanna rip my face off!
          —L.C.

This mother's face had already been "ripped off" long before she lost her file. Consciously or not, the poem appears to be attending to several psychological vulnerabilities all at once. Writing poems and making art allows us to see and feel ourselves more completely.

I am like a rainstorm, flooding everything in my path,
Thunder that roars through the sky.
A flash of lightning striking down trees and telephone poles causing damage,
Chaos everywhere nowhere to run, no place to hide.
Wind blowing, houses being destroyed
There's no end to my anger.
          —Q.S.

"The power of the image is the power of seeing resemblances," says poet Robert Bly. "That discipline is essential to the growth of intelligence" (Bly, 1990, p. 274). While one student sees herself in the weather, another finds a perfect metaphor in sports.

To make a shot.
It happens when you throw
a ball.
Keeping balance
and making sure that you
have the right aim.
It's like a motivational-at-ease.
Level yourself.

Keep the focus
and see through the right angle
and the right path.
It's like a glass, don't break it.
And in order to make that shot,
keeping the right view . . .
You can make it!
That shot!
Yeah!
　　　—L.D.

In his book A Little Course in Dreams, *psychologist Robert Bosnak tells how the old alchemists were not naive regarding the dangers of the imagining faculty. They called it Storm Bird, Dragon, Roaring Lion, Wild Mercury. Thus, imagination was also known as* pharmacon*—"the healing poison." And like the potentially "healing poison" of human incarceration, everything depends on how you use it, how you work it, your attitude, your skill, and your luck. Bosnak reminds us that in the Grimm Brothers' story "Spirit in a Bottle," Wild Mercury will not heal anybody until after he is* tricked *back into the bottle (Bosnak, 1988, p. 113). For LEAP that bottle is prison itself, and our job is to use the arts to cultivate and discipline our students' relationship with their own imagination. The imaginal avenues we offer increase the chances that our students will eventually realize the positive, life-transfiguring potential of an exile so onerous it feels like death.*

The bed opened as if it were a coffin, giant mirrors blazed
before me. I was trapped only able to see myself.
　　—N.L.

I mourn in silence, nobody hears me.
The sadness is bottled up inside,
I ache to let it out.
　　—M.M.

Very often the first image you see when you "die" is yourself.
Lips sealed, story inside.
　　—N.L.

Thus, the instant of psychological awakening entails images from the start, although not immediately recognized as such, for "inside" and "inner self" are spatial metaphors for something beyond words or time or space. The marvel of working in a prison is that almost everything we do therapeutically and artistically is brand new for the women of LEAP. Even the idea of intentionally imagining one's future, for example, of sustaining that vision long enough to describe it, feel it, and draw it out, can be a profound first foray into the artistic shaping of one's destiny.

Artistic shaping doesn't mean total control, it means working with what happens, with what you receive, even if it's "3 to 10 years." Sometimes you have to be stopped before you can see what's going on. While prison stops and "holds" our students, the Nursery and LEAP offer them dialogue, moral and therapeutic support, and imaginative forms and activities that help them self-organize their own process of reflection. We might think of these inmate mothers as simply "waking up," but when psychological pioneer Carl Jung referred to "the miracle of reflecting consciousness," he gave waking up the dignity it deserves and likened it to no less than a whole new creation of the universe, "a second cosmogony."

The artistic environment of LEAP balances the psychological and philosophical work of self-analysis with recognition of the images around us and "in" us through artistic work and play. For civilians and prisoners alike, the image world weaves in and out of ordinary days and routine consciousness. It is a kind of parallel world we hardy notice at first, a dimension intertwined with ordinary speech and internal monologues, yet rhythmically different in its manifestation from the steady onrush of habitual thought and talk. The image world is episodic, here and there. Images happen in episodes disjunctive to the mental mill wheel grinding, even disruptive like a wrench in the works. All images entangle us in some way but the more powerful images have a singularly arresting quality.

It is by attending to this image dimension in ordinary life that LEAP cultivates imaginative literacy as the basis for interactive intelligence. Nursery mothers in LEAP often begin to make use of their confinement by writing their life stories, and these narratives hold imagistic treasures that jump off the page—energetic configurations that entangle the soul and mean more than they seem to be saying:

When I was two years old I was mad at my mom because she wouldn't give me no ice cream. So I took my 14 carat gold earrings and flushed them down the toilet.
   —Q.S.

First memories can be worked with as a kind of cornerstone of one's personal myth, holding insights and new perspectives on everything that follows. Sometimes we work with these first memories by distilling the poetic image from its prose into a concentrated essence:

My mom gave me a piece of American cheese and I started throwing up
   —L.C.

Biting Nancy Scataway's cheek
   —C.L.

I remember my father and mother arguing over my mother not going to the store to get a case of Budweiser for my father and how she was too lazy to get off her ass.
          —S.H.

The earliest I remember was when I was four, boom, crash bang, my mother dragging me by whatever she could grab hold of to get me out of the inferno.
          —S.G.

I remember
I fell down the stairs at my parents' wedding.
          —M.M.

First memory: being molested
          —L.M.

Often a precise poetic image is not possible; the minute particulars are too repugnant to commit to language and share even with oneself. Yet we know by the expression on this woman's face that images are living inside her. Struck by the malaise of a single word, molested, her face and voice become the image we receive.

A first memory can be like a compressed myth of one's whole life. When I remember "how it all began," the first memory image is how my psyche says it all began. Our requirement that students write their life stories sets the stage for another kind of psychological beginning, for the external "roller-coaster ride" depicted in so many inmate autobiographies becomes the interior roller-coaster ride of emotions in a prison nursery where inability to contain oneself can lead to losing your baby. The poems I've been reading recently are manifestations of change, the effects of turning inward, of reflecting, of having the courage to suffer one's "miracle of reflecting consciousness" and then create something from that encounter.

The image is sometimes referred to as a "compressed myth," and the first function of myth, wrote Joseph Campbell, "is to waken and maintain in the individual a sense of wonder and participation in the mystery of this finally inscrutable universe" (Campbell, 1983, p. 8). Within LEAP's artistic milieu, the initial instance of wonder sometimes comes in the form of amazement to have created anything beautiful at all. "How did I do that?" asked one mother. In addition to discovering their own capacity to create things of wonder, these mothers develop—"even in prison"—an aesthetic appreciation for the beauty, weirdness, and mystery around them, in each other's art, in their own dreams and lives, and in the presence and memories of their children.

One student told me that before incarceration and her year in the LEAP program, she didn't know she had an inner self. It wasn't just creative activity in LEAP that told her this, but also the forcible separation from her family and, perhaps most of all, the profound experience of love and connection with her newborn daughter. Sometimes all she could do in class was overflow with tears of gratitude and awe.

my inter Self fill
and lister

—F.C.

The restrictive, conflicted, and isolating experience of prison is not the only source of images dominating this environment. Our days, as staff and inmates alike, are also populated with pregnancy, birth, and growing babies. Although disturbing to some outsiders, "babies in prison" can be seen with an artistic eye as a "magical juxtaposition."

> The fences are so high I look out my window
> and it makes me want to cry,
> then I look inside and see my bundle of joy,
> and the fences are far away
>   —C.L.

This contrast, contradiction even, does not go unnoticed by the inmates themselves who sooner or later surrender to the bitter ("that my baby should have to be in jail because of me") and then fruitful contemplation of their quandary.

> Red bloodshot eyes drained
> from exhaustion
> Blue sea-like eyes filled with
> joy when we play
>   —L.C.

Of course, parenting has always included its share of contrasts and extreme states, but here there are additional "juxtapositions" these women cannot ignore. Thanks to *their "second cosmogony" and this warm baby in their arms, they can no longer deny the extremely serious choice they must face: to be a mother or be that* other.

> *I never thought that it would be me smoking crack sleeping on the streets manipulating men in bars and climbing through strange windows.*
>   *—A.D.*

> *I am in two places*
> *I am there*
> *I am here*
> *And I am remembering*
>   *—N.L.*

Writing and images can put our multiple truths into a single image, poem, or piece of writing, there for contemplation—there for "owning." Art makes a place for intolerable juxtapositions, as well as the magical ones. It offers an alternative to the kind of compartmentalizing and denial that would otherwise defeat us.

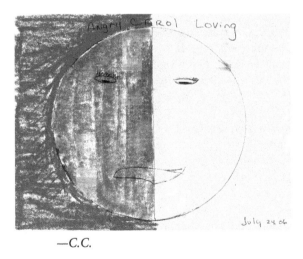

—C.C.

The tension between differing elements somehow placed together despite their disparity is appreciated by artists and humorists for its generative power. What that power generates or evokes is more images. Thus the contradictory nature of life and self propagates an infinity of visual poems when we participate in their unfolding through our imaginatively literate "beholding."

> *My house was built nice from the outside.*
> *My house looked great to by passers.*

Inside it was dirty, sadness, pain, and gritty.
My house was supposed to be perfect.
Until that sad day . . .
The Devil crept in and stole my house away.
    —S.S.

Hypocrisy and contradiction are how we find it; paradox and integrity are how we shape it. But shaping involves a willingness to receive, to accept the givens one bumps up against and begin to trust life's stubborn and changing conditions.

One student said she had buried many things in graves, and it was causing her to stagnate. She imagined herself as a tree that's "stagnating." She said, "It won't grow and it won't die. It can't feel the sun." She said when it comes time to leave prison, "I want to leave shining, with all the graves turned into one shiny memorial. I want to be a tree that's growing and can feel the sunlight."

At a different moment she wrote:

I can hear the pounding rain
Hit the jail pavement
    —S.A.

Can imaginal education be a pathway to freedom? It may be helpful to think of images as energetic configurations that entangle the senses and soul. Living energies. *(And what if we called them spirits?) Even a student's poster for a presentation about becoming a nurse entangles the soul because this was made by someone whose only career since age 14 was selling drugs. I think of images as constructs that arrest the mind. That is, they put you in a kind of trance through which something imaginal transpires in one's beholding. Inmates experience our arts-based parenting and literacy program as a kind of sanctuary from prison life, a strange ("What's a positive word for* weird?" *one student asked searching for a good way to describe LEAP), yet safe, place for real talk, tears, surprises, humor, and most of all:* making. *In LEAP, we* make *things. We make* things. *We don't just "do time," we make our time together, as in one exercise in which each student gets an opportunity to "create the moment" for the rest of us to share. Eventually a line on the wall from Robert Bly's poetry begins to make sense to the seasoned LEAP student:*

because the world is mad
the only way through the world is to learn
the arts and double the madness.

There's a new group painting on the wall that reminds one of the mothers of "Carnivaal in Brazil" and that another describes as "everything at once." Other group murals similarly draw the eye into kaleidoscopic encounters with an arresting vibrancy—*unknown worlds these mothers have made and entered into together. The mural is the* thingly *residue of an unpredictable group encounter by people who originally trust no one—and the* image *is what draws you into that mural-thing with a vitality belonging to it and awakening a vitality in us. There must be a secret message in that aliveness because it always brings inspiration and hope. Is one task of imaginal education to cultivate a sensitivity to that "secret message"? How can inscrutable combinations of shape and color in a mural of madness have any meaning at all? And yet . . .*

Through the poetic and visual images in this study—these mysteriously autonomous configurations that entangle our senses and souls—imprisoned people are touching us. And who knows, perhaps by beholding their images, we touch them back.

Today during count, Leanna woke up crying in her sleep. I picked her up and took her to the window. I said to her, "Look, mama, look." She kept on looking at the bars right in front of her. Right then I felt like my heart was bleeding. I said to her, "Look, mama!" and pointed straight ahead. But we both saw barbed wire straight ahead. I said to her again, "Look at the trees." She looked and turned and smiled at me. At that moment my heart felt pure again.
     —F.C.

     —L.L.

REFERENCES

Bly, R. (1990). *American poetry: Wildness and domesticity.* New York, NY: Harper & Row.
Bosnak, R. (1988). *A little course in dreams.* Boston, MA: Shambhala.
Campbell, J. (1983). *The atlas of world mythology, volume 1: The way of the animal powers.* London, England: Summerfield Press.

Jung, C. G. (1965). *Dreams, memories, reflections.* New York, NY: Random House.

Knill, P. J., Barba, H. N., & Fuchs, M. N. (1995). *Minstrels of soul: Intermodal expressive therapy.* Toronto, Canada: Palmerston Press.

Levine, S. (1992). *Poiesis: The language of psychology and the speech of the soul.* Toronto, Canada: Palmerston Press.

About the Editors and Contributors

SET EDITOR

DOREEN MALLER, MA, PhD, is a Licensed Marriage and Family Therapist (LMFT), and an Associate Professor and Academic Director at John F. Kennedy University's Counseling Psychology Masters Program in San Jose, CA. Dr. Maller teaches Holistic Studies and Expressive Arts, and she applies her LMFT in Private Practice in San Mateo, California. She holds a PhD in Transformative Learning and Change and a master's in Expressive Arts Counseling psychology from the California Institute of Integral Studies. She also attended a summer PhD semester at the European Graduate School where she had the honor to train with Paolo Knill and Steven and Ellen Levine. Before her transition into the academic world, Dr. Maller held an executive position at Gap, Inc. Dr. Maller's academic focus is the tension between the individual and the collective and possibilities for human transformation. Her publications and presentations represent a broad range of inquiry including academic and cultural humility, expressive arts, juvenile justice reform, postmodern feminism, and community mental health. She has presented nationally and internationally. She is a board member of IEATA, the International Expressive Arts Therapy Association.

VOLUME EDITOR

KATHY LANGSAM, MA, is a Licensed Marriage and Family Therapist. She has supervised and supported marriage and family therapists and social work trainees, interns, and licensed staff in her various roles as Director of Clinical Services, Clinical Director, Director of Training and Internship Program for 12 years in community mental health throughout the San Francisco Bay area. She has practiced and developed collaborative programs for more than 15 years in a variety of settings including milieu, schools, county mental health, county probation, clinics, and nonprofit community-service agencies. She holds a master's in clinical psychology, with a double emphasis in family therapy and child/adolescent treatment from John F. Kennedy University. Kathy is a Certified Supervisor by the California Association of Marriage Family Therapists; she facilitates consultation groups with supervisors. She is also adjunct faculty at Golden Gate University, California Institute of Integral Studies, and University of San Francisco. Her specialties include underserved populations, high-risk children and adolescents and their families.

CONTRIBUTORS

HOWARD S. ADELMAN, PhD, is a Professor of Psychology and Co-director of the School Mental Health Project and its national Center for Mental Health in Schools at University of California, Los Angeles. From the time he was a classroom teacher and then director of the Fernald Laboratory School and Clinic at the University of California at Los Angeles, his research and teaching has always focused on youngsters in school settings who manifest learning, behavior, and emotional problems. In recent years, he has been involved in systemic reforms to enhance school and community efforts to address barriers to learning and enhance healthy development.

ANNA BERG, MSW, is a Licensed Clinical Social Worker in the Tenderloin district of San Francisco, where she has worked since 2005. She is the manager of a community-building violence prevention program that trains homeless and marginally housed people in the Tenderloin to become community leaders. She specializes in individual and group work with trauma survivors, who also actively use substances, often incorporating somatic interventions in her work with clients. Ms. Berg supervises a number of community-based organizations and frontline staff who work with complex and multiply diagnosed people. She is coauthor (along with Little, Hodari, and Lavender) of *Come As You Are: Harm Reduction Drop-In Groups for Multi-Diagnosed Drug Users* and is a peer reviewer for the *Journal of Groups in Addiction & Recovery*.

NIKI BERKOWITZ, MA, is a Licensed Marriage and Family Therapist living in San Francisco. She works in the nonprofit sector providing community mental health services, including individual and group therapy, consultation, and case management to underserved youth and their families. She received her master's in expressive arts therapy at the California Institute of Integral Studies and weaves creative art therapy interventions into her systems-based work. She has an undergraduate degree in theater and has worked for 20 years with youth in a variety of contexts including community centers, public and private performances, festivals, schools, and agencies. She has worked in partnership with University of California—San Francisco's PART (Prodrome Assessment Research and Treatment) program providing individual cognitive-behavioral therapy treatment to clients with psychosis and multifamily group therapy for those clients and their families.

THERESE BOGAN, MA, is a Licensed Marriage and Family Therapist who received her master's from the California Institute of Integral Studies. Therese uses her education in community school settings while working as a therapist and consultant. Her training is focused on combining attachment theory, emotional regulation, and system theory. Her clients range from children and families to organizations facing vision change.

BERYL BRENNER, MA, has more than 30 years of experience working with the Department of Veterans in her roles as Arts Specialist/Program Director and Creative Arts/Recreation Therapist. She has received countless awards from the Department of Veterans Affairs and the Department of Army, including Performance Awards, Certificates of Achievement, and Outstanding Ratings. She obtained her bachelor's in fine arts and master's in art education from Brooklyn College.

DANIELLE CASTRO is an award-winning Trans Advocate, Educator, and Community Leader. Her efforts have successfully facilitated and supported the transformation of social service agencies, health care providing agencies, and clinical service provider agencies to be trans welcoming and affirming. Danielle is currently working for the Center of Excellence for Transgender Health in San Francisco and is completing her master's in counseling psychology with a holistic specialization and queer consciousness emphasis at John F. Kennedy University.

ANNIE FAHY, MSW, is a Registered Nurse and Licensed Clinical Social Worker. She began her career as a labor and delivery nurse. In the 1990s, Annie designed and managed substance use programs including programming for substance using women and their children, mandated court programs, and consultation to Child Protective Services. In 2001 Annie cofounded Recovery Cafe in Athens, Georgia. In 2007, she became affiliated with The MINT (Motivational Network of Trainers). In 2004, she began her affiliation and worked as a senior clinician and trainer with the Harm Reduction Therapy Center in San Francisco with Patt Denning, PhD, and Jeannie Little, LCSW. Annie offers training and professional skills development translating and implementing evidence-based practices into real-life practice. She consults with organizations and individuals regarding harm reduction. She also runs writing groups for nonwriters at the local homeless shelter.

GARDNER FAIR, PhD, is currently in private practice in Oakland, California, as a Licensed Marriage and Family Therapist. He trained at a community-based clinic and worked 9 years in a county jail with Haight-Ashbury Free Clinics. With a PhD in philosophy specializing in critical theory, he also taught at a variety of graduate programs, including New College and California Institute for Integral Studies.

PERRI FRANSKOVIAK, PhD, trained as a Clinical Psychologist and is Senior Staff Therapist and Clinical Supervisor at the Harm Reduction Therapy Center. She has been working in community mental health settings for more than 20 years, developing and delivering low-threshold treatment services to individuals with mental illness, homelessness, and substance use disorders. Her areas of interest include trauma and substance use, the integration of harm reduction principles and relational psychotherapy, identifying and working with countertransference, and using supervision as a tool for professional and personal growth. Dr. Franskoviak also has a small private practice in which she sees individuals with depression, anxiety, trauma, co-occurring disorders, and loss and has recently undertaken additional training in sensorimotor treatment of trauma. Dr. Franskoviak trains and consults with several large organizations, including housing and HIV-care agencies. She also trains community police and San Francisco Business District community guides in the management of people with mental illness. She is on the adjunct faculty at several colleges and universities and teaches courses on addiction and treatment, co-occurring disorders, and psychopharmacology. She is also coauthor of a paper on harm reduction therapy in community-based settings.

MELISSA FRITCHLE, MA, is a Licensed Marriage and Family Therapist and an active Sex Educator, Sex Therapist, and Gender Specialist. She teaches as adjunct faculty for several master's-level training programs in Northern California and coordinated the Queer Consciousness Emphasis program for John F. Kennedy University. She is passionate about positive sex education and has presented trainings for professionals internationally. In 2011, she was awarded a Sexual Intelligence Award for her work providing sex education in Uganda. She is an active member of the American Association of Sex Educators, Counselors and Therapists (AASECT), World Professional Association for Transgender Health, and California Therapists for Marriage Equality. She is a contributing expert to YourTango, a website dedicated to relationship issues, and has had articles published by *PBS: The Emotional Life* and other online media. She has a private practice in Capitola, California.

EMILY B. GERBER, PhD, is a Child Clinical and Community Psychologist with more than 20 years of experience with youth at risk or those already involved in the juvenile justice system. Trained in Prevention Science at the University of

California, Berkeley, Dr. Gerber is committed to bringing evidence-based practices to community settings where children and families need them the most. At the San Francisco Department of Public Health, she designated and now directs SF AIIM (Assess, Identity Needs, Integrate Information, Match to Services) Higher that reduces behavioral health inequities for probation-involved youth by linking and engaging them in appropriate and effective services. A noted system leader in San Francisco County for improving the city's child-serving agencies, Dr. Gerber's work has been recognized nationally and supported by the U.S. Department of Justice, the National Institutes of Health and the National Center on Minority Health and Health Disparities.

CATHERINE HOWLAND, MA, is a Licensed Marriage and Family Therapist in San Francisco. She has been working with youth who are involved in the juvenile justice system for 3 years through her position as a Clinical Case Manager with Urban Services, YMCA. She has also been a therapeutic mentor for youth transitioning home from wilderness and outpatient residential facilities. Catherine attended New College of California and Agosy University for her master's in counseling psychology, and San Francisco State University for her bachelor of arts in communications with an emphasis in gender and communication.

JAMIE LAVENDER, MA, is a Licensed Marriage and Family Therapist. He works as a staff psychotherapist and community program coordinator with the Harm Reduction Therapy Center, providing individual and group psychotherapy to people with unresolved substance use issues, in low-threshold community mental health settings and private practice. He provides training and consultation for staff at a variety of community organizations. He has worked with children and families in schools and family service agencies, with adults navigating the criminal justice system at a jail diversion program, and with opiate users accessing opiate replacement treatment. He is coauthor (along with Little, Hodarim, and Berg) of *Come As You Are: Harm Reduction Drop-In Groups for Multidiagnosed Drug Users.* With a background in transpersonal/integral and somatic psychology, music, and hospice chaplaincy, he uses dreamwork, drumming, and ritual in personal and professional practice.

JENNIFER LELAND, MA, is a Licensed Marriage and Family Therapist who has been working with system and probation involved youth for more than 15 years. She has held a variety of positions ranging from street outreach worker, substance abuse and residential counselor, case manager, home-based family therapist, mental health manager, and clinical supervisor. As a youth who was probation involved, she is especially passionate about delivering meaningful treatment and services to youth involved in forensic and residential settings. She is currently coordinating the SF AIIM Higher program, which provides specialized treatment services to youth involved in the San Francisco juvenile justice system.

JEANNIE LITTLE, MSW, a Licensed Clinical Social Worker and Certified Group Psychotherapist, is executive director of the Harm Reduction Therapy Center, a nonprofit agency providing harm reduction therapy for drug and alcohol users with complicating emotional, social, and health problems. She has worked in domestic violence and homeless shelters, group homes, homeless drop-in shelters, and private practice with children, adolescents, families, and dually diagnosed adults since 1978. In 1993, Ms. Little began developing harm reduction treatment services, beginning at Healthcare for Homeless Veterans then in private practice and at the Harm Reduction Therapy Center. She specializes in group treatment of substance use disorders and dual diagnosis. Ms. Little trains and consults with dozens of mental health, housing, and social service organizations and hundreds of clinicians and other social services staff each year in the areas of harm reduction, dual diagnosis, group work, housing, and homelessness. She is the author of several papers on harm reduction, dual diagnosis, and groups and is the coauthor of the book *Over the Influence: The Harm Reduction Guide for Managing Drugs and Alcohol* and of the second addition of *Practicing Harm Reduction Psychotherapy*.

JENNIFER PLUMMER, PsyD, has been working with the Harm Reduction Therapy Center since 2003. She currently works as a therapist, supervisor, and community program coordinator at San Francisco Pretrial Diversion: Court Accountable Homeless Services, Hospitality House Sixth Street Self-Help Center Senior Program and at the Homeless Youth Alliance in the Haight-Ashbury district of San Francisco. She has worked in social services for the past 20 years in many capacities and earned her doctorate degree in clinical psychology in 2010. Dr. Plummer is a psychodynamic practitioner who relies heavily on object-relations theory with a focus on early relational trauma and its impact on the mind. Her dissertation, "In the Arms of Addiction," focuses on the impact of trauma in the lives of injecting heroin users and their subsequent relationship to the needle.

STEVE PODRY, MA, is a writer, musician, intermodal expressive arts facilitator, and trainer who also teaches and directs an arts-based literacy and parenting program for incarcerated mothers. He earned a bachelor of arts in English at the University of Notre Dame, a master's in counseling psychology at the University of Oregon, and a Certificate of Advanced Graduate Studies at the European Graduate School in Switzerland. He also trained for 3 years with expressive arts maestro Markus Alexander. Jung, Hillman, Dylan, Bly, and other poets and shamans have been his greatest influences in opening up the healing possibilities of the human imagination.

RACHEL E. SEILER, PhD, is a Licensed Clinical Social Worker, works full-time as a social worker in the nonprofit sector, and is an adjunct professor in the Sociology Department at the College of Mount Saint Vincent. She received her master's in social work from SUNY Stony Brook and her PhD in the transdisciplinary, social justice–oriented field of transformative studies from the California Institute of Integral Studies. For more than a decade she has provided advocacy and direct services and created and managed programs for the empowerment of marginalized communities and diverse constituencies of vulnerable and underserved individuals and families both on Long Island and in New York City.

LINDA TAYLOR, PhD, is the co-director of the School Mental Health Project and its national Center for Mental Health in Schools at the University of California, Los Angeles (UCLA). Previously, she served for 13 years as assistant director of the Fernald Laboratory School and Clinic at UCLA, and then for 14 years worked in the Los Angeles Unified School District. Throughout her career, she focused on a wide range of psychosocial, mental health, and educational concerns. Currently, she is involved with systemic reform initiatives designated to weave school and community efforts together more effectively to address barriers to learning and enhance healthy development.

STEVEN TIERNEY, EdD, CAS, is Professor of Counseling Psychology and Chair of the Community Mental Health program at the California Institute of Integral Studies. He received his doctorate from Northeastern University and a postgraduate certificate in child and adolescent psychotherapy from Boston University. He is a Certified Addiction Specialist. He has worked in community mental health since 1980 and specializes in services and treatment for adolescent and transition age youth, specifically in the areas of addiction and HIV. Steven has had a lifetime commitment to expanding access to health services, particularly for adolescents and families. He was appointed to the San Francisco Health Commission in 2008 and in that role continues his efforts to increase access to comprehensive health care to all children, youth, and families. He works every week as a volunteer counselor at Magnet (San Francisco's Gay Men's Health Center) and was a lead trainer in a Centers for Disease Control and Prevention sponsored program for 6 years working in Zambia to expand the capacity of system of care to effectively deliver HIV services. Dr. Tierney was elected president of the San Francisco Public Health Commission in January 2011. He is on the Board of Directors of the American Mental Health Counselors Association and is the Co-chair of the Bay Area Marriage Family Therapist Educators Consortium.

KARINA WONG, MA, is currently completing her PsyD in clinical forensic psychology at the California School of Forensic Studies at Alliant International University, San Francisco Bay. During her doctoral studies, she is acquiring a range of clinical experiences working with underserved populations in a variety of community mental health settings. In addition, she is interning at the San Francisco Juvenile Justice Center, where she examines competency cases for the Juvenile Justice System, as well as conducting data analyses for the Juvenile Justice Department. With her passion in clinical and forensic psychology, she hopes to continue engaging in assessment, treatment, and research both nationally and internationally.

Index